THE PAT FAY METHOD

How to Manage Your Home Remodel or New Construction

Without a General Contractor

to Save Serious Money

by Pat Fay, BSME

A Construction Management Book for the Homeowner

The Pat Fay Method. How to Manage your Home Remodel or New Construction without a General Contractor to Save Serious Money.

by Pat Fay, BSME

Published by: Pat Fay, Inc.
PO Box 201
Kirkland, WA 98083-0201
www.patfay.com
patfayinc@aol.com

Printed in the United States of America by Pat Fay, Inc.

Copyright 2006 by Pat Fay
All rights reserved. No part of this book may be used or reproduced or transmitted in any form or by any means, electronic or mechanical, including photocopying, recording or by any information storage and retrieval systems without written permission from the author, except for the inclusion of brief quotations in a review.

First Edition, 2006

Library of congress Cataloging-in-Publication Data
Fay, Pat
The pat fay method. how to manage your home remodel or new construction without a general contractor to save serious money / by Pat Fay
Library of Congress Control Number: 2006906968
ISBN-0-9788364-0-5

Don't worry about people stealing your idea. If it's original, you'll have to ram it down their throats. Howard Aiken

Dedication

This book is dedicated to the homeowners of America. I have written this book so that you no longer have to put up with the high cost of home construction that is the standard today in America. The status quo is based on the false premise that American homeowners cannot manage their own projects and can be treated with disrespect. The homeowners of America deserve better options and to be treated fairly by the home construction industry. This book will provide you with the knowledge needed to guide you in the management of your remodel or new construction project without a general contractor. All that is required from you, the homeowner, is courage, steadfastness and confidence in the Pat Fay Method.

I also dedicate this book to my wife, Krista Kennelly Fay, for showing me the power and effectiveness of basic common sense combined with simple construction management techniques during the construction of our home in Kirkland, Washington in 1994.

Acknowledgements

I would like to thank my daughter, Adelle, for her help not only in editing my manuscript but also for her guidance to her engineer father on how to better write a book. She has put many hours of her time over the last few years into guiding the structure of this book as well as correcting my grammar, syntax and style. Also, since she does not work in construction her questions allowed me to understand how a typical non-construction homeowner would view and perceive the information contained in this book. It forced me to write clearer and with better explanations so the typical homeowner could better understand and use this book to help them manage their home construction project without a general contractor.

However, I did not accept all of her edits. Therefore, I am solely responsible for any grammatical or other errors found in this book.

I would also like to thank my insurance agent Joe Hughes of Farmers Insurance, Kirkland, Washington (insure4u@cnw.com). He very kindly reviewed my chapter on insurance and made excellent suggestions which I hope will greatly improve the benefit to the homeowner.

Credit to RS Means Company. I would also like to thank the RS Means Company. I will be using square foot cost data from RS Means Company in this book. They are a national leader in construction cost estimating data for residential, industrial and commercial construction. I am privileged to have their permission to use their square foot costs (on how much it should actually cost to build a house) in this book. Any data titled from RS Means comes "from Means Square Foot Cost Data, 2005. Copyright Reed Construction Data, Kingston, MA 781-585-7880; All rights reserved." Their website is www.rsmeans.com.

Disclaimer

The information and methods in this book, which are based on Pat Fay's knowledge and experience, have worked well for Pat Fay; however, readers use this book at their own risk.

Therefore, Pat Fay and Pat Fay Incorporated make no express or implied warranty of fitness for use of the information contained herein. Also, Pat Fay and Pat Fay Incorporated make no implied or express warranty or guarantee in connection with the information contained herein, including, without limitation, correctness, accuracy, completeness, and methods.

If, after reading this disclaimer and before using this book, the purchaser wishes to return this book, the purchaser may contact Pat Fay Inc. at patfayinc@aol.com for a full refund of the purchase price less shipping and handling.

Why this Book was Written

The creation of this book has taken a long and interesting route. I had no plans to write a book on what my wife and I learned when we built our new home without a general contractor in Kirkland, Washington, in 1994. At the time of our project we only thought about building a nice house and not spending too much money.

During our project my wife and I did our own planning and preliminary design. Once we had determined the floor plan and elevations pretty well, we hired an architect to produce a set of permit ready construction documents. We found an architect who took our floor plan and made it into a great floor plan.

After we received our building permit we hired and managed the many contractors needed to build our dream home. We did not use a general contractor for reasons that you will read about in the body of this book. However, the main reason is that they are too expensive for the service they provide.

Our project was both successful and unsuccessful.

It was unsuccessful because our project did not go smoothly. We had thought that because of my extensive experience as a construction manager in Industrial Construction that we would have a straight-forward house construction project.

In fact, we had an awful experience that left us mentally and emotional exhausted by the end of our project. We made many mistakes and some of our mistakes cost us a lot of money. We were treated very poorly by the majority of the contractors we hired. Only three out of about 25 contractors were ethical and did what they said they would do, when they said they would do it and for the price agreed upon initially.

More importantly, however, building our home was a successful project because we finished our home and we stayed married. In fact, our relationship grew stronger because of this shared, difficult experience. My respect for my wife grew because of her knowledge, skill, great ideas, and ability to keep her wits about her through the thick and thin of our project (which I was not always able to do).

Another reason we had a successful project is because our cost to build was only $65 per square foot (SF). We built a brand new 3,000 square foot, two story house with a two car detached garage. The house also has a 1500 square foot unfinished basement and the garage has a 500 square foot living space above. Therefore, the finished living space is 3500 SF. In 1994 the cost for new construction in Seattle was about $120 per square foot.

By managing our new home project without a general contractor we saved approximately $192,500 ($120-$65=$55/SF x 3500 SF = $192,500).

Actually, we had budgeted $50 per square foot based on the cost data in the RS Means Cost Estimating Manuals. The problems we encountered with our contractors drove the price up to $65 per SF.

RS Means Company produces excellent cost estimating manuals that define the amount of labor and materials needed to build houses. Their square foot cost manual defined that in 1994 the cost to build a new house including the general contractor's overhead and profit was $62.50 per SF. The contractor overhead and profit is typically about 25%. If one subtracts 25% from the $62.50 you get about $50 per SF.

At the time of this project, I had over 20 years of experience in all phases of industrial construction and even two years of building houses in the deserts of Saudi Arabia. Despite my professional experience, I was barely up to the challenges that presented themselves during this project. I learned the hard way that the rules of the industrial construction world are not followed in the home construction world. The home construction world has no rules - except what seems to be made up by the contractors as they go along.

If a person with my extensive construction knowledge and experience could be run through the wringer by the current home construction process then I can completely understand why this process can ruin a family's finances and even destroy a couple's marriage. It need not be that way.

Part of the problem is that the typical homeowner does not know what they need to know before they do a remodel or build a new house. They go into their project with excitement, happiness and joyful anticipation. By the time their project is complete many wish they had never started their project. They feel beaten up and have a lot of anger towards their contractors. Most feel cheated.

The ordinary homeowner thinks little of the planning, preliminary design and final design phases of their project because they mostly focus upon the construction phase. That is partially correct because the greatest cost of their project will be in construction. However, we learned that to be in command of your construction phase you must fully understand the details of what makes up your planning and design phases. By knowing everything that comes before construction, you will be able to answer the vast majority of questions that come up when you are deep in the jungle of the construction phase.

After we had lived in our new home for a time we felt better about our home construction process. However, at the same time I became angry whenever I thought about how the home construction process was so complicated. I felt it should be more like the industrial construction process where the owners really are in charge of their projects. I thought to myself why not try to teach other homeowners how to be in charge of their project as well as teach them how to avoid the pitfalls we encountered. So I decided to teach a seminar. I titled it "How to be Your Own General Contractor". My seminar was a three-hour lecture covering all the phases of the home remodel and new construction process.

Unfortunately, the seminar was a failure! I could not convince enough homeowners that they should trust in the power of the contract not their contractor. Nor could I convince them that their money should stay in their pocket and to not pay their contractor up to 50% of the money at the time they signed a contract!

In fact, I did not get enough students to pay for my expenses. Interestingly enough, most of the people who most responded to my advertisements were women. They would be very interested in taking my seminar, only, in the end, decide not to attend.

Upon follow up, I found two reasons why they decided not to attend my class. The most common reason was because their husband said he knew everything there was to know about construction and contracting and that he would tell his wife what to do. The second reason was that they had spoken to their contractor who told them my class would be a total waste of time.

I felt sorry for these women because, being a man, I know how a husband will react when things go poorly on a home remodel project even when a wife was just doing what she believed her husband had instructed her to do. He will usually blame his wife. Men will go to great lengths not to blame themselves, especially when there is someone else to blame instead.

As for the second reason, I was dismayed that women would actually believe their contractor that my class was without value. Taking their contractors advice in this case was as bad as letting the fox guard the hen house.

I had just about decided to give up on the seminar when I had a conversation with my friend, Steve Hale. He suggested rather than giving up on my seminar that I teach it at Discover U in Seattle. Discover U (www.discoveru.org), as I found, was and is a lifelong learning organization that holds classes mostly in the evenings and weekends. The classes they hold are unique and range from how to become a private detective, to how not to stay single in Seattle, to computer training classes, to how to be a blacksmith, and, of course, how to be your own general contractor.

I have taught my class three or four times per year at Discover U since 1996. I have thoroughly enjoyed myself even though the attendance, in the early years, was quite small, often as few as three to five students.

My students were ordinary men and women who wanted to remodel their existing home or even build a new home. Some had built before and they generally had poor experiences with their contractors and wanted to do a better job the second time around. They also wanted to be in charge of the process. Others had never done any remodeling before but they wanted to build without experiencing the terrors they had experienced vicariously through their friends and associates.

In 2002 my class sizes unexpectedly jumped to 15 to 25 students. Obviously, something in the market place was changing. So I sat down and began to write this book. I wanted to be able to reach homeowners throughout America not just those who could attend my class in Seattle. I believe I have something unique and valuable to teach ordinary homeowners about how to manage their home construction projects.

I have written this book so that you, the ordinary American homeowner, can read it and understand the dangers and pitfalls before you act. When you have the information and knowledge from this book available to you before construction starts then you have an excellent chance of not succumbing to the many problems that have caused such problems for other homeowners, including me.

I want to teach you what my wife and I learned in the difficult world of homeowner remodel and new construction. I believe, with this knowledge, good planning, and by following good, basic, project management techniques, the homeowner can manage their home remodel or new construction project to a successful completion without a general contractor. I define success to mean quality materials, superior workmanship, a reasonable price, lower personal stress levels, and staying married.

This book is not written for the financially elite of our society (even though they could put it to good use). They have enough money so they can just write a check for double the original bid – a problem that they can reluctantly, but easily make go away.

However, for the vast majority of us solving the problem this way is a pipe dream. We work very hard for the limited amount of money we have. Doubling the cost of a project can spell the financial ruin of the family involved. They can even end up having to sell their home because they cannot afford to make the payments on a mortgage that is twice as large as was originally planned. Then the finger pointing starts and spouses begin to fight. Even the best marriages can fail under such pressure. In cases such as this it would have been better if the remodel had never occurred.

I believe the time is right for this book because there is a shift in the thinking of the American homeowner. I believe they are awakening to the realization that they can have better quality construction for a reasonable price. They realize that it is their home, their money, and after all, the contractor is just someone that has been hired to perform a service. It is a vital service but it does not mean that the contractor is in charge of either the project or the homeowner's money. They are hired to perform specific work that is defined in a written contract.

Now is a good time to ask what new innovations have taken place in recent years that have benefited the homeowner with better quality and lower prices? Not many. There are the Home Depot and Loews home construction super stores that have brought reasonable prices to construction materials. The stores are also expanding into installing many of the products they sell. This is a good thing. Besides these super stores I don't know of anything that brings innovation and lower prices to homeowners except for the Pat Fay Method.

Stagnation is a good way to describe home construction in America today. The price of building and remodeling in all areas of America has reached absurd levels that in no way reflect the actual cost of materials and labor needed to build or remodel. The Pat Fay Method will allow homeowners to use their imagination, energy and enthusiasm in a positive way to build or remodel their home for a reasonable price with high quality materials and workmanship.

In this book I have dedicated myself to teaching homeowners a better way to do home remodel and new construction. The methods I teach are those common to industrial construction but in the homeowner construction world they are considered unorthodox and controversial.

The homeowners who buy this book and then implements the ideas and methods found herein will be told that what I teach cannot be done! Do not believe it because what I teach is nothing more than good, basic, construction and project management techniques, principles and methods. I have added my own knowledge and experience to create a unique 21st century method of how to become a home construction project manager and successfully manage your remodel or new construction without a general contractor to save serious money and still stay married.

What is the Pat Fay Method? The Pat Fay Method is a home construction process where the homeowner is in charge of their home construction project instead of turning all responsibility and money over to a general contractor.

The homeowner can manage their remodel or new home construction process while maintaining their present full time employment. All you need is the ability to be organized, dedicated to your goals, a good plan, and most importantly believe what the Pat Fay Method teaches rather than what the contractors say you should do.

Instead of hiring one general contractor the Pat Fay Method has the homeowner hiring separate contractors to build the different phases of the construction. The homeowner becomes the project manager eliminating the general contractor. The homeowner manages the construction process by hiring contractors who are experts in their field for each phase of construction. It is the responsibility of these experts to do the work they know how to do.

Therefore, the homeowner does not even need to know that much about construction except in which order things should be done. The knowledge of the construction process gained from this book will teach you that information and much more.

The reason the Pat Fay Method does not use a general contractor to manage the home construction process is because they add too large a fee to all their subcontractor charges. This results in home construction projects that are far too expensive.

The general contractor also typically asks for change orders for work that should be included in their original price. They also charge too much for legitimate change orders. This causes the homeowner much anxiety, unhappiness, and personal and financial stress.

There are risks in working with all contractors and this book addresses those issues of how to manage your contractors and your home construction project. However, the financial savings are so great that the risks are offset by the amount of money that can be saved.

The most important rule in the Pat Fay Method is that the homeowner keeps their money in their account rather than turning over large sums of money to the contractor. The standard practice today is the homeowner is told they need to pay the contractor 50% of the money at the time the contract is signed. Why do this when the contractor has done no work? There is no law or rule that states this must be done. It is just a common and unfair practice that the Pat Fay Method intends to greatly reduce if not eliminate.

Paying the contractor before work is done is the root cause of the majority of problems found in home construction in America today. Every year, thousands of normal American homeowners pay some general contractor a large sum of money only to see the general contractor and their money leave town without accomplishing any work. Another common problem is that the general contractor will take the homeowner's money and finish someone else's project with it. Then there is no money left for your construction project.

In the Pat Fay Method, the homeowner signs a contract but no money should change hands until actual work is accomplished.

I have formulated a set of rules that define the Pat Fay Method. The chapters of this book expand upon these rules.

The Pat Fay Method is:

1. The homeowner takes the role of the project manager. The homeowner is in charge of their home construction project – not the contractors. The contractors work for the homeowner. The homeowner does not pay large sums of money to the contractor at the time the contract is signed.

2. The homeowner is responsible for their planning and preliminary design.

3. The homeowner hires an architect or building designer to perform the final design and produce a construction and permit-ready set of construction documents.

4. The homeowner is the first point of contact with the permitting agency. The architect/building designer supports the homeowner in the permit process as needed.

5. The homeowner buys adequate liability insurance before construction begins.

6. The homeowner signs a contract that defines at a minimum what work is to be done by the contractor, when the work is to be started and finished, what quality of workmanship and materials is acceptable, how much the work will cost and when payment is to be made.

7. The homeowner hires different contractors to do the different phases of construction without a general contractor. Each contractor is responsible for completing the work they contracted to do. The homeowner is responsible for paying the contractor when the work is completed, inspected and, when applicable, signed off by the building inspector. The contractor signs a lien release at the time payment is made.

8. The homeowner avoids hiring anyone to help them manage their project. The home construction industry is full of people willing to manage your project for $2,000 per week. Do not hire them unless it is a lending requirement or you just know that you need assistance. Be beware though because you may be disappointed by their performance and by the amount their fee increases your project's cost. If you do hire a consultant it should be for a fixed fee.

9. The homeowner is responsible for daily inspection of the work. The homeowner inspects for quality workmanship, installation of correct materials, and that the work is being done according to the building plans.

10. The homeowner and contractor will use the services of a professional arbitrator to resolve disagreements. The homeowner and the contractor may agree to disagree on various aspects of the work, such as quality of workmanship, types of materials, adherence to the plans, cost, or any other general disagreement. The homeowner selects an arbitration firm before construction begins.

11. The homeowner pays top dollar for the work they contract out. In return they expect the contractor to use the best materials available and to install those materials with extraordinary workmanship.

12. There are no change orders allowed, unless defined in writing on the homeowner's no verbal changes form (NVC). The NVC must be made out at the time of the change with a description of the change with a defined cost. It is not acceptable for the contractor to ask for additional money for minor errors and omissions on the drawings or due to requirements of the building code or the building inspector. The contractors are hired because they are experts in their work and they know all the applicable rules, codes, and regulations that guide and govern their work.

13. The homeowner treats the contractor and their workers with respect. Likewise, the contractor and their workers treat the homeowner and the homeowner's property with respect. Both parties work toward a win-win relationship: the contractor does all the work they agreed to do at the price agreed to and the homeowner pays the contractor when that work is satisfactorily completed.

14. The Pat Fay Method empowers the homeowner to have the home remodel or construction done as they like, at the price they originally agreed upon and even to enjoy the process of getting there.

Have fun doing your home construction project. The Pat Fay Method enables you, the homeowner, to tell the contractor what you will accept or not accept. Try it by looking a contractor in the eye and telling them that since they will not work according to the Pat Fay Method you will not be using them on your project. Tell them you will find a different contractor that wants to earn excellent money for a well performed job according to the Pat Fay Method. Some contractors will walk away from your work but many others will want your work because you pay top dollar.

By following the Pat Fay Method it is possible to remodel your home or build a new home in the price range of $100 per square foot not $150 to $250 per square foot as the homeowner is quoted in the year 2006.

If the homeowner decides to hire a general contractor.

I cannot expect every homeowner to follow the Pat Fay Method and to manage their home construction project without a general contractor. If you fall into that category then there are still many parts of the Pat Fay Method that can help you have a more successful and less expensive home construction project.

The homeowner can use a modified version of the Pat Fay Method to plan their project and select their general contractor. The planning, preliminary design and final design phases are well covered in this book and can help any homeowner. The chapter on conducting home construction meetings will be vital to managing the project even if you hire a general contractor. The chapter on scheduling will allow the homeowner to understand how long a project should take and how to track the project and the general contractor's progress.

No homeowner should go into home construction without adequate insurance coverage separate from what the general contractor carries and chapter 7 will help the homeowner understand insurance issues. The chapter on safety will also help the homeowner limit their liability by understanding the many safety issues inherent to construction.

The chapter on change orders is vital to every homeowner. This issue is a recurring nightmare in home construction because the change order can add tens of thousands of dollars in unexpected costs to a project. What will the homeowner do when their general contractor presents a change order asking for more money? What hourly rate for change orders did the homeowner agree to before the contract was signed? These and other questions about change orders are addressed in this book.

Once construction is underway how does the homeowner ensure that quality materials and workmanship are being employed on their home construction project? The chapters on the construction phase and construction materials will help the homeowner be sure that high quality materials and excellent workmanship are used on their project.

What will the homeowner do when the contractor and the homeowner cannot resolve a dispute? What methods will be employed to resolve the dispute?

How will the homeowner protect themselves from material supplier liens? This situation occurs when the homeowner pays the general contractor but the general contractor does not pay the material suppliers. The material supplier must be paid or they have a legitimate reason to place a lien on the homeowner's property. How is it done?

As you can see this book is not only for homeowner who will follow the Pat Fay Method but also for the homeowners who will be hiring a general contractor. There is much to know and this book will help the homeowner to understand these issues before they get into trouble on their home construction project. The homeowner who is prepared and knowledgeable will be able to manage their home construction project to a more successful and less costly conclusion than the homeowner who is not prepared.

The issues presented above are common to all home construction projects. This book has answers and solutions to these issues. These issues need to be understood and defined before hiring a general contractor.

If managing your home construction project without a general contractor is not for you then give yourself a fighting chance to succeed by reading the Pat Fay Method before you hire a general contractor.

Experience/Resume of Pat Fay, PE, BSME

Education: High School diploma, Mercer Island High School, 1969
Bachelor of Science in Mechanical Engineering, University of Washington, 1973
Professional Engineering License: July 2000

Work Experience;

Hydraulic Design Engineer, the Boeing Commercial Airplane Company, November 1973 to March 1975. Designed hydraulic power systems for the 747SP airplane program.

Manufacturing Engineer, April 1975 to February 1976. Started a company manufacturing wooden rocking horses and selling them to daycare centers.

Mechanical Engineer, Formost Packaging Machines March 1976 to December 1976. Designed mechanisms, conveyors and moving components for bread bagging machines.

Field Construction Engineer, Arabian Sundt Limited, Dhahran, Saudi Arabia, April 1977 to May 1979. Field engineer coordinating between office/warehouse and construction supervision. Assisted and ran construction crews in the building of approximately 800 houses for ARAMCO.

Mechanical Field Engineer & Mechanical Superintendent, The Austin Company, June 1979 to April 1981, Seattle, WA & St. Louis, MO. Responsible for managing and directing all mechanical contractors in the construction of industrial facilities for the Boeing Company and McDonald Douglas.

Principal Mechanical Engineer, Metcalf & Eddy in Riyadh, Saudi Arabia, May 1981 to June 1985. Responsible for the resolution of all mechanical design revisions and construction issues relating to the $1.1 billion Royal Saudi Air Force Airbase Upgrade at four airbases to support the Peace Sun F-15 jet fighter program in Saudi Arabia.

Construction & Mechanical Superintendent, the Austin Company, Seattle, WA. October 1985 to May 1986. Responsible for directing and coordinating all subcontractors in the construction of industrial facilities for the Boeing Company.

Project Engineer, Construction Management, Facilities Mechanical Engineer, Cost Estimator, the Boeing Company, Seattle, WA. May 1986 to Present. Responsible for design, construction, operation and cost estimating of facilities for the Boeing Company.

Home Construction Manager, 1992 to 1994. Managed and directed all subcontractors in the construction of our 3500 SF house in Kirkland, WA without a general contractor.

Table of Contents-Overview

i. Dedication
ii. Acknowledgements
iii. Disclaimer
iv. Why this book was written
v. What is the Pat Fay Method?
vi. If the homeowner decides to hire a general contractor
vi. Pat Fay's experience/resume
vii. Table of Contents-Overview
viii. Table of Contents-Detailed

Chapter 1-Introduction to the Pat Fay Method of Home Remodeling and New Construction.. 18

Chapter 2-Planning and Preliminary Design by the Homeowner...................... 33

Chapter 3-The Home Construction Meeting.. 48

Chapter 4-The Final Design Process by your Architect or Building Designer...... 56

Chapter 5-Scheduling.. 70

Chapter 6-Working with your City; Permitting and The Building Inspector......... 77

Chapter 7-Insurance.. 89

Chapter 8-Project Safety.. 92

Chapter 9-Contract Documents... 99

Chapter 10-The Change Order.. 121

Chapter 11-The Contractor.. 130

Chapter 12-Managing and Using Competition to Drive Down the Cost of the Home Construction Project... 150

Chapter 13-Construction Materials... 156

Chapter 14-The Construction Phase: Monitoring and Inspection..................... 164

Chapter 15-Home Construction Pricing & Cost Estimating............................. 178

Chapter 16- Lessons Learned from Homeowners... 220

Chapter 17-Summary of the Advantages and Disadvantages of the Pat Fay Method 226

Chapter 18-Contractor Licensing and Control by State…………………………… 229

Chapter 19-Construction Management forms………………………………………… 234

Table of Contents-Detailed

- i. Dedication
- ii Acknowledgements
- iii. Disclaimer
- iv. Why this book was written
- v. What is the Pat Fay Method?
- vi. If the homeowner decides to hire a general contractor
- vi. Pat Fay's experience/resume
- vii. Table of Contents-Overview
- viii. Table of Contents-Detailed

Chapter 1-Introduction to the Pat Fay Method of Home Remodeling and New Construction.. 18

What the homeowner will learn
What the homeowner will not learn
Pat Fay's class
The standard contractor method of home construction and why they are so expensive
    The best scenario offered by the general contractor
    The surprise change order
    Unpaid suppliers
    Not included in the contract
    Change orders for minor errors and omissions in the plans
    The building inspector caused additional work
    The homeowner pays for excellent quality materials but the general contractor installs the cheapest materials possible
    The homeowner expects high quality workmanship but only poor or average quality workmanship is delivered
    General contractor says the work is completed but it is not
    Excessive subcontractor markup by the general contractor
    The worst scenario offered by the general contractor
The differences and advantages of the Pat Fay Method
No method can provide you with complete protection
Why manage your project yourself?
    Reduced stress
    Quality of workmanship
    Quality of materials
    Control
    Lower overall construction cost
Arbitration, not lawsuits, to settle differences
Be wary of construction management books meant for industrial or commercial projects
Qualifications & time needed to manage according to the Pat Fay Method
    Skills needed: communication, organization, records and knowledge
    Know what you want
How the remodel or new construction process will affect your life and your relationship with your spouse or significant other

      Work as a team to build respect in your family relationship
      Select one person to be the final decision maker (preferably not the man)
      New construction is a hard project; a remodel is even harder
      Where to live while construction is underway
You will feel one of two ways at the end of this book – empowered or overwhelmed
This is a new method; we can expect push back from those vested in the status quo

Chapter 2-Planning and Preliminary Design by the Homeowner……………………….. 33

Your house theme or project mission statement
For the homeowner the planning & preliminary design is one process
What is the planning process?
      Planning is fun
      What kind of project is it?
            Minor projects
            Major projects
      Defining the work you want to accomplish
      Examples of the planning process
            Kitchen, bathroom, family room
What is the preliminary design process?
      Preliminary design is not as much fun
            Cost considerations
      Doing your preliminary design
            Sketching
            Floor layouts
            Let the ideas grow in your mind
            Plan and elevation views
            The use of pictures to define the design
The 3-ring binder is the backbone of your planning & preliminary design process
      What should go into your design binder?
      How to organize your 3-ring binder
            The section tabs you may want to use to organize your design binder
                  Write you ideas down on a piece of paper, date and file
Your first call and visit to the city about your building permit
      The city's permitting requirements
      Review the requirements only; do not try to understand them
      You want a building permit
            The best reason to have a permit
            Having a permit affects your house resale value
            Small projects may not need a permit
Make your major changes in the planning/preliminary design phase
Purchasing pre-designed plans
Finalizing your planning and preliminary design
      Copy for your architect or building designer
How long should your planning and preliminary design take?
      List of section tabs for 3-ring binder organization

Chapter 3-The Home Construction Meeting……………………………………….. 48

Why to have meetings
The five types of meetings under the Pat Fay Method
Where to have the meetings
When to have the meetings
Who should be at the meetings?
How often should you have the meetings?
The meeting agenda with a time limit
How to conduct the meetings
Take meeting minutes
How to behave in the meetings
      You and your spouse are a team of professionals
      There is no room for pointing fingers of blame
How to respond to controversial ideas or proposals
Closing the meeting
Brainstorming
Problems that happen in meetings
Guidelines
Sample of agenda
Sample of meeting minutes

Chapter 4-The Final Design Process by your Architect or Building Designer………. 56

Does the homeowner need an architect or building designer?
    Why you need an architect or building designer
        The architect is the expert in the building code
    What is an architect?
    What is a building designer?
Do you need a structural engineer?
    Why you need a structural engineer
Do you need a civil, electrical, or mechanical engineer?
Do you need an interior designer?
The design build contractor
Finding an architect/designer
    Interviewing the architect/designer
    The second interview
    Final selection of the architect/designer
Negotiating with the architect/designer
    The most important thing to negotiate with your architect/designer
    Other terms to negotiate with your architect/designer
    The design schedule
What you can expect to pay for design services
    Lump sum fee vs. an hourly rate for design services
Signing a contract for design services
    The drawings you should receive from the architect/designer
    Have specifications and material requirements on the drawings

  Purchasing pre-designed plans
Working with your architect/designer
  How to interact with the architect/designer
  The preliminary design phase
  Increase to the design fee as a result of late owner changes
  The final design phase
  You are the final decision maker
Other services provided by your architect/designer for an additional fee

Chapter 5-Scheduling... 70

What is a schedule?
  The Gantt chart
Two types of schedules
  High level schedule, low level detailed schedule
The two kinds of schedules
  Straight line activity schedule
  Modified straight line activity schedule
Common tracking elements
What goes into your schedule?
  The elements of a schedule
Where does the homeowner find out how long a construction activity should take to accomplish?
Is scheduling difficult?
  Build in buffer times
How to make your project schedule
  Draw your own schedules
The use of the schedule during your project for time and cost
  The biggest scheduling issue Pat Fay encountered
    One contractor on site at a time
What to do when a schedule is not being met by the contractor
What to do when a contractor is way behind schedule
  Contractor is about a week behind schedule but on site daily
  Contractor is several weeks behind schedule and on site only infrequently
  Contractor started the project but only worked a few days and then disappeared
Schedule disadvantage of the Pat Fay Method
The realities of scheduling in the homeowner construction world
How long will your project take?
How long did Pat Fay's new house project take?
Example schedules
  High level straight line schedule, SCH-1
  High level modified straight line schedule, SCH-2
Schedule of project activities in building Pat Fay's house, SCH-3

Chapter 6-Working with your City; Permitting and the Building Inspector............ 77

What is a building permit?

Why you want a building permit
    Why your city wants you to have a permit
The homeowner's responsibility in regards to the permit
The homeowner's responsibility in regards to the building code
What is the building code?
    Why there is a code
    The building code is a minimum requirement only
    The code is a science and an art
    Your state has a building code
    Your city's amendments to the code
Working with your city to get your permit
    The building official's role in applying the code to your project
    The personality and attitude of your city
    The Pat Fay Method is allowed by the building code
        A word about the State of Louisiana
Pat Fay's permitting experience
Keeping notes and your cool when dealing with the city
    Questions you do not ask your city
    Questions you do ask your city
    Legal complaints against your city regarding your permit
    There are different departments in the city
What to do when your permit seems to be lost in the city
When you do not use your architect/designer in the permit process
When you do use your architect/designer in the permit process
Be wary of beginning your project with only a demolition permit
What to do while your project is in permitting
What to do when you receive your construction permit from the city
The Building Inspector
    The inspection department is not the building department
    The role of the city in the enforcement of the code
    The building inspector's right to inspect
    The work must remain accessible
    What work needs to be inspected by the city inspector?
    The homeowner's inspection duties

Chapter 7-Insurance.. 89

Speak to your personal homeowner insurance agent
    Your homeowner's insurance & the extended umbrella policy
Homeowner's construction insurance
    Coverage for liability, material theft and vandalism
    Discount available before construction starts
The contractor's insurance coverage
    Have your name listed on the contractor's insurance
State industrial insurance and workers compensation
On site construction safety and the construction safety plan
    A fence helps

Chapter 8-Project Safety.. **92**

Why is safety important?
Who is responsible for safety?
    The homeowner's role in safety
        Safety for the homeowner's family and friends
    The contractor's role in safety
What is safety?
    Safe work environment
    Unsafe behavior
    Personal protective equipment (PPE)
Safety for the homeowner on their own construction site
Contractor safety
    The contractor's safety meeting and safety plan
Providing hardhats and safety glasses
General safety rules for the homeowner
General safety rules for the contractor

Chapter 9-Contract Documents.. **99**

What are contract documents?
Contract law and the home construction project
What is a contract?
What is a contract versus what is a proposal?
The contract is a document for both the homeowner and the contractor
    The intent of the contract agreement
    Honoring the intent of the contract by the homeowner
    Honoring the intent of the contract by the contractor
What should not be in the contract: paying 50% of the money at the time the contract is
    signed
    Why the homeowner should not pay 50% of the money
    The contractor states they need the money to buy materials.
    Material can be sent to the homeowner's project on credit.
    The contractor can go to their banker.
    The contractor can pay for the materials themselves as their bond
    Exceptions to the rule of not paying 50%
What should be in the contract?
How long and complicated should the contract be?
When to sign the contract
    Do not follow mainstream construction management books
How to modify the contractor's contract
    What is an addendum to the contract?
    The addendum is a simple way to modify the contractor's contract
    How to attach the addendum to the contractor's contract
    Mark up the contractor's contract proposal
What is a scope of work?

What are specifications?
    How to use specifications to define materials and quality
Types of contracts to use in home construction
    Fixed price contract
    Time and material contract
    Offered price contract
Material and labor costs can be broken out
    Equipment costs
    Why the homeowner wants to see costs broken out
How to control change order costs
    Use of the No Verbal Changes form
    Understanding liens
        What is a notice to lien?
        What is a lien?
        What is a lien release?
    The importance of receiving the lien release
How to resolve an impasse between the homeowner and the contractor
    When the homeowner and the contractor agree to disagree
    Arbitration
    The arbitrator agrees with the homeowner and the contractor fixes the problem
    The arbitrator agrees with the homeowner but will not allow the contractor to fix
        the problem
    Arbitrator agrees with the contractor
Contact an arbitration firm before the first contractor is hired.
    What kind of arbitrator does the homeowner hire?
Avoid lawsuits
Paying the contractor
    When to pay the contractor
    How to pay the contractor
        Use the two party check
    Getting the lien release from the contractor's material suppliers
There is no room for trust in the home construction contracting world
A word of encouragement to the homeowner that feels overwhelmed
A sample contract and a sample addendum

Chapter 10-The Change Order... 121

What is a change order?
How the change order can ruin the homeowner's project
Legitimate change orders
    Example of a legitimate change order
What are not legitimate change orders
    Minor errors and omissions on the plans
    Answering questions or clarifying something in the plans
    The surprise change order at the end of the project
    The building or site conditions are different
    The building inspector's requirements have caused additional costs

    Any change that does not increase labor or material costs.
    Expensive materials that are shown on the drawings or were agreed to in writing.
    The increase in cost change order for no legitimate reason
 How to respond to a change order request from the contractor
 How to control change orders on your project
    Use the No Verbal Orders (NVC) change order form
    The use of the NVC form must be negotiated into the contract
    Define the hourly rate to be charged for change order work
    When to use the NVC form
      Increases to the cost change order
      Decreases to the cost change order
      No cost change order
    How to use the NVC form
    Example of how to fill out a NVC form for a new door
      If you cannot come to an agreement on the price
    Sample NVC form

Chapter 11-The Contractor.. 130

Why is a contractor called a contractor?
What is a contractor?
Definition of the terms: general contractor, builder, contractor, and subcontractor
Pat Fay's opinion of contractors
How to find contractors
    It is a myth that contractors are hard to find
    Look in the yellow pages
    Talk to your friends and associates
    Look on the Internet
    Contact local material supply houses
    Do not pass up building sites
    Look in the smaller outlying town newspapers
    Place your own advertisement in the newspaper
    Go to a freeway overpass
    Home Depot and Lowe's
      Advantages and disadvantages of Lowe's and Home Depot
      Pat Fay used Home Depot to install a roof
    Costco and other companies
    If you do have difficulty finding contractors in your area
      Move down the contractor food chain
      Pay a premium or bonus
How to screen contractors during the selection process
    Remember you are forming a business partnership
    Discuss your project and what you are planning to do
    Two questions the homeowner must ask the contractor
      Are you an expert in your field of construction?
      Why should the homeowner use your company?
    Review the contractor's project 3-ring binder

      Look at the contractor's current project
      Look at the contractor's previous work
      Contact your State Department of Labor and Industries
Getting pricing from the contractor
      Ask the contractor if they charge for an estimate
      The detailed price breakdown will cost money
Final selection of your contractors
      Negotiating construction start date
      Negotiating price
            Comparison to the homeowner's cost estimate
            Comparison to other prices or bids
      Negotiating contract terms with the contractor
      When to sign the contract
Problems contractors have in conducting business
      Knowledge and experience
      Education
      Business issues
      Construction labor issues
      Material issues
      Quality and workmanship issues
      Mistakes
Guidelines for contractors who want to work according to the Pat Fay Method
Conversation between Pat Fay and a successful general contractor
      Homeowners need to come on site daily
      There should only be one decision maker in the construction process
      The issue of change orders and charging the homeowner additional money
      Contractors are builders first and businessmen second
The con man contractor
      There is no room for trust in home construction
      The key to the con man contractor
      The con man contractor and the law
      About the con man contractor
      What motivates the con man contractor?
      How to identify the con man contractor
      Legitimate contractors act insulted
      The Pat Fay Method is a new idea
      Pat Fay's two experiences with the con man contractor

Chapter 12-Managing and Using Competition to Drive Down the Cost of the Home Construction Project... 150

The pure Pat Fay Method for managing the home construction project
      Hire a different contractor for each phase of the project
      Who are the different contractors the homeowner needs to hire?
Acceptable modification from the pure Pat Fay Method
Two methods of driving down the project cost
      Competition drives down the project cost

    Bidding out project work packages
      The pre-bid walk through
      Contractors see the actual work site
      Contractors see each other. Therefore, they compete
      An interesting thing happens at the pre-bid walk through
      How to conduct the pre-bid walk through
        A simple example: replace kitchen cabinets
        A more complex example: concrete foundation
      Other details for the pre-bid walk through
Request for proposal (RFP)
    How to issue the request for proposal
    A sample RFP letter

Chapter 13-Construction Materials... 156

Material quality is important.
    Strength and grade type materials
    Finish materials
Methods of acquiring the materials needed to build your project
    The homeowner buys the materials
      Getting good pricing for materials
    Having the contractor supply the materials
      The contractor discount
      Does the homeowner share in the contractor discount?
    Where to buy the materials
      The advantage of Lowe's and Home Depot warehouses
      Home Depot and Lowe's install the materials they sell
      Disadvantage of Lowe's and Home Depot
      Pat Fay used Home Depot to install a roof
Paying for materials
    When the homeowner buys the material
    When the contractor buys the material
      The two party check
      What if you never received a notice to lien from a supplier?
      Get your material lien release
      Review of notice to lien, liens and lien release
Inspection and counting of delivered material
    Incorrect or damaged material

Chapter 14-The Construction Phase: Monitoring and Inspection.................. 164

What is the construction phase?
Being prepared for the construction phase
A few steps to get started
    Step 1: Build the construction phase 3-ring binder
    Step 2: Take pictures before, during and after
    Step 3: Have an arbitrator lined up

- Step 4: Have insurance coverage updated
- Step 5: Call before digging underground
- Step 6: The homeowner hires their first contractor and turns them loose

A review of construction safety
- What to do if the contractor is not following their safety plan

Managing relationship with the contractor during the construction process
- The homeowner visits the site daily.
- Working and negotiating with the contractor on site
- Have a single point of contact
- This is a business relationship
- Short construction coordination meetings when the homeowner comes on site
    - Leaving notes for the contractor
- Maintain communication
    - Allow the contractor to vent
    - Do not embarrass the contractor in front of their workers
    - The homeowner's behavior
    - When to call the police

Managing the quality of the work by monitoring and inspecting the work
- Why should the homeowner inspect daily?
- An example of what can happen if the homeowner does not inspect
- Carry the construction 3-ring binder
- Use the daily construction log
- Use of the request for information form (RFI)
- What to do if the contractor will not sign the RFI form?
- When the homeowner does not feel qualified to inspect a phase of construction

Monitoring and inspecting the materials used on site

Managing the inspections by the city building inspector
- Post the building permit on site
- Call for inspection per the city's requirements
- Working with the building inspector
- The building inspector only inspects per the requirements of the code
- Exceptions to the completed work by the inspector
- Contractor's responsibility to fix or repair
- Inspector signs off on a phase of construction

Monitoring and tracking the construction schedule
- Measuring or determining the amount of completed work

Controlling change orders in the construction phase
- The homeowner has a right to make changes
- With this right comes the responsibility to pay
- Use the no verbal changes form (NVC)
- What to do when the contractor suggests a change
- Changes the homeowner wants
- Changes the homeowner does not want
- What to do when the contractor asks for more money for no reason
- Are there changes driven by the building inspector? This is a trick question

Paying the contractor

Project money management

      How to use the cost control form
      Project money management must be kept up daily

Chapter 15-Home Construction Pricing & Cost Estimating.............................. 178

Pat Fay's goal in the home construction pricing and estimating chapter
What is home construction pricing?
Three methods of arriving at construction pricing
      Gathering home construction pricing from contactors
            Contact 6 to 10 contractors
                  An example in pricing a new 200 amp electrical panel
      Use Home Depot, Lowe's and Costco for comparative pricing
            Contractors must beat Costco, Lowe's and Home Depot pricing by 20%
What is cost estimating?
      Cost estimating for the homeowner
            Budgetary estimating
                  Residential SF costs from RS Means Company
            Detailed takeoff from drawings
            What does square foot costs mean?
            Determining square footage
            Square foot cost by activity
            Square foot costs go down for larger jobs, up for smaller jobs
            Cost by lineal foot
The Pat Fay Method of how to think about estimating
      Think in terms of labor, material, equipment, contractor profit
            Estimating labor according to crew size
                  What hourly rate to pay for labor
            Estimating material cost for an activity
            Estimating equipment cost for an activity
Adding contingency or risk to the estimate
Overtime will destroy a homeowner's budget
Contractor profit
      What is a reasonable profit for the contractor?

Detailed cost estimating sections.. 189

1. Design, structural engineering, civil engineering, surveying, permit fees, scaffolding, portable toilets

2. Utility trench by trencher, utility trench by backhoe, excavation for a basement, exterior grading.

3. Underground Utilities; water, sewer, electrical power, natural gas, telephone

4. Concrete foundations; spread footings & concrete walls

5. Framing & insulation.

6. Drywall/sheetrock; tape & mud, PVA coating, texture

7. Roofing & flashing, gutters & downspouts.

8. Exterior siding.

9. Finishes; doors & hardware, windows, flooring, kitchen cabinets, counters

10. Appliances

11. Plumbing; underground plumbing, above ground rough-in plumbing, finish plumbing: kitchen sink with garbage disposal, all other sinks, kitchen appliances, toilets, showers, bathtubs, laundry room, hot water tank, and hot water recirculation system.

12. Heating Ventilating and Air Conditioning (HVAC)

13. Electrical and Communications. Detailed costs; electrical panel, dedicated 120V outlet for a microwave or furnace, 6 outlets on one circuit, light switch, light, stove, electric clothes dryer, air conditioning compressor, hot water heater, telephone/data outlet.

14. Concrete flatwork; sidewalks, driveways, patios.

15. Decks

Chapter 16- Lessons Learned from Homeowners………………………… 220

Situation 1: Planning for a kitchen remodel
    Lesson learned #1-Do not hire a designer before deciding what you want
    Lesson learned #2-Do not remove scope of work to reduce cost of project
    Lesson learned #3-Get pricing from 6 to 10 contractors
    Lesson learned #4-Homeowner's mistaken feelings of trust
    Lesson learned #5-Homeowner's mistaken feelings of obligation
    Lesson learned #6-Homeowner not wanting to hurt the contractor's feelings
    Lesson learned #7-Homeowner is afraid to say "No, I will not use you on this project!"
Situation 2: Work on a backyard garden structure
    Lesson learned #8- Do not pay the contractor until project is complete
    Lesson learned #9- Do not give contractor any money to buy materials
    Lesson learned #10-Homeowner mistakenly concerned about being fair to the contractor
    Lesson learned #11-Trust in the Pat Fay Method

Chapter 17-Summary of the Advantages and Disadvantages of the Pat Fay Method.. 226

Advantages
      Cost savings
      Reduced stress
      Better quality material and workmanship
Disadvantages
      Planning and scheduling
      Coordination
      Time
      Length of construction
To use the Pat Fay Method or not?

Chapter 18-Contractor Licensing and Control by State...................... 229

Chapter 19-Pat Fay Method Home Construction Management Forms................. 234

      Project Log-Planning
      Project Log-Construction
      No Verbal Changes (NVC)
      Cost Control
      Contract for Construction Services
      Addendum to the Contract for Construction Services
      Daily Construction Record
      Request for Information (RFI)
      Telephone Conversation Record
      Transmittal Form
      Meeting Minutes
      Contractor Information Sheet
      Lien Release and Claim Waiver Form
      Contractor Bid or Price Review Form
      Schedule Form-High Level
      Schedule Form-Low Level Detailed

Chapter 1-Introduction to the Pat Fay Method of Home Remodeling and New Construction

What the homeowner will learn
What the homeowner will not learn
Pat Fay's class
The standard contractor method of home construction and why they are so expensive
- The best scenario offered by the general contractor
- The general contractor rarely shows up on the construction site
- The surprise change order
- Unpaid suppliers
- Not included in the contract
- Change orders for minor errors and omissions in the plans
- The building inspector caused additional work
- The homeowner pays for excellent quality materials but the general contractor installs the cheapest materials possible
- The homeowner expects high quality workmanship but only poor or average quality workmanship is delivered
- General contractor says the work is completed but it is not
- Excessive subcontractor markup by the general contractor
- The worst scenario offered by the general contractor

The differences and advantages of the Pat Fay Method
No method can provide you with complete protection
Why manage your project yourself?
- Reduced stress
- Quality of workmanship
- Quality of materials
- Control
- Lower overall construction cost

Arbitration, not lawsuits, to settle differences
Be wary of construction management books meant for industrial or commercial projects
Qualifications & time needed to manage according to the Pat Fay Method
- Skills needed: communication, organization, records and knowledge
- Know what you want

How the remodel or new construction process will affect your life and your relationship with your spouse or significant other
- Work as a team to build respect in your family relationship
- Select one person to be the final decision maker (preferably not the man)
- New construction is a hard project; a remodel is even harder
- Where to live while construction is underway

You will feel one of two ways at the end of this book – empowered or overwhelmed
This is a new method; we can expect push back from those vested in the status quo

Chapter 1-Introduction to the Pat Fay Method of Home Remodeling and New Construction

What the homeowner will learn. The homeowner will learn that by managing your own project you will not only greatly reduce the cost to build but you will also learn that your frustration and stress level will also be greatly reduced. You will learn how to define exactly what you want by establishing a theme (your hearts desire) and planning your remodel or new construction around it. You will learn how to define what you want and how to confidently make decisions that make your project happen. You will learn how to deal effectively with contractors because you possess what they desire most: money. Most importantly you will learn from Pat Fay's mistakes and other common errors made by homeowners before you build so that you do not have to repeat them. You will learn how to manage and be in control of your project, particularly in control of your money. You will learn the most powerful tool you possess is the power of your checkbook. Give it away needlessly and will learn the hard way what the true meaning of regret is.

You will learn that it is easier to be in charge of your project then to turn over the responsibility to a general contractor. You have a personal commitment to see your project is done well. A general contractor has a money incentive to see it done as quickly as possible. You will not cut corners but a general contractor will. It is true that the responsibility for your project will be yours. Remember though, it is not that you have to do all phases of the construction process yourself but it is your responsibility to see that all phases of the construction process are accomplished by the contractors you hire.

What the homeowner will not learn. You will not learn how to become a general contractor and go into business for yourself building houses. That is not the intent of this book. This book teaches homeowners how to manage their home construction or remodel, and how to manage the contractors they hire to do that work.

This book is not a cookbook with set steps for the homeowner to follow. It is a book that informs and empowers the homeowner to become a project manager in the management of the construction of their new home or in the remodel of their existing home.

Pat Fay's Class. During the body of this and other chapters I often mention 'my class'. I am referring to a 3.5 hour class that I have taught since 1996 where I teach homeowners how to manage their home construction projects without a general contractor. That is where the idea for this book originated.

The standard general contractor method of home construction and why they are so expensive. The standard of home remodel or new construction in America today is for the homeowner to hire a general contractor to do their whole remodel or all of their new construction project. Some homeowners hire their own architect or designer and some hire the architect/designer who is employed by the general contractor. The general contractors with inhouse design capability typically call themselves design build contractors. Either way, once the design is complete the typical homeowner then turns over the responsibility of the construction project completely to a general contractor.

The next step is for the homeowner to sign a construction contract and to pay up to 50% of the total cost at the time the contract is signed. The typical homeowner does this even though *no work has been accomplished*. On larger projects the 50% may be replaced by a large sum of money that changes hands in the range of $40,000 to $100,000 as a down payment to get the project started.

This is when the vast majority of home construction projects start going bad. Once the contract is signed and money has been given to the general contractor, the standard contractor method can branch out into a number of scenarios. These are:

The best scenario offered by the general contractor. The best scenario that can occur is where the homeowner has hired the best general contractor to be found. The general contractor uses your down payment money to pay for the building permit and to buy materials for your project, puts their workers to work doing their specialties and hires subcontractors to do those work packages most suitable for subcontracting. They work diligently, ask clarification questions when needed of the homeowner but do not charge the homeowner any money for these questions. They ignore the minor omissions and errors found in all drawings, they have the building inspector sign off on all the those portions of the work that require the building inspector's signature, and complete the project on time. They submit a bill for their final payment and sign a lien release. If subcontractors and suppliers have filed a notice to lean the general contractor gets them to sign a lien release as well.

The homeowner then makes the final payment to the general contractor, the general contractor pays off all the subcontractors and suppliers, the homeowner receives the final occupancy permit and the keys to the completed project. The homeowner is happy because their project is completed and it has cost what was agreed to all those months ago when the contract was signed. The contractor goes away happy because they have received the money due for the work.

The only negative to this scenario is that the homeowner will be paying too much money for the service the general contractor provides. Anything over $100/SF for a new home or major remodel is too much.

The general contractor rarely shows up on the construction site. The general contractor will rarely show up on your construction site because they send their workers and subcontractors to do the work for them. Once a phase of construction is complete most general contractors don't even bother to show up on your construction site to check the quality of the work by their employees and subcontractors. They act just as a broker. Why bother using them when the homeowner can act as the broker themselves.

The surprise change order. Everything on your home construction projects goes as described in the best scenario except that at the end of the project when the homeowner makes their final payment to the general contractor they are handed a change order detailing all of the changes supposedly requested by the owner. This will take the homeowner completely by surprise and the cost can be tens or hundreds of thousands of dollars.

Unpaid suppliers. Everything on your home construction projects goes as described in the best scenario, the homeowner makes their final payment to the general contractor and both parties go away happy. Then a few weeks later letters from suppliers begin to arrive asking for payment for the materials supplied to your project that have not been paid for by the general contractor. If the general contractor does not pay these bills then it is the homeowner who must pay for the material a second time. This will also take the homeowner completely by surprise and the cost can be tens or hundreds of thousands of dollars, depending on how many suppliers are left unpaid.

Not included in the contract. In this scenario the homeowner and contractor have agreed that the project will cost a certain amount of money. At some point in the construction the general contractor will claim that some portion of the work was not included in the contract. The homeowner had believed all of the work needed to be done to accomplish the contracted scope of work was to be included in the original price. Now that the contract is signed, the project is underway and payments have been made, the homeowner is surprised by the general contractor's claim that the plumbing or electrical or the finish work was not included in the agreed to price.

Change orders for minor errors and omissions in the plans. During construction there will always be questions that the general contractor needs to ask the homeowner to clarify the intent of the drawings. The very best drawings are about 90% complete and there are always some minor errors and omissions in the plans. Therefore, it is legitimate for the contractor to ask questions. It is not legitimate to ask for additional compensation just because the homeowner has answered questions. For example, if a wall is not yet built and the contractor asks a question about the location of the window opening and the homeowner decides to move it a few feet from where the plans indicate, then making a change of this type should not require extra payment.

An example of an error in the plans is if the drawings do not show a header for a window or door. This is an error but it is not a legitimate reason for the contractor to claim that they need additional labor and material to install the header. This is because the general contractor knows that there is always a header installed above a door or window. This is their responsibility as an expert builder.

An example of an omission error in the plans would be where no anchor bolts were shown on the foundation drawing for holding down the framing bottom plate. This would not be an extra cost because the code requires the anchor bolts and an expert general contractor will know this.

The building inspector caused additional work. In this scenario the general contractor claims that the building inspector caused them to do additional work resulting in additional charges to the homeowner. The building inspector is never the cause of changes. The building inspector only inspects per the requirements of the building code. The building code is a minimum requirement that the general contractor is supposed to know inside and out. It is never legitimate to charge the homeowner for mistakes made by the general contractor or their poorly trained employees. It is always their responsibility to build according to the requirements of the building code. The building code is the contractor's construction rule book.

The homeowner pays for excellent quality materials but the general contractor installs the cheapest materials possible. In this scenario the homeowner, during negotiations with the general contractor, will have specified that they only want the highest quality materials installed in their house. The contractor typically states that will cost more money. The homeowner agrees to pay additional money. Then during construction an inferior, low grade product will show up on site and be installed.

This issue is really a significant problem. The typical homeowner usually does not even notice that the inferior product is installed until after the fact. Then it is really a fight to get it changed out. The contractor will claim all sorts of excuses.

One example is from an experience one of my students related to me when they had a deck installed. They had specified in the written contract that only 2x4 cedar boards were to be used for the deck planking. She was on site when the decking material was delivered and it was not 2x4 but rather ¾ cedar decking. She spoke to the contractor about the wrong material being delivered and she was told that the delivery company had just delivered the wrong material. Don't worry we will send it back and get the 2x4 cedar decking. The next day when she came back all of the ¾" material was installed and the contractor refused to replace it. He even had the nerve to say that the 2x4 cedar would cost too much money. This was after the homeowner had already paid a premium for the 2x4 cedar decking. If the contractor will not change out the incorrect material you will need the services of your arbitrator.

Often though the homeowner will have only verbally told the contractor that they wanted 2x4 cedar decking. In this case you will want something in writing that you directed the contractor to remove the material from the site. You will need to fill out an RFI form (request for information). You will write out the fact that the wrong material was delivered, that you want it removed from the site, and that you want 2x4 cedar decking to be installed as agreed to. Then you sign it and also have the contractor sign it. Now you have documentation. Just the mere fact that you knew to go the RFI route will more than likely convince the contractor to install the correct material. If not then you have documentation to help the arbitrator establish fault.

The homeowner expects high quality workmanship but only poor or average quality workmanship is delivered. The best example I can give is from a couple who took my class. They had the front of their house remodeled to remove several small windows and install a large single piece window to take advantage of the view. After the project was complete they were enjoying dinner and admiring the view when the wife noticed that the window looked crooked. They set a carpenters level on the window and found that it was indeed not level. When they called the general contractor to come and fix the window they were told that they had only paid for average quality workmanship. If they wanted excellent workmanship they would have to pay an additional fee.

General contractor says the work is completed but it is not. In this scenario the general contractor will say the work is complete and that they want their money. You know the work is not complete. The contractor will not listen to reason. What to do? Simply call your arbitrator. They will know how to handle the situation and they will help the homeowner resolve the situation.

Excessive subcontractor markup by the general contractor. A standard practice by general contractors is to take a subcontractors bill and mark it up by 200% to 500%. For example if the plumber charges $8,000 to plumb a new house the general contractor will actually charge the homeowner $16,000 to $40,000. They then take the difference between what the plumber actually cost and what they charge the homeowner as pure profit. A generation ago the general contractors would only markup a subcontractor's bill by 25%.

The worst scenario offered by the general contractor. The worst scenario that can occur is where the homeowner has hired what they consider to be a good general contractor. They sign the contractor's contract and at the same time hand the contractor a check for say $60,000 because the general contractor told them they need it to buy materials and get started. Besides that is how it is done.

The contractor goes straight to their bank deposits your check into their corporate account. Once it clears they have the funds transferred to their personal account, have a certified check made out to them from the bank, close their checking accounts and leave town.

Don't think this cannot happen because it does all too often. When I was first teaching my classes I used to tell my students that one way to eliminate the worst scenario from occurring was to only use contractors off their banks recommended list. After I said that in a class, years ago, a woman raised her hand and told how her neighbor had used a general contractor from the bank's list, signed a contract for their new house to be built, gave the contractor a check for $75,000 and then he disappeared. I did not use that statement again in my class.

The scenarios that actually happen to homeowners may be one or more of the scenarios described above. There may also be novel and new ways for the homeowner to be treated poorly by their general contractor.

The typical homeowner hasn't had much of a choice before the Pat Fay Method because the home construction process is so confusing. I believe that there really has been no one to inform the homeowner about what is the best process to follow, in what order to do the work, how long each phase of the work will take and how much each phase should cost.

The differences and advantages of the Pat Fay Method. The main difference of the Pat Fay Method is to eliminate the general contractor completely by hiring specialty contractors to do each different phase of the work.

The advantage of this is that if the homeowner is unfortunate enough to hire a bad contractor it will not be for the whole project. The homeowner can either limp through that phase of the project with the problem contractor, call their arbitrator or fire them. Either way, you will soon be rid of the problem contractor. Then you and your project can move on to the next phase of your project.

Also, your financial risk is greatly reduced. Since there are about 20 phases to your construction project, you only risk about 5% of your project cost on any one contractor. By limiting the size of the contracts you further reduce the financial risk. Rather than sign a contract for your entire project, the Pat Fay Method recommends that you contract out smaller phases of your project. If a contractor does well on the first contract then you can use them on the next or other phases of your construction.

Another advantage of the Pat Fay Method is that merely by reading this book the homeowner is now aware of what can go wrong. Then they can take steps to ensure that they are not one of the homeowners taken by bad contractors.

The single most important difference and advantage to the homeowner from the Pat Fay Method is the knowledge that they do not have to give the contractor any money at the time they sign the contract.

Last but not least, the homeowner can build for a much lower price than that offered by the general contractor even if they make a lot of mistakes.

No method can provide you with complete protection. No method, including the Pat Fay Method, can completely shield you from the bad contractor. Bad contractors are just too resourceful and unscrupulous to be stopped. However, one of the goals of the Pat Fay Method is to make the homeowner aware ahead of time what some of the potential pitfalls are. It also can help you limit the size of your risk and financial exposure. Then you can still have a successful project in spite of the fact that you encounter a bad contractor or two in the home construction process.

Why manage your project yourself?

    Reduced stress. Money is typically what most people believe to be the main reason for managing their project themselves. However, to me it is the reduced level of frustration and stress once into construction. The homeowner is always dismayed by how frustrating the construction process is with a general contracting company that promises a comprehensive construction service but actually delivers something far less. The result is the homeowner gets frustrated, then angry, and as a result their stress level increases dramatically. Increased stress can cause both health problems and marital relationship problems. Sadly, I know of many instances where couples almost divorced as a result of their remodel or new home construction project.
    Don't misunderstand me though because managing the home construction project is stressful. The point I am making though is that the stress level you will experience managing the process yourself will be far less than if you hired a general contractor to do the work.

    Quality of workmanship. The quality of the construction workmanship is critical in all phases of construction. The homeowner will have greater control over the quality of the workmanship by subcontracting out each phase of the work than they will have if they hire a general contractor. In my opinion, most general contractors have their own standard of quality. If a homeowner wants a higher level of quality then the contractor will either ask for more money or just ignore the homeowner.
    In the Pat Fay Method you have more influence over quality because you do not pay the contractor to get started so your money stays in your account. When you inspect the construction work you have the influence of not paying the contractor until the work is done correctly and with excellent quality to your satisfaction. If they do not provide quality workmanship you bring in your arbitrator to help you. If the contractor still will not fix the quality issue even after the arbitrator has ruled in your favor then the arbitrator can bring in one of their contractors to repair and complete the work.

    Quality of materials. The quality of the construction materials is another critical component to the overall quality and long life of your home. If you subcontract out the work you can buy many of the materials yourself to ensure that the quality is as you want it. Then you hire a subcontractor to install the material. If you allow a general contractor complete control they will try to buy the least expensive materials and finishes to put into your house thereby reducing their material cost and increasing their overall profit at your expense.

    Control. If you subcontract out all the work you will be in charge of when the work gets done. It is true that the homeowner will have the increased burden of finding the subcontractors to hire where the general contractor has a list of contractors that he has built up over the years. However, even this should not discourage the homeowner because there are so many contractors and excellent skilled craftsman looking for your work. Another feature of control is that you have the ability to stop the project if you are too stressed out and start it up again after a two week vacation. Not so when you have a general contractor.

In my classes, I have spoken to many homeowners who went on vacation and when they came home their construction project had advanced but they were unhappy with what had been accomplished. Walls were in the wrong place, poor quality materials were installed, and the overall quality of workmanship was poor. They regretted having gone on vacation during their home construction project. If you manage your own project with the Pat Fay Method, you can determine the timeline of your project.

Lower overall construction cost. The homeowner can manage their own project, make just as many mistakes as my wife and I did, and still pay far less than you would if you hired a general contractor. General contractors today are charging extremely high dollar values for low value skills and expertise. Yes, it is hard to build houses properly according to the building code, but it is not difficult. The building code is a minimum standard not a maximum standard.

People have been building houses for centuries. This expertise is common knowledge among general contractors, subcontractors, inspectors, city building departments and suppliers. The only persons who are mystified by the process are homeowners. Remember, this is not commercial or industrial construction. It is just wood framed houses built on concrete foundations assembled largely by young men without high school educations.

There is a way to prove what houses should cost. One is to see chapter 15 and review the cost estimating section. This is Pat Fay's version of house construction estimating. It shows in great detail the cost for each phase of home construction.

Another way is to use cost estimating and construction costs from a highly respected national estimating company. Their name is RS Means and they have cost estimating manuals with all current material and labor costs for industrial, commercial and residential construction. Their employees survey material suppliers, gather labor rates, and measure the productivity of construction workers using the latest tools. They know how long it takes to install a foundation, build walls, install doors and windows, install the electrical systems and everything else that goes into a house. They then publish their data for everyone to see. They know how much the material costs that goes into a house and they know how much labor it actually takes to install all of that material. They then divide the total cost of all labor and material by the square footage of a house to determine the square footage cost.

Any data titled from RS Means comes *"from Means Square Foot Cost Data, 2005. Copyright Reed Construction Data, Kingston, MA 781-585-7880; All rights reserved."* Their website is www.resmeans.com.

First, however, a review of what general contractors are charging for home construction in the Seattle area is useful. I believe these costs are indicative of what is being charged in most of the major cities in America today: too much!

A custom, two story, 3200 SF house with wood siding built by a general contractor in Seattle will be a minimum of $150 to $200 per SF (not including land prices). The homeowner may get quotes for less than this but by the time the house is completed the cost will be in the $150 to $200 per SF range due to change orders and increases to the scope of work that the general contractor says was not included in their original price.

Means Estimating states that this custom, two story, 3200 SF house with wood siding should cost $79.15 per SF in 2005. What is more startling about this number is that it also includes the general contractor's overhead and profit.

A luxury house built by a general contractor in Seattle will be a minimum of $250 to $300 per SF (not including land prices). Once again the homeowner may get quotes for less than this but by the time the house is complete the cost will be in the $250 to $300 per SF range due to change orders and increases to the scope of work that the general contractor says was not included in their original price.

Means Estimating states that this luxury, two story, 3200 SF house, with wood siding should cost $91.05 per SF in 2005. Once again this number includes the general contractor's overhead and profit. Why is there such a large difference between what RS Means says a house should cost and what general contractors charge? It is because the general contractors are charging too much for their services. Where does the extra money go? It goes into the general contractor's pocket as pure profit. Who pays for all that profit? The homeowner does. See the last column of the following charts to see how much money the homeowner is losing to a general contractor.

The following charts show how much extra profit the general contractors of America are receiving per house. These charts show how much a house should cost based on RS Means cost estimating data compared to what the general contractors charge.

Custom House			Low Cost Range-$150/SF		
Square Footage (SF)	RS Means Cost per SF	Final Cost by RS Means	Contractor Cost per SF	Final Cost from the Contractor	Difference (Excess GC Profit)
2400 SF	$88.30/ SF	$211,920	$150/ SF	$360,000	$148,080
3200 SF	$79.15/ SF	$253,280	$150/ SF	$480,000	$226,720
4400 SF	$72.80/ SF	$320,320	$150/ SF	$660,000	$339,680

Luxury House			Low Cost Range-$250/SF		
Square Footage (SF)	RS Means Cost per SF	Final Cost by RS Means	Contractor Cost per SF	Final Cost from the Contractor	Difference (Excess GC Profit)
2400 SF	$101.80/ SF	$244,320	$250/ SF	$600,000	$355,680
3200 SF	$91.05/ SF	$291,360	$250/ SF	$800,000	$508,640
4400 SF	$83.55/ SF	$367,620	$250/ SF	$1,100,000	$732,380

Custom House			High Cost Range-$200/SF		
Square Footage (SF)	RS Means Cost per SF	Final Cost by RS Means	Contractor Cost per SF	Final Cost from the Contractor	Difference (Excess GC Profit)
2400 SF	$88.30/ SF	$211,920	$200/ SF	$480,000	$268,080
3200 SF	$79.15/ SF	$253,280	$200/ SF	$640,000	$386,720
4400 SF	$72.80/ SF	$320,320	$200/ SF	$880,000	$559,680

Luxury House			High Cost Range-$300/SF		
Square Footage (SF)	RS Means Cost per SF	Final Cost by RS Means	Contractor Cost per SF	Final Cost from the Contractor	Difference (Excess GC Profit)
2400 SF	$101.80/ SF	$244,320	$300/ SF	$720,000	$475,680
3200 SF	$91.05/ SF	$291,360	$300/ SF	$960,000	$668,640
4400 SF	$83.55/ SF	$367,620	$300/ SF	$1,320,000	$952,380

Note: The difference between the custom and luxury houses is in the quality of the materials and workmanship. The custom house will have materials and workmanship above average. The luxury house will have extraordinary materials and workmanship as well as many special features.

You will notice that as the size of the house gets larger the cost to build it per SF goes down. This is true because as you build a larger house the cost of the labor and material needed to build decreases per square foot. You just don't use as much material and labor per square foot to build a large house as a smaller house. This is very useful information to the homeowner because they typically do not know this. General contractors do not tell the homeowner this detail.

As you can see the dollar incentive to manage your own project without a general contractor is high. The homeowner can save serious money by managing their home construction project without a general contractor.

Arbitration not lawsuits to settle differences. In the Pat Fay Method the goal is to complete the home construction project. It is not to punish the bad contractors you run into along the way. Therefore, I do not recommend suing any of your contractors. Rather you will want to hire an experienced arbitrator to help resolve whatever problem you have with your contractors.

Civil lawsuits in our society are just not effective. Even if you are 100% sure that you will win your case it will still cost you a lot of money to prosecute. Lawyers charge $250 to $300 per hour. You could easily estimate 120 hours of work by your attorney for a simple lawsuit. This would be $30,000. It will also take a long time; probably about 2 years.

Also, even if you win your lawsuit there is no guarantee that your bad contractor will have any money. The typical contractor will have either spent your money on another project or spent it going on vacation. It is gone. If you spend money on a lawsuit you will be throwing good money after bad. Besides you need that money to finish your project.

Your arbitrator also charges about $250 per hour but the amount of time to resolve the situation will be much less. The arbitrator will come to your construction site, interview you, take a look at the problem, interview the contractor, and make his/her judgment. For a simple issue you are probably looking at 4 hours. For a complicated issue it may take up to 16 hours. This is a range of $1,000 to $4,000. This is still expensive but much less expensive than a civil lawsuit and it will be resolved more quickly. Then you can get back to your home construction project.

Be wary of construction management books meant for industrial or commercial projects. The typical construction management book is written for commercial and industrial projects. They are not appropriate to the home construction project. They will tell you all of the complicated steps needed to plan and manage a commercial or industrial project. They are wonderful resources for the construction management graduate from a university but they are not, I believe, for use by the homeowner. The commercial and industrial construction worlds are too different from the home construction world.

The most dangerous misapplication is where they state that all of your contracts must be written and signed before you start your project. They recommend this to have your contractors prepared for a tight construction schedule. Also, they say that you will then know what the final cost of your project will be because you have all your contracts lined up and executed. Do this only if you want an unsuccessful home construction project.

In the Pat Fay Method you will typically have only one contract signed at a time. Sometimes you may have two contracts signed if one is just about complete. The problem with having all of your contracts signed ahead of time in the home construction world is two fold.

The first is your project will probably be behind schedule. Being behind schedule is standard operating procedure for almost all construction projects. Therefore, your finish contractor, for example, cannot get started on the day stipulated in your contract. If you have a tough contractor they can claim that your delay has cost them money because they could have been working on another job. You may have to pay them for their losses.

The second is that the conditions of your project will not be exactly as described in your drawings or contract. The contractor will be able to legitimately claim an extra cost because of the different conditions from what they originally bid.

I had an acquaintance who thought my class was a waste of time because he had read a couple of construction management books. He and his wife had their old house torn down and a new one built. They decided to manage the construction themselves but they followed the guidelines given in the construction management books. Both of the above scenarios occurred. They ended up having to sell their lovely new home because they could not afford the second mortgage they took out to pay the contractors for their change orders and delays. They ended up paying about $200,000 in change orders. What home construction project can afford an extra charge of $200,000?

Qualifications & time needed to manage according to the Pat Fay Method. If you have a high school or college education you are qualified to manage your home construction project. Most of the general contractors and their construction workers building your house or remodel do not have a high school diploma. You are more than qualified.

My wife had a part time job and I had a full time job. We worked at managing our new house project before and after work and on the weekends. Occasionally I would take a day of vacation to attend to the project. The point is that you do not have to quit your job to manage your project according to the Pat Fay Method. The reason for this is because you are hiring contractors that are experts in their field to do the work they contracted to do. Your job is not to babysit them but to hold them accountable to do what they agreed to do. Your job is to manage, monitor, coordinate, and inspect.

Skills needed: communication, organization, records, knowledge. The ability to communicate is the skill most needed to successfully manage your home construction project. You will need to be able to communicate with a diverse range of people with varying educational backgrounds. Honesty and sincerity have always been the best communication tools for dealing well with people.

Do not expect every conversation or negotiation to go your way because they won't. However, if you know what you want you will be able to determine early in a business relationship whether the person you are speaking to will be able to help you or not.

Organizational and record keeping skills are very much needed to be able to stay on top of your project. A 3-ring binder will help you immensely in these endeavors. If you can file the information you gather into an appropriate place so that you can retrieve it easily then you will be ahead of most homeowners. (You will learn how to set up your binder in the next chapter.)

Knowledge is a fairly critical requirement in construction. However, the lack of home construction knowledge should not deter you from managing your home construction project. Although you probably do not have the knowledge you need now, your ability to read, discuss with experts, and to learn will allow you to gain the knowledge you need. If you have some construction experience that is great. If you do not have construction experience that is fine also because we are not doing construction. We are managing contractors in the construction process.

Know what you want. Knowing what you want seems to be such a simple concept that we all give lip service to it. However, if you actually know what you want then you should be able to write it down on a piece of paper in a simple paragraph. Then do so please.

Try to write down what you want to build or remodel and what it should look like when the contractors are complete. You will find this is not quite as easy or simple as it seems. However, it is a critical skill that you must be able to do if you want to succeed in your home construction project. I suggest you start today with a blank piece of paper and write out what you want because if you cannot write it out on a piece of paper how can you communicate what you want to an architect/designer or contractor?

How the remodel or new construction process will affect your life and your relationship with your spouse or significant other. Construction is very stressful. Your relationship with your wife, husband, significant other, and children can be at risk because it is so stressful. Be very aware that this is not an easy process. If you allow yourself to be consumed by the stress and anger you will become a very difficult person to be around.

Your attitude and behavior in the face of the problems and stress presented by home construction will define whether it will strengthen your relationship with your spouse or tear it apart.

Work as a team to build respect in your family relationship. If you take a hard process and you share it with your spouse or significant other then you will build a stronger relationship than you had before. This is done by working as a team with your spouse. If the two of you decide that you will not allow finger-pointing and blame but rather acknowledgement that it is a difficult process and that everything does not get done on time and that it is no one's fault. Then you will be able to work through the problems together. You will find yourself having more respect and admiration for your spouse than you had before. The result of working together as a team will be a better relationship with your spouse and a stronger marriage because you shared a common hard experience and were successful.

Select one person to be the final decision maker (preferably not the man). In the Pat Fay Method one person has the final decision making power. In the Pat Fay Method we highly recommend that that person be the woman. The reason for this is because most contractors are men and they will become chummy with the husband. They often have an uncanny sense of knowing how to flatter a fellow man so that he feels like one of the gang. When this happens the man may be susceptible to making decisions that are favorable to the contractor but unfavorable to the best interests of the project.

On the other hand, a contractor will be less likely to be able to convince a woman to do something that is not in the best interest of her project. If the man has to get the final OK from the woman then when he tries to explain the situation to her she can pop the bubble of temporary insanity cast by the contractor over her husband.

New construction is a hard project, a remodel is even harder. A new construction project is a difficult project because there is a lot of planning, design and construction to manage and accomplish.

The remodel is even more difficult because there is three times as much work to do. Also, many homeowners fall into the trap of thinking that a remodel is not that hard of a project and thereby go about it casually. Don't fall into that trap.

In a remodel, there is planning & design, discovery, and new construction. The planning & design is pretty much the same as in the new construction. Discovery is where your demolition takes place and when the sheetrock or siding is removed (or whatever it is that you demolish to make way for the new construction) and the homeowner discovers the actual conditions of the structure.

Discovery almost always reveals something of which you were unaware, such as, rot or different conditions than what is shown on your plans. If you already have your contracts signed before discovery takes place then you will probably be hit with a change order at the very start.

In the Pat Fay Method you hire a contractor to do the demolition as a separate phase or activity. The contractor may even be the one who is going to do the new construction. Then once the actual conditions are revealed you finalize your price and then sign the construction contract. You have the opportunity to not sign a contract if the price goes up too much as a result of the new conditions and find a different contractor.

Where to live while construction is underway. Where to live is something the homeowner needs to consider. In a remodel, many people start out living in the house as it is being remodeled but then are driven crazy by the noise, dust, and chaos. The homeowner then has to scramble to find another place to live and to add a line item for temporary housing to their budget.

I have heard of a number of interesting alternatives to renting an apartment or a hotel room. One client was completely remodeling the upstairs of their split level house. They decided to seal off the lower level. They tore out the sliding glass doors and installed an entry door. They had a plumber build in a kitchenette for a cooking space on the other side of their downstairs bathroom. They had a carpenter frame in the stairwell and put a plywood floor across it to seal off the upstairs so that the basement was like a separate apartment. They did have quite a bit of noise but since the remodel took about 6 months they saved the cost of renting a different place to live.

Another client bought two nice tents and set them up in the backyard; one for the parents and one for their two children and the family dog. They camped out while the remodel was going on. I thought that was quite resourceful.

You will feel one of two ways by the end of this book.

Empowered. After reading this book, many homeowners will feel completely empowered to manage their own home construction project without a general contractor. The Pat Fay Method is just what they needed to be in charge of their project. Many of these individuals will have already done a project or two and will have experienced first hand how much money they had to pay to get their project completed and how poorly they were treated by the contractors they hired. The Pat Fay Method is what they have been searching for to help them effectively deal with home construction contractors.

Overwhelmed. Other homeowners will read this book and a feeling of being completely overwhelmed will descend upon them. The thought of managing their own home construction project looks so intimidating and difficult that it leaves them with a feeling of dread. If this happens to you do not despair because this is a temporary feeling. Continue to read (even reread) all the sections of this book, start your planning and preliminary design binder, go through the planning and preliminary design process and get enough sleep at night. In about two weeks you will become a person that will feel as if they always knew this information and this process.

This is a new method; we can expect push back from those vested in the status quo. The Pat Fay Method is a new process in the home construction industry. As of 2005, Pat Fay has trained about 500 people in the last ten years in this process. This has been done by teaching classes held in private homes, in hotel meeting centers, senior centers, and other venues in the Seattle area. This is not very many but it is a start.

I have received feedback from former students who have gone home and built their new homes by following the Pat Fay Method. They have had very successful projects. They were able to build as recently as 2005 for $80 to $90 per square foot and have luxury style homes. They were able to find contractors to work according to the Pat Fay Method. They also told me how many contractors refused to work for them because that is not how it is done.

My goal is to sell this book to homeowners so they will have the tools and knowledge of what I have learned in a lifetime of experience in construction. I envision tens of thousands of ordinary homeowner using this book to help them save literally hundreds of thousands of dollars in their home construction projects.

We can expect push back from those vested in maintaining the status quo. Why should they accept the Pat Fay Method? It puts them in a position of being responsible for the work they have contracted to do at a reasonable price. It is much more advantageous for them to take the homeowner's money up front and then continue to work on other people's projects and only show up on your job when it suits them. They also enjoy the benefits of charging too much for their services. It has been this way for a long time now. It is time for the status quo to end.

It will not be an easy process. For instance, look at the State of Louisiana. In Louisiana it is actually against the law for a homeowner to be their own general contractor and subcontract out the work. Why should that be? It would be one thing if the state regulated contractors so they would act ethically, honestly, and with integrity. Instead, they have a state law that forbids the homeowner from receiving a building permit unless they have a general contractor.

When I spoke to a state official about this they said they do allow a homeowner to get a permit if they plan to physically do all the work themselves but not if they plan to subcontract the work out. "Why is that?" I asked. "Because it is the law" he replied. To whose benefit is a law like that?

However, the citizens of the State of Louisiana can still benefit from the Pat Fay Method by following the principals and methods found herein when dealing with a general contractor.

Each section has tremendously useful information on what you should and should not do. With this knowledge and information the homeowner has a much better chance to manage their home remodel or new construction project so that they receive high quality workmanship, excellent quality materials, and that it costs a reasonable amount of money.

In short, with the Pat Fay Method the homeowner will prove that they can manage their home remodel or new construction without a general contractor, save serious money and still stay married.

Chapter 2-Planning and Preliminary Design by the Homeowner

Your house theme or project mission statement
For the homeowner the planning & preliminary design is one process
What is the planning process?
    Planning is fun
        What kind of project is it?
            Minor projects
            Major projects
        Defining the work you want to accomplish
        Examples of the planning process
            Kitchen, bathroom, family room
What is the preliminary design process?
        Preliminary design is not as much fun
            Cost considerations
        Doing your preliminary design
            Sketching
            Floor layouts
            Let the ideas grow in your mind
            Plan and elevation views
            The use of pictures to define the design
The 3-ring binder is the backbone of your planning & preliminary design process
        What should go into your design binder?
        How to organize your 3-ring binder
            The section tabs you may want to use to organize your design binder
                Write you ideas down on a piece of paper, date and file
Your first call and visit to the city about your building permit
        The city's permitting requirements
        Review the requirements only; do not try to understand them
        You want a building permit
            The best reason to have a permit
            Having a permit affects your house resale value
            Small projects may not need a permit
Make your major changes in the planning/preliminary design phase
Purchasing pre-designed plans
Finalizing your planning and preliminary design
        Copy for your architect or building designer
How long should your planning and preliminary design take?
        List of section tabs for 3-ring binder organization

Chapter 2-Planning and Preliminary Design by the Homeowner

Your house theme or project mission statement. The most important single step in the entire home construction process is to define your house theme statement. Without this step your project is like a ship without a rudder or a life without a goal. It will meander anywhere wasting time and losing money hand over fist.

Your theme or mission statement is just like the statement all successful companies have that defines what they are trying to accomplish. If you do not have a theme then anything is possible and anything can happen on your project. If that is the case you will spend a lot of money and you may not be happy with the results.

You must write a simple one or two sentence statement that defines what you are trying to achieve in your project. Then whatever you do and whatever decisions you make can be bounced off this theme and judged whether it supports your theme or not.

The theme will allow you to stay focused on the correct path for your project. It will allow you to avoid the pitfalls of loosing sight of your objective and building something that you will find does not meet your desires. Unfortunately, this discovery is usually made during the construction phase where it is going to cost you a lot of money to fix the problem.

The best theme example I can give is the simple theme my wife set for our new house project; openness and spaciousness. These three words governed our decisions in all phases of our project.

In fact, we had been lost in our planning and preliminary design phase. We had reams of information on floor plans, elevations, interior designs and all sorts of information that basically overwhelmed us. We just kept gathering information and filing it away and did not know what to do with it.

When we defined our theme of openness and spaciousness everything fell into place. Now we could bounce each idea and piece of information off the bedrock of our theme and it either fit and was kept or it did not fit and was discarded.

My wife and I used this simple theme to guide our project. Our theme went to the heart of what we wanted to create in our new home. As a result our main floor is a grand and open room of 1500 SF that has no interior walls except for the small powder room in the northwest corner.

Therefore, in the Pat Fay Method, the very first thing you do is to write out your house theme.

For the homeowner the planning & preliminary design is one process. The planning & preliminary design must be one process because of the limited manpower the homeowners have; themselves. The homeowner will take on the responsibility of the industrial planner and the preliminary designer.

It is a good responsibility for the homeowner to have because they know best what it is they want. They only lack the experience and knowledge of how to do the planning and preliminary design.

What is the planning process? Planning is the act of describing in words what you would like built or modified in your house. This is called the project requirements.

In the Industrial construction world we have planners who's only job is to gather and define the requirements needed to build a facility. They speak to the customer, ask a million questions, take notes, and then write out the project requirements. They may even do some space planning.

They turn these requirements over to a project administrator who hires engineers and designers. They in turn are responsible for generating the drawings that meet the intent of the requirements and the building code.

Planning is fun. Planning is not difficult and can actually be fun. It is fun because you get to consider having all the things you would like to have in your remodel or new construction. Everything is in during the planning stage. Do not limit yourself. A free flow of ideas is needed to really find out just what you want. Besides you may find an expensive, nice to have item that you thought you could not afford may actually work after all. Of course, the cost of some of your ideas may eventually force you to remove them during the preliminary design stage but why limit yourself in the beginning?

What kind of project is it? You will need to understand size of your project and therefore its complexity. You do not want to fall into the trap of thinking you have a minor project when it is really a major project. Minor projects are those that have few interdependent activities. Major projects are those that have many activities with different trades.

Minor projects. Minor projects are those projects that are simple both in concept and execution. They are such things as living and bedroom remodels, repainting, and even when you are removing all the sheetrock in a room and replacing it with new, then tape, mud, texture and paint. It may include changing out the carpet. A new roof is a minor project also even if you are removing shakes, adding plywood sheathing, and composition roofing. Window and door replacements, removing non-load bearing walls, and changing flooring or finishes out are all considered minor projects. Decks would also be a minor project even if your deck is very large.

Major projects. Major projects are those projects that have many interlocking activities that require multiple trades and contractors to work upon them. These require thoughtful planning to be sure the homeowner considers all the work activities needed to accomplish their major project.

Major projects are such things as adding another floor to your house, adding a new room where a new foundation has to be installed, installing a basement where there was only a crawlspace, completely gutting a house and remodeling, a kitchen remodel, a bathroom remodel where new plumbing fixtures are installed, installing a new bathroom, and of course a new house. Kitchen and bathroom remodels are included because of the complexity. There are many trades that have to be involved; plumbing, electrical, flooring, sheetrock, exhaust systems, natural gas, cabinets, and finishes.

Defining the work you want to accomplish. In the planning process you will want to end up with a paragraph with your explanations of exactly what it is that you want. It is amazing to see the simple planning documents that have resulted in very large facilities that cost in the tens of millions of dollars. Planning does not have to complicated, it just has to be thorough.

Examples of the planning process. Let us define the requirements for a few rooms. Perhaps you want a new kitchen, a new bathroom or just more room for the family to be together. The act of planning is to state in simple terms what you want in those rooms.

Kitchen. You may want a larger kitchen, a quiet dishwasher, hardwood floors, granite counter tops, more shelf space, windows in your cabinets so you can see your dishes, a wider refrigerator to accommodate large cookie sheets, a plate warmer, a deeper sink, a ventilation system that takes away the fumes from cooking, soft lighting for parties (because everyone seems to group in the kitchen) yet bright lights for cooking and meal preparation.

This simple paragraph now defines your kitchen requirements. You can also call it your kitchen specifications. All of these things are possible but will remain in your head until you put pen to paper or sit down in front of your PC and type it out. Some people are intimidated by the thought of writing their ideas down on paper. If that is the case with you then buy a small voice recorder. Dictate to the recorder and then copy your dictation down later.

Bathroom. A new bathroom may include things such as a soaking tub built for two, a phone built in by the tub, a light switch by the tub, a separate shower, a closet for the towels, double sinks so you do not have to share, tile on the floor and walls, a low water usage toilet, a high powered exhaust fan, and a sound system for when you have champagne together in the tub.

Family room. A large family room would be better defined as more room for certain activities. This may be a room where the family can gather with an entertainment system, solid core doors with good seals to isolate the sound from the rest of the house, your very large sofa, 2 easy chairs, a nook for the computer, and a space for your son to play video games to ensure his inclusion in family gatherings instead of allowing him to hide out in his room.

These three examples are simple but good statements that define the project requirements for the three respective rooms. You are finished with your planning. Planning does not have to be complicated. However, for the homeowner to write these simple paragraphs often takes much time and thought. You could easily spend several months to write these requirements out because your ideas in the beginning are fluid and it takes time to solidify ideas into a simple paragraph. It is time well spent.

What is the preliminary design process? Preliminary design is nothing more than taking the planning requirements and turning those words into drawings. For the homeowner it is more appropriate to say taking the requirements and turn them into sketches. Good sketches but not drawings. Drawings are for your architect or designer to produce.

Preliminary design is not as much fun. The preliminary design process is not quite as much fun as the planning process because this is where you realize that all the things considered in your planning phase may not fit into the space you have available. Also, it may prove to be too expensive.

Cost considerations. Everything we do in construction costs money. The problem for the homeowner has been to determine what a reasonable price is to pay to have construction activities performed. How much should the material cost, how many labor hours are required to install the material, what labor rate should be paid, and how much profit should be added to it all? It is the homeowner's job to put a price to each of the items they want included in their construction.

How does a homeowner do this? You go to chapter 15 and read about how much the material should cost, how many labor hours are required to install the material, what labor rate should be paid, and how much profit should be added to it all.

Doing your preliminary design. Now the homeowner gets to take a pencil and paper and start sketching because this is where space planning occurs. We call it preliminary design but in essence the end of planning and the beginning of preliminary design flows together.

You now get to define the size of the rooms and then place the furniture and equipment, if any, in those spaces to see how it all fits. You will need to see how your furniture fits in the room spaces you've sketched and how the room spaces fit into the house as a whole.

Sketching. At this point a word of encouragement may be appropriate. Do not be apprehensive about sketching out room spaces. I know from experience that it is difficult for the normal homeowner. Not that I have any difficulty with sketching because you wouldn't either if your first mechanical drafting course occurred in the 9th grade.

However, in my early classes I had an exercise where I asked my students to take a few moments and sketch up their dream floor plan. You would have thought I had asked them to take poison. The looks of apprehension on their faces was startling. After this same reaction occurred in several consecutive classes I had to drop that part of the class. My student's reaction taught me how difficult sketching is for the typical homeowner.

The homeowner following the Pat Fay Method must make sketches of their floor plans so they have floor plans to give to their architect or building designer.

Floor layouts. The first sketch of a room I want you to make is a square. Just get out a sheet of paper and draw a square. Imagine this is a room and you are looking down from above. Each line of the square represents a wall. Label this sketch SK-1 and date it. You are finished for today.

Let the ideas grow in your mind. The next day, take a separate sheet of paper and draw the exact same square but this time add a door in one wall and make marks on the other 3 walls denoting windows. Label this sketch SK-2 and date it. You are finished for today.

The next day, take another sheet of paper draw the exact same square with the doors and windows. Now sketch in a sofa, a table and chairs, a stereo, a TV, and a bookshelf. Now I hope you realize that you are only drawing a two dimensional outline of these objects. If you look down on your table it will look like a rectangle. That is what you sketch when looking from above or in architect and engineer language this is a plan view. Label this sketch SK-3.

Do this for one full week, adding features, new walls, closets, hallways, and whatever takes your fancy. What will happen is that your imaginary room will grow into a much larger space and you will begin experimenting.

Two things will happen. One you will overcome any apprehension you may have had about your ability to sketch. Two you will witness the power of your subconscious mind in the design process.

Each person has a conscious and subconscious mind. For design, we use the conscious mind to feed information and data to the subconscious mind. Unbeknownst to us our subconscious mind will take that data and start processing it. I find this process works best for me after a night's sleep. The next day design problems that I had found difficult the day before had been solved without my conscious thought. This is the subconscious mind at work. Put this innate ability to work for you.

Plan and elevation views. You will be sketching in either the plan or elevation views. A plan view is as if you were standing above the room and looking down at it. The elevation view is as if you are standing in front of your house and looking at the whole front of your house from top to bottom or standing in front of your kitchen cabinets so you can see them from floor to ceiling. The plan and elevation sketches represent what you see in two dimensions.

The best scale for the homeowner to use is ¼ inch is equal to one foot. The reason for this is that this scale allows you to do your sketches and layouts on a standard 11 ½" x 17" piece of paper. This size paper will allow you to sketch a floor plan of 40' x 60'. The 40' length in 1/4 scale measures out to 10" and the 60' measures out to 15". 40' x 60' is 2400 SF. This should be ample for 99% of all home construction projects.

Engineers and architects make their drawings to scale. This means that the size of the objects in a drawing represent the actual size of the object as they would be in a full scale setting. To make this easier for ourselves architects and engineers use triangular shaped scales that have not only a ¼" to 1' scale but many others for a total of 12 different scales. Go to a stationary store and buy an inexpensive architect's scale and use it. The sketching and layout is actually quite interesting.

Laying out furniture in your room sketches can be tedious if you sketch your furniture in one position and then to experiment you change it by erasing or sketching it all over again. An easier way to do this is to make to scale cut outs of your furniture, cabinets, TV's or any type of equipment you will be installing in a room. Of course, you will want to use the same scale for your cutouts as you do for your room floor plans.

This means that if your sofa is 6' long by 3' wide then on your paper cut out you will have a miniature sofa that is 1 1/2" long by 3/4" long. This is 1/4 scale. You make up miniature cutouts for everything. Then you lay them out in the room where they go and you can rearrange them until you get everything to fit. If you cannot get them to fit then you may have to make the room larger. Then you see if the larger room fits in your overall house footprint. If you can make it fit then great. If it will not fit then you must make a decision about what furniture you will not have in that room or make the decision to make the room larger.

For a brand new house you work the sketching from two directions. First you sketch the size of the overall house footprint. Second you sketch what each individual room should look like. You cut out the rooms and lay them over the house footprint. Of course, they are not going to match up at first but the point here is you do not want the overall footprint to dictate the shape and character of the individual rooms. Rather you want the requirements of the individual rooms to dictate the final outline of the house footprint.

For a remodel you really are more limited by the footprint of your existing home in dictating what the size and shape of the remodeled rooms will be. The exception to this is if you already plan to move walls to make more room.

The use of pictures to define the design. You many want to cut pictures out of magazines of the kind of elevations you want for your house. If you have taken a picture of an elevation or a house floor plan that you like then use it as your sketch. You won't need to spend as much time sketching because the picture will tell your architect/designer just what you want. Using pictures is an excellent way to define what you want.

The 3-ring binder is the backbone of your planning & preliminary design process. The next step is to build a planning and preliminary design 3-ring binder. This is going to be the backbone of your planning and design process. Buy yourself a 3" thick binder. You will need a large binder because you will find that it will fill up rather quickly. In fact you will find that it will not hold everything.

Therefore, you will also use a filing cabinet with folders matching the titles in your binder. When the binder gets too thick you can take some of the older information and archive it in the folders in your file cabinet. Throw nothing away while you are still working your project. Once the project is complete then will be the time to clean up your files by purging information that is no longer needed.

However, during the project you cannot judge what is needed and what is not. There is nothing as frustrating as knowing that you tossed something out last week that you need today.

What should go into your design binder? Everything. All of your sketches, all of your ideas, all of your pictures, and everything else that is a part of your planning and preliminary design process. You will want to eliminate that pile of papers on your desk that sits there and grows into a dragon that you are afraid to touch. For once you will be an organized professional project manager. Stay on top of your project by being organized.

How to organize your 3-ring binder. You will want to divide up your binder into major subject headings with file dividers. Then there will be breakdown dividers under each major heading. I would recommend you buy quite a few dividers.

We've all probably put binders together before for school or projects and it is no different now. You will find that as you get into your planning and preliminary design that you will be adding lots of tabs that will make your binder unique to your project and your way of project management. Have fun with this. Keep extra blank dividers in your binder so you can easily make new subject headings as you need.

To start with you can have these dividers titled with the sections of this book; planning, design, permitting, meetings, cost estimating, etc. You will find that each of these sections will grow into many subtitles. Or you can use my list or parts of my list found at the end of this chapter. Remember you are the project manager now and you get to organize the way you decide is best for your project.

The section tabs you may want to use to organize your design binder. Please see the end of this chapter for a list of subject headings that can assist you in organizing and dividing up your design binder. This list is the major headings with many of the breakouts that divide a subject heading into its components. This is not intended to be a complete list but rather a list to get you started. As project manager you are responsible for managing your project and growing your 3-ring binder to meet your own requirements.

Write you ideas down on a piece of paper, date and file. It is important that all of your ideas and plans are written down and filed in the appropriate tab in the 3-ring binder. I can't emphasize enough how important this is.

It is important because if you can take all of your ideas and use them to help you accomplish your construction goals then you will be head and shoulders above the typical homeowner. Your ideas are the beginning of great things for your house. If you do not write them down you will be constantly recreating things you could have completed earlier.

Your first call and visit to the city about your building permit. A phone call is the first contact you want to have with your town, city, county or state. Once you decide that you are going to do a home construction project give them a call to discuss the project with the planning or permitting department.

No matter how small the project I recommend that you discuss it with your permitting agency. From now on I will call the permit department 'the city' for ease of use. (I briefly go over the subject of permitting here because Chapter 6 has been devoted to this subject).

Typically when you call a city you will get a receptionist. Just briefly explain your situation and they will transfer you to either the permits or planning department. Take out one of the Project Log sheets and write down the date and the phone number you called and the name of the person you speak to. Take notes on the phone conversation so you can remember what was said two weeks from now.

The city's permitting requirements. The city's permitting requirements are usually a combination of the adopted national building code and local amendments. The national code until recently has been the uniform building code (UBC). In 2003 the international building code replaced the UBC. Your city has to formally adopt the new code before it can be applied. The local amendments are requirements that your community and building department have decided are an improvement to the national code or they reflect unique community standards.

Review the requirements only; do not try to understand them. When you go to the city they will typically have a set of requirements to give you. I have seen them consist of a single page to a thick folder of papers. Either way you will accept them and then casually look them over. Do not try to read all of the requirements unless you are lucky enough to live in a city that has a single sheet of requirements.

The reason for this is because it is not your responsibility to know and understand the requirements of the building code. That is the responsibility of your architect/designer and contractors. One of the reasons you hire these people is because they are experts in their field. As experts they are responsible for knowing how the building code and city's requirements apply to their specialty.

You want a building permit. Many homeowners mistakenly think that it is better to build without the city getting involved. Please do not believe this. In the Pat Fay Method we want a building permit.

The best reason to have a permit. The best reason for getting a permit is that for the price of the permit you will get a wonderful person who works for the city, who will come out to your house and inspect the contractor's work. Your inspector may not always look all that professional because of they way they dress and look. Actually they look a lot like contractors. In fact, many of them were contractors so they know the tricks of the trade. Also, they may be a little rough around the edges. However, they are the only person you are going to encounter on your project that is on your side. They may not seem like it but they are. They will insist that that your house is built properly according to the building code.

Having a permit affects your house resale value. Another reason you want to be sure to have a permit is because you want to be able to get the value of your remodel plus appreciation out of your house when you sell it. Your real estate agent will want to know how you have upgraded your home in the years you have been there to help establish the resale value. If you say you did a kitchen or bath remodel they may ask you if you had it permitted. Many prospective buyers do not want to buy a house that has had unpermitted work done on it. The liability that a mistake may have been made and not corrected is too great. This may cause many potential buyers to walk away from your home. After all there are probably many houses available in the area to choose from.

Another scenario is that you may find a buyer but they will make a lower offer on your home due to the unpermitted remodel work. It is just not a good risk to do anything on your home without a permit.

Small projects may not need a permit. Your project may be small and if so it may not need a permit. When you call the city explain that you are doing a small project and would like to know if it needs to be permitted. Now if your project is just changing out your cabinets or changing from carpet to tile you may be told you do not need a permit. However, do not assume this. Call them and make a log of the conversation and file it in your 3 ring binder.

You are still not finished. We have all heard the stories about people being told one thing by 'someone' in the city that said a permit was not needed. Once the project was underway they find out this was a mistake. You must write a short letter to the city's permits department. You will state you spoke to Mr. Jones on July 15th and you were made to understand that your home construction project does not need a permit for the following reasons. Keep a copy and mail it. This is your official record.

Make your major changes in the planning and preliminary design phase. The planning and preliminary design phase is where you want to let your imagination run wild with ideas and possibilities. Consider everything and anything. Get your experimenting done during this phase because it costs nothing but your time.

Once you get into final design with an architect/designer you do not want to exercise them trying out all the wonderful ideas you can think of because it will be expensive. You are paying the bill. The point is that you need to work through your process and come to a point where you have your floor plan and elevations worked out or you have a maximum of two or three options that you will let your architect/designer help you to finalize.

Purchasing pre-designed plans. There are companies that will sell you architectural plans fully completed for the house of your dreams. I don't believe you should waste your money on these plans unless you only have to spend $20 or so. Spending any more is a waste of your money. The only use for these plans is if you would like to copy them.

Don't think you can use these already designed house plans and submit them to your city and get them approved. Your city will ask where your plot plan is that locates the house on your lot and in your neighborhood. What about the location of utilities? What about meeting the conditions of your building lot not to mention the local amendments to the national code.

If you do buy these plans, you will still need to hire an architect/designer to finish them and make them ready for permit submittal. Why waste your money on pre-designed plans that will not really save you any time or money.

Finalizing your planning and preliminary design. Deciding when you are finished with your planning and preliminary design is difficult. If you are still revising rooms, changing the footprint of your exterior walls, still clipping pictures of elevations then you are not finished. If, on the other hand, you have your floor plan pretty worked out but not wholly complete and you have a good idea of what you want the elevations to look like or at least narrowed down to two or three options, then you might be close.

Also, if you are just plan tired of sketching and laying out rooms and your 3-ring binder is full then you are finished. Or you may have reached your scheduled deadline and ready or not you are turning it over to your architect/designer. Almost.

Copy for your architect or building designer. Your last step is to make copies of all your sketches of floor plans and all your pictures and sketches of elevations. Now you are ready to hand this package to your architect or building designer. Keep the copy for yourself and give the originals to your designer.

Don't worry that it isn't neat enough or organized properly. All that matters is that you give this information to your design professional. Remember they are only interested in your floor plans and elevations. However, your other information contained in you 3-ring binder is useful to them as reference. Therefore, always bring your 3-ring binder with you when meeting with your architect/designer because they may have questions about finishes.

How long should your planning and preliminary design take? This really depends on two things; the size of your project and you.

The size of your project really matters. If you are just remodeling your bathroom you can probably get your planning done in a week or two. If it is a whole house remodel you may need anywhere from two to six months. For a brand new house you may need three to seven months.

The next variable is you. No one can make you do anything but yourself. How quickly you get done with your planning really depends on the amount of effort and time you expend. What kind of project manager will you be? Industrious or lazy? Only you can answer that question.

We spent about one year in our planning and preliminary design. We took that long because that was what was right for us. Besides we had not yet developed the Pat Fay Method. If we had known then what is in this book we could easily have cut our planning & preliminary design time in half.

List of section tabs for the 3-ring planning and preliminary design binder.

1. Theme or project mission statement

2. Planning and preliminary design
    (See the detailed list on the next page)

4. Meetings

5. Final Design by architect or building designer
    Preliminary design
    Final design

6. Interior designer
    Draperies
    Upholstery
    Wall decorations
    Display cases
    Window coverings, shades
    Planters

6. Cost Estimating and construction pricing

7. Scheduling

8. Permitting

9. Insurance

10. Construction materials

2. Planning & Preliminary Design (expanded list)

    Floor plans
        Main floor
        Second floor
        Bathrooms
        Kitchen
        Pantry
        Living room
        Bedrooms
        Library
        Office
        Rec room
        Dining room
        Music room
        Sauna, steam bath
        Exercise room
        Shooting range
        Entry way
        Elevator
        Closets
        Decks
        Patio
        Yard, garden, fence, swimming/lap pool

    Elevations
        Front elevation
        Side elevations
        Back elevation
        Room elevations

    Basement
        Floor plan
        Laundry room; washer, dryer, dryer vent
        Storage areas
        Bedrooms
        Bathroom
        Dark room
        Wine cellar
        Wall construction, recommend concrete not CMU blocks
            waterproofing

    Garage
        Floor plan
        Elevations
        Garage door, door opener
        Storage above; disappearing stairway

    Shop area

Bathroom details
    Cabinets
    Sink
    Bathtub
    Shower
    Faucets, drain hardware
    Toilet
    Floor finishes
    Wall finishes
    Paint colors

Kitchen details
    Cabinets; doors, hinges, drawer pulls
    Island
    Sink; faucet, soap dispenser, garbage disposal

    Kitchen appliances
        Dishwasher
        Oven; gas, electric
        Cooktop/range: exhaust system
        Plate warmer
        Refrigerator
        Freezer
        Microwave
        Garbage compactor
        Kitchen ventilation
            Exhaust system
            Location of heating vents

    Kitchen finishes
        Flooring
        Counter tops; formica, tile, granite, marble
        Trim; base, ceiling
        Hardware
        Paint colors

Bedrooms
    Closets; shelving, clothes racks, doors
    Bookshelves
    Flooring
    Location of bed

Fireplaces
    Wood burning

    Gas
    Fireplace vent

Doors
    Door list
      Exterior; threshold, weatherstripping
      Interior
    Door frames
    Door hardware; hinges, locksets
    Door trim

Windows
    Window type; vinyl, wood, metal
      Define how they open
    Double pane, triple pane, low E glass

Flooring finishes
    Hardwood
    Carpet
    Tile
    Colored concrete
    Baseboard trim

Stairs
    Handrails
    Railings
    Finishes

Heating and air conditioning
    Furnace; gas, electric
    A/C; type
    Grilles, vents
    Water heater; electric, gas

Electrical & Communications
    Telephone
    Cable
    Internet
    Fiber Optics
    Alarm system
    Electrical wiring; only allow copper wire, no aluminum

Exterior Materials

    Siding
      Type; cedar, vinyl, aluminum
      Paint, stain

        Plastic wrap (beneath)
        Bubble insulation (beneath)

Roofing
        Composition
        Cedar shakes
        Metal
        Tile
        Flashing
        Gutters

Chapter 3-The Home Construction Meeting

Why to have meetings
The five types of meetings under the Pat Fay Method
Where to have the meetings
When to have the meetings
Who should be at the meetings?
How often should you have the meetings?
The meeting agenda with a time limit
How to conduct the meetings
Take meeting minutes
How to behave in the meetings
    You and your spouse are a team of professionals
    There is no room for pointing fingers of blame
How to respond to controversial ideas or proposals
Closing the meeting
Brainstorming
Problems that happen in meetings
Guidelines
Sample of agenda
Sample of meeting minutes

Chapter 3-The Home Construction Meeting

Why to have meetings. Meetings are a necessary and vital part of the home construction process. The homeowner will be using them to accomplish their goals during all phases of the construction project. Without them there is no effective method of accomplishing what needs to be done. In construction, you will soon have more on your plate to coordinate and understand than you initially anticipated. To understand, control, direct, and accomplish these tasks in a coordinated fashion will require the homeowner to conduct effective meetings.

    There is no secret to understanding how to conduct an effective meeting because all you need to remember is three things:
1. Review what you have done
2. Discuss what you are doing now
3. Plan the things you need to do in the future

    Many homeowners are professional people and they fully understand why they have meetings at work. However, I have found it interesting that the professional person leaves this skill and knowledge at work instead of applying it to their home construction projects. Please do not be a lazy project manager on your own project. Hold meetings and conduct them professionally.

    We have meetings to coordinate between the different people working on the project. Through meetings we share information so that all people involved have the same knowledge. We make decisions at the meeting which allow the players to all work in the same direction and as a team. Also, we have meetings to resolve an issue or problem.

When you have regular meetings you will be in charge of your project. There is nothing worse for the homeowner to have the architect/designer or the contractor making decisions on their behalf without consulting the owner, particularly if the result does not reflect what the homeowner wants. Meetings will reduce the likelihood of this happening or, if it does happen, you will be aware of it sooner than you would be without a meeting. Then you at least have the chance of reversing a decision before it is too late.

The types of meetings. In the Pat Fay Method there are five types of meetings. They are:

1. The sit down/formal meeting
2. The telephone meeting
3. The standup meeting
4. The shopping meeting
5. The confrontational meeting

The sit down/formal meeting is used during your planning at home, with your architect/designer, scheduled meetings with the city, contract negotiations, signing of the contract, and major problem resolution with the contractor.

The telephone meeting is used when you do not have time to meet face to face but it is critical to communicate. You run a telephone meeting the same way you would a face-to-face meeting: professionally and with an agenda. Be sure to document your telephone meetings on the telephone log sheet just as you would document a sit down meeting (forms are in chapter 19). You should consider your phone calls to suppliers, potential contractors and architect/designer as mini-meetings.

The standup meeting is what you will be holding daily on site to coordinate with the contractor. You don't need to show the contractor the agenda but be sure you go through it yourself in your discussion with the contractor. Take notes on what is discussed to be included in your more formal write up of this meeting.

The shopping meeting is when you are out visiting supply houses and you speak with a sales agent or are gathering product information sheets. Keep records of these meeting on the project log because you will want to use this information to compare against different potential suppliers.

The last and most problematic meeting is the confrontational meeting. The confrontational meeting is usually held when you have a problem contractor. It can either be a sit down or a standup meeting but it must be face to face and in private. Do not have this meeting over the telephone. For this one you need to look your adversary in the eye, otherwise, it will not be effective. You hold this meeting when you are unhappy or dissatisfied with something (quality, material, schedule, safety, etc.) and the standup meeting has not resolved the issue. Avoid being angry or shouting in this meeting. You do need to approach this meeting as if this were a problem at work that you are confronting firmly but professionally.

In the confrontational meeting you discuss one issue and one issue only with your problem contractor: the problem. Do not let your problem contractor fog the issue by bringing in unrelated subjects. If they do, firmly and politely bring them back to the subject you want to discuss. If there are two or more contractors to deal with, allow only one adversary person to be the spokesman otherwise you will be answering questions from multiple directions and you will become overwhelmed. Remember that getting angry will cloud your judgment and will not help resolve the problem. As with all other types of meetings, being professional and in control of the meeting will allow you to accomplish your goals.

You may not resolve the issue in a single meeting. If you do solve the problem then you can just move on in your project. However, the main goal of this meeting is to determine where the contractor stands and what he plans to do or not do. Then you will know one way or the other. This counters the technique contractors have of stringing the homeowner along indefinitely. However, once it becomes clear that the contractor is not going to cooperate to satisfy your issue/concern, end the meeting.

What comes next depends on the issue. Perhaps you will need to write a letter and send it certified mail with return receipt requested. Perhaps it is time to call in arbitration. Arbitration is covered in more detail in chapter 9 on contract documents. However, now you know, one way or the other, where the contractor stands in regards to your issue.

Take meeting minutes. You will need to keep written minutes of your meetings. Minutes are just a written record of what was discussed, the actions needed to be accomplished, who is assigned to each action and what will be discussed at the next meeting. You can use the meeting minutes template at the end of this chapter for your first meeting. Don't be locked into this form because you can use any format that works for you.

Standard topics to be covered are schedule, design issues, current action items, problems, cost, and material selection. You will also want to track commitments that are not kept. You need this not so much to beat up on the person that is not completing their actions but it is an indication of their commitment to the process and perhaps their ability to follow through. This is good information to know sooner rather than later. When the meeting is over it is best to type the meetings minutes immediately while it is still fresh in your mind. It is easy to remember great detail from your notes right after the meeting but very difficult even the next day. Also, before you know it the next meeting will be upon you.

Where to have the meetings. The location depends on where you need to conduct the meeting. During the planning phase you will probably meet at the kitchen table. During the design phase you will still be meeting at the kitchen table to review drawings you have received from your architect/designer. You will also have meetings at your architect/designer's office to review the design. During the permitting phase you will be meeting at the city's offices and, yes, still at the kitchen table. During the contractor selection and contract negotiation phase you will be meeting at the jobsite which very well may be your kitchen table and at least one time at the selected contractor's address of record. During construction you will have many meetings at the kitchen table as well as standup meetings with the contractor in the construction area. Meetings during job closeout and review of final payments will be done from the kitchen table.

The confrontational meeting more than likely will be held at the jobsite. If so, make this as private as possible. By this I mean do not have this meeting with the contractor foreman or owner in front of his men. Be sure that the workers cannot even hear the conversation. The reason for this is because you do not want to embarrass this individual in front of his workers. In public he will be forced into taking an aggressive stance, rather than a conciliatory position if he has privacy.

When to have the meetings. Hold the meetings at convenient times for the people that attend. The meetings need to be scheduled and put into your calendar with the date, time and who will attend. During the planning phase it may be just yourself and your spouse. If you are a single person you will still hold meetings. It is a little more difficult because you do not have someone with which to discuss your issues and ideas.

Who should be at the meetings? Who attends depends on what kind of meeting it is. The point I wish to make is that you do not invite people who are not necessary to the meeting. Remember that other people's time is important also. If someone doesn't need to be at the meeting do not invite them. However, do not fail to invite someone who is vital to questions that have to be answered just so that you do not inconvenience them.

If someone is taking the time to attend your meeting and they do not need to be there for the whole meeting, adjust your agenda so the subject that involves them can be discussed first and allow them to go on their way. Don't forget that sometimes someone can attend effectively by simply telephoning in at the meeting or you call them at a specific time.

How often should you have meetings? During the planning phase I recommend a minimum of three per week; two during the week and once on the weekend. You can do more if you can schedule them or if there is a reason. However, there must be time allowed for you to accomplish the work assigned at the meetings.

During the design phase you should have meetings with your architect/designer at least once every two weeks. During the permitting phase you will have more telephone meetings than face-to-face meetings with your permitting agency. You should have a face to face with the city in the beginning of the permit process and another if the permit gets stalled somewhere inside the city bureaucracy. You will always want a face to face meeting with the city if they are requiring of you something that you do not understand and it will cost you a significant amount of money.

During the construction phase I recommend a minimum of one daily standup meeting with the contractor on site and two would be better. The best would be one meeting in the morning and one in the afternoon. This allows you to discuss what needs to be accomplished that day during your morning meeting and to check-in on how much has been accomplished by the end of the day. Sometimes two is difficult to schedule.

Also, if you have hired one contractor to do multiple phases of your project you will want a more formal meeting once every two weeks with the contractor to review all issues such as progress, schedule, quality, problems, and billing.

The Meeting Agenda with a Time Limit. You always want to have an agenda made up before you start your meeting. The agenda is nothing more than a list of the subjects you want to cover in your meeting. See the example at the end of this chapter. However, you also want the outcome of each agenda item defined. I believe it is not enough to have an agenda item of, for example, status of rough plumbing. It should be status of rough plumbing for the kitchen sink to be completed on Tuesday. The agenda guides the meeting, keeps you on track, and helps you cover subjects you want discussed.

Set a start time and finish time. Open-ended meetings always end up taking too much time. The planning and design review meetings will be about one hour. The telephone meeting will naturally be shorter and to the point. The standup meeting with your contractor on site will usually be only 10 to 15 minutes. The shopping meetings are the amount of time it takes to coordinate with a salesman at a supply store. The confrontational meeting will be short – probably less than 5 minutes.

How to Conduct the Meetings. All you need to say to start a meeting is, "It's seven o'clock, let's get the meeting started. First let's review the notes from the last meeting." Then you go through the last meeting minutes as a quick review. This exercise primes everyone's mind to what happened at the last meeting and brings forward why you are having this meeting.

Then progress through the agenda one item at a time. Remember the agenda is there as your guide. Refer to it often and follow it. It allows you to stay focused on what is important in this meeting.

Don't forget to create the right atmosphere in the meeting. If you are open to ideas then people will feel free to bring them up. If you are negative when new ideas are brought up then people will learn not to say anything in your meetings.

How to Behave in the Meetings. Always be professional in your meetings. By professional I do not mean for you to be bossy and without humor. Professional means allowing people to feel safe in discussing what they feel is important so they can speak their mind. During the planning phase you are there to work cooperatively with your partner, not to be dominating or intimidating. You are holding meetings so that important subjects can be discussed. Arguing and fighting are not allowed. Never allow alcohol to be consumed before or during a meeting. This sets the wrong tone and you will regret it if you do not follow this rule.

Being prepared for your meetings is critical. You define for yourself what you should do in preparation for the meeting. If you have an action item be sure you have it completed or have progressed toward completing it. I cannot tell you how many times I have heard young engineers on very large projects say, "I haven't been able to get to that yet". This is unacceptable. The fact is that they put off important work until the last minute, which often means that it will be done with lower quality or will not get done in time and will hold up your entire project. Set the example of how you want work done on your project: Do your work in a timely manner!

Remember to be positive but not Pollyannaish. If someone has done a good job then say thank you and tell them what a great job they did (particularly to spouses). Be simple and straightforward. Remembering to say thank you goes a long way in the design and construction world just as it does everywhere else. However, never feign affection. If you have a contractor you do not care for do not pretend that you do. People can spot insincerity. Be civil but not chummy.

Also, when an individual presents a new idea take time to think; do not immediately become negative. Look for the positive. This idea that you do not like at first may contain something that you do like. You do not have to like the idea but at least let the person present it before you bite their head off. There is no reason why you cannot simply state that you do not like that idea without filling your voice with emotion. Reject the idea, not the person presenting it.

How to respond to controversial ideas or proposals. Respond with aplomb. Try not to be rattled by what you hear. Try to keep yourself under control and do not let your emotions run wild. In the home remodel/construction world a really controversial idea usually stems from a change order, surprise bill or the schedule being slipped. I recommend that the first thing you say in such cases is, "Is this according to the contract?" Then see how they respond. If nothing else this question will allow you the time to gather your wits.

Closing the Meeting. The end of the meeting should have a time where the meeting leader turns to each attendee and asks them if they have any further input. Use each person's first name. For example, you could say, "Before we close the meeting let's go around the table and ask for any further input or items we may have forgotten. John, do have anything you would like to bring up before we close the meeting?" Also, do not forget to confirm the time and date of the next meeting.

Common problems in meetings.
-The meeting wanders. To counter this just follow the agenda. Do not let the topic under discussion jump from subject to subject. Finish each topic in the order found on the agenda.
-The meeting degenerates into just a reporting session. You need to remember that you are managing a construction project and you need to hold people accountable for completing their assigned work.
-The meeting is nothing but arguments. Don't allow the meeting to be a means for attacking someone because the person getting attacked will probably never attend another meeting. Hard words are for the confrontational meeting.
-The side bar conversation. Do not allow two conversations to go on in your meeting. If there is one then stop the meeting and ask them to share their discussion.
-The rambling participant. This is someone who needs to tell you the history of the world before they get to the point. In some cases they just like to hear themselves speak. You may have to interrupt them to get them to stop. Remember that everyone's time is valuable and should not be wasted. A way to counter a rambling participant is to ask them questions that require a yes or no answer.
-The dominating member. Do not allow someone to intimidate or boss around the other team members. Cooperation on the project will die as a result. There is nothing wrong with having a meeting leader but do not allow someone to dominate the meeting negatively.

Guidelines: Remember why you are having the meeting. It is to coordinate and accomplish the work. Consider this your theme and guide your actions in the meetings accordingly. I recommend that you schedule your planning meeting after dinner is finished and the dishes put away. No alcoholic beverages are to be consumed before or during the meeting. This is to prevent tempers from getting out of control. There is work to be done. Conduct yourself in a professional manner.

Each member must be prepared by having their work complete. If you have an assignment from the previous meeting then you are expected to have worked on that issue and all others for which you are responsible. For example, if it was to contact the city about your permit then you should have a log of the telephone conversation and a written log of the visit you made to the city.

A well run meeting fosters a feeling of esprit de corps among the members and results in personal commitments to perform better on the project. When this happens the people involved know what to do, how to do it, when to do it, and feel empowered that what they do will be well accepted. This will help to drive construction costs down.

Sample Agenda

Example of Planning Meeting Agenda

1. **Review last meeting minutes**
2. **Review the Agenda for this meeting**
3. **Design Review**
4. **Permit Issues**
5. **Construction Planning**
6. **Project Schedule**
7. **Field Work at the job site**
8. **New Topics of Discussion**
9. **Finances/Budget/Costs**
10. **Action Items**
11. **Go around table and ask for final comments from all**
12. **Next Meeting date and time**

Sample of Meeting Minutes

Example of Meeting Minutes for Our Project
Date

Attendees: List the names and companies of all that attended.

Review last meeting minutes: Just review the topics from the last meeting. Do not read verbatim. Just hit the highlights. No responses are expected.

Review the Agenda for this meeting: The agenda is on a separate sheet of paper. It may be the exact list of items to be gone over as the last meeting but typically new items are included because you are farther on in your project. Give everyone a copy of the agenda.

Design Review: If you are in the design phase you will want to discuss where you are in the design. Perhaps you have just received the 60% complete drawings from your architect/designer. It is appropriate to go over them in this meeting. You will want to look at each line and each word on the drawings. Are the floor plans as you want, are the closets and stairwell where you want them, do the plans show finish call outs for tile, carpet, or hardwood?

Permit Issues: You will give an update on your latest understanding of the requirements of your city. What is the cost of the permit? Are there deposits required? When will you or the architect/designer be ready to submit to the city?

Construction Planning: List the specialty contractors that you have lined up because you are planning to act as your own general contractor.

Project Schedule: Review the schedule. Are you on schedule or is it slipping? Discuss the impact to your project. What do we need to do to fix this issue?

Field Work at the job site: Discuss what is currently happening on the job site.

New Topics of Discussion: List the new items that have come up for the first time that need to be tracked in the meeting minutes.

Finances/Budget/Costs: Every meeting should have time spent on the budget and tracking your costs spent and what will be spent. Stay on top of your finances, who you have paid, and who you need to pay. Receive lien releases at time of payment.

Action Items: List each action item separately. Include what it is, who is working it, when it is to be completed. There should be quite a few of these.

Round Table: Ask everyone for their final comments. Take notes.

Next Meeting date and time: Set the time, date and place for the next meeting.

Chapter 4-The Final Design Process by your Architect or Building Designer

Does the homeowner need an architect or building designer?
    Why you need an architect or building designer
        The architect is the expert in the building code
    What is an architect?
    What is a building designer?
Do you need a structural engineer?
    Why you need a structural engineer
Do you need a civil, electrical, or mechanical engineer?
Do you need an interior designer?
The design build contractor
Finding an architect/designer
    Interviewing the architect/designer
    The second interview
    Final selection of the architect/designer
Negotiating with the architect/designer
    The most important thing to negotiate with your architect/designer
    Other terms to negotiate with your architect/designer
    The design schedule
What you can expect to pay for design services
    Lump sum fee vs. an hourly rate for design services
Signing a contract for design services
    The drawings you should receive from the architect/designer
    Have specifications and material requirements on the drawings
    Purchasing pre-designed plans
Working with your architect/designer
    How to interact with the architect/designer
    The preliminary design phase
    Increase to the design fee as a result of late owner changes
    The final design phase
    You are the final decision maker
Other services provided by your architect/designer for an additional fee

---

Chapter 4-The Final Design Process by your Architect or Building Designer

Does the homeowner need an architect or building designer? Yes, the homeowner needs an architect or a building designer to do the final design. Under the Pat Fay Method, you are responsible for the planning and preliminary design phase of your project. Then you hire a professional to produce a permit-ready set of construction documents. You take all of your planning and preliminary design information, such as floor plans, elevations, and your planning binder and turn it over to your Architect/Designer.

    Hiring an architect/designer does two things for you. It gives you drawings that you can submit to your city for permitting that represent your needs, as well as the requirements of the national building code and the local amendments to the national code. It also allows you to bid the project out to contractors. A well defined set of construction documents is essential and critical for your construction planning, for scope of work definition, and for good contractor pricing.

Why you need an architect or building designer. I have had many discussions with homeowners who say they know people who just had some sketches and general layouts to define their project. They say these sketches were given to a contractor and the project turned out great. These stories are everywhere and some may even be true. For every story like that, there are thousands of more common stories where the project did not turn out well and the homeowner was forced to pay thousands of dollars more than anticipated to complete the project.

To think you can just do your own layout of a project and give it to a contractor and have it come out just the way you want is a misunderstanding of the home construction process. Many projects are done this informal way but this method can lead to projects that result in an unhappy ending.

Of course, a little common sense goes a long way in home construction and there are exceptions to every rule. This is because the skill level of the individual homeowner varies so much. Maybe you are a really great interior designer. If that is the case, then by all means use your own layout for smaller remodels such as redoing the bathroom, finishing off the basement, or a smaller kitchen remodel where you are just changing out the cabinets or some of the appliances. However, once you get into the size or complexity of a project where you are completely gutting the entire upstairs, adding additional rooms, or adding a second floor to an existing house, then please do yourself the favor of hiring an architect/designer. A new house absolutely needs the expertise of an architect/designer.

The architect is the expert in the building code. Another reason why you need an architect/designer is that we do not live in a society where you can build anything you want. In our modern society you must temper your ideas based upon the building code adopted by your city. This building code is usually amended by local codes that reflect the collective covenants of your community and your building department.

Understanding the code is very difficult because it is an art not a science. Therefore, do your planning and your preliminary design, but when you get to the point where you know what you want to build, then it is time to ask for help. This help will be found by hiring an architect or a building designer. These professionals know their way through the building code and how your city wants it applied to your house design. They are your hired experts in the building code.

The final design will be the responsibility of your architect/designer. The architect/designer will know what the maximum size the house can be based on the overall size of your building lot. In my case the house footprint could be no larger than 35% of the overall lot size. Also, there will be a height restriction. In the Seattle area this is 25 to 35 feet depending on the jurisdiction. The final design will also include a plot plan which shows your house as it fits on your building lot with certain set backs from the edges of your building lot. The lot will usually be shown with how it fits into your neighborhood with the adjacent streets. Some areas even require an accurate elevation of your lot. There will be many other specifications that your city and the code require to be reflected in you plans. Adhering to these requirements will be the responsibility of your architect/designer.

What is an architect? An architect is a professional with at least five years of college/university education who is expert in building design. It may be houses, commercial buildings or even industrial buildings. As with all professionals they specialize in some area of design. You want one that has specialized in house design. Architects are licensed after passing an examination and meeting educational and experience requirements set by the state in which they reside. These requirements vary by state. To be able to use the title 'architect' they must be licensed by the state in which they work. The American Institute of Architects can also help in your understanding of architects (www.aia.org).

What is a building designer? A building designer is also a professional with a four year education but not usually five years as with an architect. They are qualified to design houses. They usually have some expertise that sets them apart such as energy efficient, green houses, or solar heated homes. They can be certified by the National Council of Building Designer Certification (www.ncbdc.com).

Do you need a structural engineer? Yes you need a structural engineer to ensure your house is structurally sound. However, do not hire a structural engineer yourself. In the Pat Fay Method you will ensure that a structural engineer is a part of the design process but let your architect/designer hire the structural engineer. You will pay for this service through your architect/designer but you do not need to have any contact with the structural engineer. Your architect/designer will manage that portion of the work for you. Your architect/designer will have structural engineers with whom they already work.

The cost to your project will be about $600 for a simple structural design to about $2000 for a larger, full house project. If you hire a structural engineer yourself you will be charged far more than that – probably in the $6,000 range.

The reason for the $6000 price is because if you go directly to the structural engineer they will need to have a meeting with you to determine your requirements. Then a site visit will be made, as-built drawings produced, computer aided drafting (CAD) time spent, structural calculations made for load and shear forces, and seismic considerations. They may double check the work perhaps with another field check, and then give you the finished product.

Once you receive this information you will look at it and wonder what it all means. Unless you are an engineer yourself it will look like Greek. Meaningless. Now you have spent thousand dollars for something you do not understand. It is also something your architect/designer doesn't need either. This is because the architect does not create by the input of the structural engineer. Rather, the structural engineer takes what the architect creates and determines the method to make it structurally sound. If you do go to this expense your architect will glance at the drawings, ignore the structural calculations, throw the whole package in the corner and go back to work on the building design. You will have wasted the money you spent for the structural engineer.

I had a client who did just that. They had hired a structural engineer to produce as-built drawings of their home with a request for his recommendation on what to do to bring their existing house into compliance with the latest building and seismic codes. When I was brought into the picture the homeowners were at the stage where they had paid several thousand dollars on a $6,000 contract. They had received some very preliminary drawings with the prospect of spending several thousand dollars more to complete the work. They did not want to continue with the structural engineer and wanted to know how to get out of the contract. There was nothing I could do for them because they had signed a contract with the structural engineer to perform the complete as-built drawings. Several thousand more dollars were needed to complete the work per the terms of the contract. I told them they were responsible for paying the bill. They were not very happy people.

If you sign a contract you are responsible for performing your part of what is defined in the contract. For homeowners the responsibility is almost always to pay money for delivered services. If you do not pay, you will have problems ranging from a lawsuit to a lien on your property.

The unfortunate homeowner who hired the structural engineer had the right idea but did not understand the correct process to follow. If you have a similar remodel situation you will know better because you will follow the Pat Fay Method. Just let your architect hire the structural engineer and save yourself $6,000 and a lot of frustration.

Why you need a structural engineer. It is a requirement now in many states to have a seismic analysis done on a new home and on remodels. Those of us who live in the West really want the structural engineer's expertise because we live in active seismic zones. No one wants their home to fall down or suffer major damage in a seismic event. Even if your state does not require it, please request that your architect hire a structural engineer to review your drawings and to do the structural calculations. It is cheap insurance and worth the money.

Earthquakes are not the only reason you want a structural analysis performed. The problem of high winds is another very good reason. Wind loads can rack a house out of alignment if the interior walls do not properly counteract the shear forces transmitted through your house structure by the wind. Winds of 30 mph are common and gusts can go to 40 to 60 mph easily. If you are living in tornado or hurricane country they can be far higher. You really want your house to be structurally sound and well inspected.

During hurricane Andrew in Florida in 1992 we saw the results of poor workmanship, improper inspection, and probably lack of structural engineering design. Whole rows of houses would be tinder except for an occasional house here and there that withstood the terrible forces exerted by the hurricane. It was not just luck that those houses survived. They were properly designed and built and no doubt well inspected.

To withstand the external forces of wind, earthquake, and storm your house and particularly your remodel needs to be tied together structurally. That means there needs to be a solid foundation with a spread footing with reinforcing bar and anchor bolts and straps secured into the foundation. Then those straps and anchor bolts must be tied into the flooring and framing. If you have a second story it must be tied into the first so the forces and loads from above can be transmitted to the foundation. Then the roof trusses must be tied in properly to the top plates of the upper framing. If these steps are completed then your house will be well on the way to being a good, solid house able to withstand the forces presented by nature.

Do you need a civil, electrical or mechanical engineer? If your project is a remodel you will probably not need the services of any of these engineers. For a new house project you may need the civil engineer.

The skills these engineers bring to projects are more important to large commercial and industrial projects than in home construction. Your architect/designer and contractors working on your project will provide the services these engineers provide on industrial projects.

A civil engineer is the most likely of the three engineers to be required. They design septic systems, drainage systems and do surveys. They also do things such as property division where you break one large lot into smaller lots. I had to hire a civil engineer to design a drainage system for all the rain downspouts at my house. The city required this because there is no storm drainage system in my neighborhood. The civil engineer did a perk test on our property to determine a dissipation flow rate for the soil on our property. They then used the flow data to design the size of an underground drain field. I paid them a fee and they handed me a design for a drain field much like a septic system. Then I was required to install 4" diameter PVC piping from each downspout on my house to a catch basin in our backyard which then drained all the rain water into the properly sized underground drain field.

An electrical engineer is used in commercial and industrial buildings to design the electrical systems and produce drawings that can be used to bid and construct the electrical systems. In home construction the electrical systems are not typically designed but rather laid-out. Most design elements in a house are already defined in the building code.

A mechanical engineer is used in commercial and industrial buildings to design the heating, ventilating, and air conditioning systems (HVAC) as well as the plumbing systems. The elements of house plumbing systems are defined in the building code with rates of slope for the piping and the types of piping allowed for drain, waste, vent applications and potable water. Your architect/designer will show the locations of sinks, bathtubs, showers, and toilets. Then it is your plumber's responsibility to install the piping to meet the building code. Heating and air conditioning systems are designed and installed by heating/air conditioning contractors. You might need to hire a mechanical engineer to do a heat load calculation for your house, but typically that is handled by your heating contractor.

Rely on your architect/designer to help you decide whether these types of engineers are needed or not. Your architect/designer knows the requirements of your city.

Do you need an interior designer? Whether you hire an interior designer or not depends on your own abilities. If you know exactly what you want and are good with finishes, then by all means, do it yourself. If you are not great with interior finishes, colors, fabrics, and bringing it all together into a beautiful rendition of the theme in your home, then do hire an interior designer. In my classes I teach my students that all houses have the same basics underneath but the finishes are what make a house into a beautiful home. Here you must be honest and critical with yourself. My wife is a natural interior designer and knows how to decorate beautifully and tastefully. We did not put an allowance into our budget for interior design. Other people will.

The design build contractor. The design build concept is where a construction company will also have a design capability so that they will do both the design and the construction phases for the homeowner. They also state that since they know the design so well they can give the homeowner the best construction price. It is a good idea in theory but the experiences I have learned about from the homeowners who have dealt with design build contractors is not good.

In the last ten years of teaching my class I have seen literally hundreds of sets of drawings from my students who brought in their drawings for my review. The best construction drawings were those drawn by architects and building designers who had no interest in the construction phase. Their responsibility was to produce a construction and permit ready set of drawings.

A construction and permit ready set of drawings means that the documents will have a foundation, main floor, second floor, and roof plans with section cuts that take you to an elevation. There also will be the four exterior elevations. All of these elements will have enough detail and dimensions so that a clear definition of the work can be found in the construction documents. Then a third party contractor can read the drawings and clearly understand what is to be built.

The poorest construction drawings I have ever seen have been those produced by design build contractors. They had few if any dimensions on either their plan or elevation views. They typically did not have section cuts or if they did they were not properly labeled so a third party could find their way from the section cut to the actual detail of that section cut on another drawing. They also rarely had any structural members called out or had not taken shear forces into account.

My conclusion is that the design build construction companies do not produce good construction documents so that only they can build from the drawings. Their drawings are poor on purpose so that the homeowner who tries to take the drawings and bid out their project will find that other contractors must bid high because the drawings leave so much to the imagination.

This wouldn't be so bad if the construction prices from the design build contractors were reasonable but they are not! The prices my homeowner students were given to build by the design build contractors were very, very high. For example, one couple had a set of these design build construction drawings to remodel their existing 2,200 SF split level house. There were no new exterior walls to be built or modified. It was just gutting the interior and building it out new. Interior finishes were nice but not that expensive. They had two proposals from the same company who drew the drawings. The reason there were two proposals is because the first one was so high that the couple complained and they were then given a second, lower proposal. The first cost was $800,000 and the second was $695,000. That is $364 per SF and $316 per SF respectively for a remodel! They could have built 3 new houses for those prices.

A second example is from a man who wanted to take his 400 SF garage (20' x 20') and convert it into a manufacturing space. The scope of work was to replace the garage door with windows, add 4 other windows, raise the level of the ceiling joists because they were too low for walking, and relocate the electrical panel. He had paid $3,000 for the drawings and they were the worst drawings I had ever seen. They consisted of one plan view without a single dimension, no section cuts and no elevations. There were several isometric views of the garage from different directions showing elevations but they had no construction details by which to build. The price proposal was a flat $60,000 with no detail breaking out why the project was to cost $60,000. That is $150 per SF. I recommended that instead of modifying the roof trusses with a beam to get height that he should just rip the old roof off, build a 2' stub wall and put on a new roof. My cost estimate to do this, add the windows, relocate the electrical panel, and add flooring was $25,000 or $62.50 per SF. I could write a book just on the examples of how badly homeowners have been treated by the design build contractor.

The homeowner following the Pat Fay Method will want to use architects and building designers unaffiliated with a construction company.

Finding an architect/designer. One of the best ways to find an architect/designer is to speak to your friends – particularly those that have done projects similar to yours. Other sources are to look in your yellow pages or to read the real estate section of the newspaper. Ask the recommendation of any builders you know. One of the largest concentrations of architects will be at a home show in your area. You might even put an ad in the newspaper. Also, check the internet for listings of architects and building designers in your area. The American Institute of Architects can also help find architects in your area (aia.org). Another resource on the web is e-architects.com.

Building Designers can also be found through the National Council of Building Designer Certification (NCBDC): NCBDC, 2962 Saklan Indian Drive, Walnut Creek, CA 94595; 888-726-7659; www.ncbdc.com. Another source for building designers is the American Institute of Building Design: 2505 Main Street, Suite 209B, Stratford, Connecticut 06615; 800-366-2423; www.aibd.org.

Interviewing the architect/designer. Once you have about five to ten leads, the next step is to go through an interview and selection process. Telephone calls are a good way to start instead of spending the time and going to see them personally. Many times a call will reveal that the architect's schedule cannot accommodate you. Don't be discouraged if this happens. Use it as an opportunity to ask for their recommendation for another architect/designer. They will know many other architects and/or designers that may have the time for your project.

When you do find an interested architect/designer you will want to explain to them that you have done your planning, preliminary design and that you have a 3-ring binder with all of your research and a preliminary floor plan. You hire the architect to take your preliminary design and make it into a great design so you have a beautiful yet functional home that meets the current building codes.

You'll find that many architect/designers are intrigued by a homeowner that has done their planning and a preliminary design. However, some will not.

Once you have five to ten architect/designers on your short list, then move to the second interview.

The second interview. The second interview must be conducted face-to-face. You have two goals in the second interview. The first is to look at examples of their other projects to see if you like their style of design. The second is to determine if you can communicate easily with them.

Your conversation topics should be focused on your project. Gauge their reaction to your floor plans and your planning binder. It is a plus if they are interested in what you have done already. Likewise, it is a minus if they dismiss your work. Later when you are alone, add up the positives and negatives to compare one architect/designer against another. Then choose the one who you think will work the best with you and do a good job on your project.

In our case we found a great architect with whom we just hit it off. He was easy to speak to, he listened to our ideas, and was very impressed with our floor plan and the amount of preliminary work we had already done. He said what we had done made his job so much easier because we could skip the phase where he would try to determine what his new client wanted. We liked him: not because he said flattering words, but because he listened to us, looked us in the eye, laughed a little with us, and then he made a good critique of our floor plan. He noted that we had forgotten closets and where was the stairwell? He took our floor plan, laid it on his table, overlaid a large sheet of onion paper (thin paper that allowed our floor plan to show through) over our floor plan and right there he began making modifications and improvements. He added a number of closets, the stairwell, a mechanical chase, rearranged where our fireplaces were and even relocated some of the exterior walls to add better ventilation for individual rooms. We knew we had found our architect.

Final selection of the architect/designer. As in all relationships, you are looking for someone with whom you can work well. One of the main criteria is to be able to speak easily to the architect/designer and know that he or she is listening to you. You need to be sure the architect will accept and use your ideas and take into account the information you have gathered in your planning. Look at the previous projects the architect/designer has designed and see if you like their work. Have they done any projects similar to yours? This is nice to have, but not critical because the architect/designer has the skill to handle almost any house remodel or new construction.

You may find that you are interviewing an architect/designer recently graduated from the university. The younger architect/designer will not have a large portfolio but do not write them off because of this. This should not stop you from using them because they may be young but they are not inexperienced. They all have four to five years of formal college education and more than likely many years of practical training. Also, the younger architect may not charge as high a fee.

My wife and I interviewed a number of architect/designers. One architect came very highly recommended from some personal friends. He was a well respected architect in Seattle and he wouldn't even look at our binder or our floor plan. He told us that he would create a masterpiece for us that would fit our lot, take advantage of the view, and it would be beautiful. However, he wasn't interested in our ideas. If we wanted to use him then those were the terms by which he would work with us. Also, his fee was $40,000. I'm sure he would have designed a beautiful house for us but it would not have been our home. We did not use him because he would not involve us in the design process and his fee was too high.

In the final analysis you tally up the positive and negative marks for each architect/designer and then compare them against each other. Then make a decision on who you will hire.

Negotiating with the architect/designer. When you negotiate with an architect/designer you are stating what it is you want and listening to what they have to say in return. You are not trying to take advantage of them but rather you have certain things you want them to do for you in their role as your architect/designer. Tell them what you want and see what they say in reply. Take notes.

The most important thing to negotiate with your architect/designer. The most important thing that you want is a complete set of drawings that reflects what you want built for your remodel or new construction. The drawings should reflect the latest building code adopted by your city as well as the local amendments to the building code. You will want a permit ready set of drawings that are required by your city for your use for the permit application and for your use in bidding out the project to contractors.

Other terms to negotiate with your architect/designer. Have your architect include as part of their fee working with the city permitting department to satisfy their requirements and exceptions. When your drawings come back from the city they will typically have markups and exceptions noted on the drawings (usually in red). This is normal and does reflect negatively on your architect/designer.

There is not a permitting department anywhere in America that will not have markups and exceptions on a new set of drawings. In fact, the experienced architect/designer will leave out some minor details that will be easily discovered by the plans reviewer at the city. If they do not then the plans reviewer will dig deeper and deeper until he does find something to markup. The deeper they dig into the code to find exceptions the more expensive it will be to fix. However, you need to negotiate with your architect/designer so they will not charge you additional to revise the drawings according to the plan reviewer's markups.

You will also want to negotiate two site visits to your project while it is under construction. I recommend that the first visit be before the concrete is poured for the foundation and preferably before the concrete forms are completed. This way they can look at the foundation forming to be sure it matches the plans. On the second site visit you will want your architect/designer to come out to speak to the framing foreman. Have them come out when the main floor is having the plywood flooring nailed and glued down. If you were to ask the framing foreman if he has any questions he will just tell you no. However, when your architect shows up they will be deep in conversation discussing the plans. There are always questions.

The design schedule. Normally you can expect a design package ready for permit submittal in three to four months. We received ours in about six months. However, in exchange for a longer schedule we negotiated a lower fee. Being flexible on how quickly your project is completed is one way for you to negotiate a lower fee from your architect/designer. If, however, you wanted your design in an accelerated schedule of two months expect to pay a higher fee.

When we negotiated the schedule with our architect he told us how busy he was with other houses and commercial projects but that he would like to do our job. (By the way, it seems to be a standard with everyone in the home construction industry, designers and contractors alike, to tell you how busy they are even if they are not. I think it is a technique so that you are inclined to think they are doing you a favor for taking your job.) We told him we would like to use him but that his initial fee was higher than what we wanted to pay. We asked if there was any way he could lower it. He told us he did not like to lower his fee but if we were willing to have him work our project as a secondary or filler job he could lower his fee a little.

You need to understand how the mind of an architect/designer or engineer works. When we work on a project there comes a point when we cannot make any more progress on it. We need to set it aside and work on a totally different project. A second or filler project clears our mind from whatever has us stuck on the first project. When we get stuck on the second project, we go back to the first project and our minds will have worked the problem out without conscious thought and the design can then continue.

What you can expect to pay for design services. In 2005, a reasonable fee for final design services is $5,000 if the homeowner follows the Pat Fay Method. This low a fee is only possible if the homeowner has actually done their planning and preliminary design. Without this preparation you should pay your architect/designer $10,000. Structural and civil engineering fees are additional.

These prices are good for all of the major cities in the United States. In smaller towns outside of the major metropolitan areas you can find pricing down to $1 per square foot. There are also architects who will not consider a fee of less than 15% of the construction cost.

The reason the design fee should be $10,000 for a standard design (non-Pat Fay Method preparation) is because 40 to 50 hours of the architect/designers time will be taken up by trying to understand what the homeowner wants. Then 40 hours is needed for the final design. The typical homeowner goes to see the architect/designer and has almost nothing prepared before hand. Even if they do, it is not typically well enough organized so they can instantly use that information in support of their ideas.

If we were to listen in on a first conversation between an architect/designer and a homeowner it might go like this:

Architect: How many square feet would you like to add to your house?
Homeowner: I'm not sure but we would like more room, maybe even a second floor or perhaps push the side of the house out because our lot is bigger there.
Architect: Great. What are you trying to create in your home space?
Homeowner: More room.
Architect: Yes I understand but what about the overall feel of the house, are you satisfied with it?
Homeowner. No, we want more room.
A. Of course, but why do you want more room? What is driving your need for more room?
Homeowner. I don't know we just thought it would be nice. And so on.

This simple conversation shows the difficulty the architect will encounter in trying to determine the design requirements from a homeowner who only knows in general what they want. This is why the architect/designer deserves to be paid an additional $5,000 for discovering project requirements.

Let's break down the cost of design under the Pat Fay Method. At a fee of $5,000 you will typically see a proposal from your architect that breaks the total cost down into 40 hours of design work at $100/hour = $4,000. Two 2-hour site visits at $100/hour = $400. Six hours of coordination with the permitting department at $100/hour = $600, for a total of $5,000.

Six hours does not seem like much for dealing with the city and it is not. This is because the first point of contact with the city is not going to be your architect. In the Pat Fay method, you are the first point of contact with the city! The architect's six hours will be coordination by phone with the city and for reviewing the comments on the drawings and specifications that you have picked up from the city and delivered to your architect's office. It will also allow for some redesign work to satisfy the city's markups.

However, the six hours does not include time to have a face-to-face meeting with the city personnel to work out the issues that have come to an impasse. This is because a meeting will take at least four hours of the architect's time; one hour of travel each way and two for the meeting. If you are unable to resolve the issues with the city yourself then you will need the architect/designer. Pay them an additional $400 per meeting with the city. Also, if your contractor needs a third meeting with your architect/designer you can figure on that also costing an additional $400.

Lump sum fee vs. an hourly rate for design services. In the Pat Fay Method you will want to negotiate a fixed lump sum fee for the architect/designer's services. I do not recommend an hourly rate for design services. The reason for this is that you cannot put a firm figure down in your budget for design services. When I have stated this idea at my classes some students mistakenly assumed this was because the architect/designer might run up the cost of the design by spending more hours than needed. There is no reason to believe that your architect/designer would do such a thing. These are professional people that have the highest standards and ethics to be found in the entire home construction process. Lump sum fee is a way to have a well defined cost for design services.

Signing a contract for design services. I recommend that you have your architect/designer prepare the contract that you will eventually sign. You will want to edit the contract to include the conditions discussed in this chapter that you feel are appropriate for your project. Remember the contract is nothing more than a proposal until you sign it. While it is in the proposal stage you have the right and the responsibility to modify it to meet your needs and concerns. Once the document is complete to your satisfaction and to the architect/designer's then sign it. Both of you should receive an original signed copy (so you'll have to sign two copies).

The drawings you should receive from the architect/designer. You should receive a drawing for the foundation, basement/crawl space, main floor, second & third floors (if any), roof plan, north, south, west and east elevations, and sections and details. The cover drawing is typically the plot plan. Some architects will have one floor to a drawing and some show two floors on one drawing. Either way is acceptable. The only difference is that the scale of the drawings is smaller with two floors to a sheet, making it a little harder to read. None of our contractors complained about drawings with two floors to a sheet.

Have specifications and material requirements on the drawings. If you have a certain material and quality requirements for your project then you will want them written out on your drawings.

Specifications are written requirements that the contractor must follow. Material requirement define what materials you want on your project. For the homeowner these requirements are almost always calling out specific material to be used and quality of workmanship issues that you want.

For example, if you want granite countertops in the kitchen you can call that out on your drawings. This callout and careful coordination between you and your finish contractor will insure that you actually have granite countertops installed not formica.

Purchasing pre-designed plans. There are companies that will sell you architectural plans fully completed for the house of your dreams. I don't believe you should waste your money on these plans unless you only have to spend $20 or so. Spending any more is a waste of your money. The only use for these plans is if you would like to copy them.

Don't think you can use these already designed house plans and submit them to your city and get them approved. Your city will ask where your plot plan is that locates the house on your lot and in your neighborhood. What about the location of utilities? What about meeting the conditions of your building lot not to mention the local amendments to the national code.

If you do buy these plans, you will still need to hire an architect/designer to finish them and make them ready for permit submittal. Knowing this can prevent you from wasting your money on pre-designed plans that will not really save you any time or money.

Working with your architect/designer. To work well with your architect/designer all you need to do is act as you would in any professional relationship. Be on time for your meetings, come prepared, make decisions when it is time to make them, do your homework, and pay your bill.

How to interact with the architect/designer. The architect/designer is a professional person who deserves your respect. You can expect excellent and professional work. However, this is a business relationship and you are hiring the architect/designer to work for you. The thing to remember is that you are paying money for the architect's service. Therefore, it is a professional relationship and your behavior should reflect that.

This means to be on time for your appointments and be prepared. If you are one of those people whose life is so busy and you are never on time to anything then please modify your behavior when it comes to meetings with your architect/designer. It is the least you can do if you successfully negotiated an excellent (reduced) fee.

Also you are not there to make friends with your architect/designer. This doesn't mean that you can't be on friendly terms. You can. In fact, being able to get along and enjoy the time you spend with your architect/designer is one of the better parts of the home construction process. There are times when you will laugh and will really be enjoying yourself but do not forget the nature of your relationship to your architect/designer. You are not family and you are not buddies. If you allow the relationship to fall into this mindset then you will be personally hurt if a deadline is not met or if you have a professional disagreement with your architect/designer. Do not bake them a cake or bring them cookies. However, after a successful project there is no reason why you cannot send your architect/designer a nice note thanking them for their services and, if you mean it, offering to act as a recommendation for them.

The preliminary design phase. Turning your floor plan and planning/preliminary design binder over to your architect is the beginning of the architect/designer's preliminary design. This consists of taking your floor plan and checking how it fits on your lot, taking into consideration the setbacks required by the city. Then your architect/designer will adjust your interior layout and flesh it out with details.

In our case our architect added closets, stairwells, refined the flow of the rooms to each other, and added a sunken dining room. These changes contributed to exterior wall changes. This process took a few weeks and two meetings. The drawings still were mostly sketches attached to an overall main and upstairs floor plan with a hint of what we would do in the basement and with the roofline. A little time was spent on helping us make decisions on the types of finishes in each room

Then came the day we had to make the decision that graduated our preliminary design into the final design phase. We had to freeze the exterior footprint of our house. Freezing the exterior footprint of your house plan is the most important final step in the preliminary design. Up until this point we could still make changes with exterior walls and not worry about additional cost. At some point though your architect/designer will request that you buy off on the final exterior footprint so the final design can begin.

Increase to the design fee as a result of late owner changes. The reason freezing your exterior footprint is significant is because now there will be no more exterior wall changes without an additional fee paid to your architect/designer. In the Pat Fay Method an additional fee of 40 hours of design time or $4000 is to be paid to the architect/designer for an exterior wall change. Yes, expect changes after this point to cost four thousand dollars. So make sure you have what you want when you sign off on the preliminary design.

This is how it works. Once the exterior wall layout is frozen, all the footprints will be finalized: foundation, main floor, second floor, the roof plan, and structural components. The elevations will also be finalized. To change any exterior wall after it is frozen will result in all the other plans and elevations being affected. The layperson just thinks an exterior wall change is just redrawing a few lines. To those that know and understand the design process it is a major redesign effort that has significant time implications and cost. That is why the architect/designer deserves an additional fee for a wall change after the exterior footprint is frozen.

However, it is your right as a homeowner under the Pat Fay Method to make late changes if it is important to you. Just don't think you can do it for free.

The final design phase. Now that the footprint is frozen the architect/designer can now feel confident that what they draw is the final rendition. It is not your responsibility to know everything that has to be done to produce the final design because it is your architect/designer's responsibility. That is why you hired them.

The final design phase goes somewhat like this: interior walls can be changed easily in the early part of the final design but they too quickly become frozen in place. When the room sizes are frozen this freezes the doors and the hallways. The bathroom layouts are finalized and the finishes defined. The exterior elevations take their final form with windows, doors and exterior trim and soffits. Section cuts are shown that reference wall construction to the detail sheets, code requirements are shown such as handrails and whole house fans. Locations of appliances for power, water, and drain locations are shown and all the drawings are finalized. Copies are made and a submittal package for the city is prepared. The design is then complete, awaiting the city's comments.

You are the final decision maker. In the Pat Fay Method your architect/designer works for you. If you feel strongly about an idea that you want incorporated in your house then insist upon it whether the architect likes it or not.

One example of not accepting our architect's suggestion is when the design of our second floor was being worked. My wife and I had defined that the room on the second floor at the front of the house was to be our living room. We wanted to be able to pick up the view from this room of Lake Washington. Our architect told us he believed this space should actually be the master bedroom. This seems to be a popular style but not for us. Also, by moving the master bedroom we would also have had to relocate the master bathroom which added a lot of complications. We liked our floor plan better than the architect's version.

However, it was something our architect felt very strongly about and he revisited it several times with us. My wife and I discussed his recommendation and we agreed to disagree with our architect.

At our next meeting I calmly stated that the matter was over and the living room would remain at the front of the house. He told us his professional opinion was being ignored but he accepted our decision (with a bit of irritation). Then his professionalism took over and he said if we insisted on having our way then we need to clean up the front elevation to bring out the best look for the living room/deck combination and for the overall look of the entire front elevation. He then sketched a reduced width elevation for the living room/deck, opened up a side section to the master bedroom so a nice 24"x 36" window could fit in the new 4' wall and voila we had a view of the lake from our bedroom. He won after all, but in a way that acknowledged our priorities.

However, be sure of what you want and be ready to accept their recommendations because they often do know best. In fact, we lost count of the many great suggestions made by our architect that we did accept because of their obvious superiority over our initial floor plan.

A second example of disagreeing with your designer comes from a conversation I had with a family friend in 1970. She had a cabin in northern Minnesota that had been built a few years earlier. She told me she was very unhappy with her kitchen. During the design phase she had stated that she did not want a conventional kitchen with an oven because she did not like to bake. She told her designer she wanted to have a lot of counter space with many outlets because she would just use plug in appliances to do her cooking.

I looked around her kitchen and it was just your basic kitchen with oven and all the other standard features with very little counter space. When I asked her why there was an oven and not very much counter space she stated, "I was told you could not do that". How sad. If there are features that are especially important to you, be sure to insist on them. Just be sure to do it professionally.

The essential point is that in the Pat Fay Method you are in charge of your overall project not your architect/designer. You have hired them to work for you. You are the master of your home and its design. If you want something in your house don't let anyone tell you that you cannot do it. As long as it is not a code/safety type issue there is no reason you should not have your way.

Even when it is a code issue there are ways to mitigate it because the code is full of exceptions. For example, we wanted to have a laundry chute from the second floor to the basement so we would not have to carry laundry down the stairs. Our architect added it to the plans and the city vetoed it because it was a fire path. Never mind that it was adjacent to the stairwell. We had to argue and insist. When our architect dug into the code he found that the chute was allowed if there was a one hour fire barrier at each end. We added a lid with sheetrock at the top and a fire damper at the bottom. Since we met the requirements of the code the city had to accept it. And I will say, a laundry chute is a very nice feature to have in one's home.

Other services provided by your architect/designer for an additional fee. The architect/designer can provide more services than just design. Additional services include planning, preliminary design, final design, cost estimates, write and issue bid proposals, review and analyze contractor bid proposals, writing contracts, selecting contractors, contract management, construction/project management, construction supervision and inspection. These services cost an additional fee. Perhaps following the Pat Fay Method of doing all the management yourself does not appeal to you. If that is the case, speak to your architect/designer about providing some of these additional services. The decision is for you to make.

Chapter 5-Scheduling

What is a schedule?
    The Gantt chart
Two types of schedules
    High level schedule, low level detailed schedule
The two kinds of schedules
    Straight line activity schedule
    Modified straight line activity schedule
Common tracking elements
What goes into your schedule?
    The elements of a schedule
Where does the homeowner find out how long a construction activity should take to accomplish?
Is scheduling difficult?
    Build in buffer times
How to make your project schedule
    Draw your own schedules
The use of the schedule during your project for time and cost
    The biggest scheduling issue Pat Fay encountered
        One contractor on site at a time
What to do when a schedule is not being met by the contractor
What to do when a contractor is way behind schedule
    Contractor is about a week behind schedule but on site daily
    Contractor is several weeks behind schedule and on site only infrequently
    Contractor started the project but only worked a few days and then disappeared
Schedule disadvantage of the Pat Fay Method
The realities of scheduling in the homeowner construction world
How long will your project take?
How long did Pat Fay's new house project take?
Example schedules
    High level straight line schedule, SCH-1
    High level modified straight line schedule, SCH-2
Schedule of project activities in building Pat Fay's house, SCH-3

Chapter 5-Scheduling

What is a schedule? There are many forms schedules can take but in the Pat Fay Method we will keep it simple. A schedule is a chart that graphically shows the activities to be accomplished during a project from beginning to end. The information shown for each activity will be a start date, finish date and duration of the task.

    The Gantt chart. The Gantt chart is the original of all graphic schedules. It was invented in 1917 by a mechanical engineer by the name of Henry Gantt. He wanted a simple graphic way to convey a project timeline from start to finish in a simple picture. All graphic schedules in use today are adaptations of Mr. Gantt's idea.

The disadvantage of the Gantt chart is that they get cumbersome to write, update, and maintain without a computer. You can end up with several sheets of paper because you need the extra room to show the activities in their proper time position. That is why in the Pat Fay Method we use the straight line chart.

Two types of schedules. The two types of schedules are the high level and the low level detailed schedules.

High level schedule. A high level schedule will show the time it takes to do the major activities in a project from start to finish. This is a useful schedule from an overall planning point of view because it will show all major activities on one or two sheets of paper.

Low level detailed schedule. A low level detailed schedule (also called a break down schedule) will show all of the activities that make up each of the major activities shown in the high level schedule. This is useful because one can see all of the many steps needed to accomplish a particular phase of construction.

The homeowner will need both of these schedules because they show your project in different levels of detail. For example, on the high level schedule the construction activity will be a single line or bar. On the low level detailed schedule the construction activity will be made up of dozens of lines detailing out each step that must occur to do all the construction activities.

The two kinds of schedules. The two kinds of schedules are the straight line activity schedule and the modified straight line schedule. The information on each line is made up of the start date, the finish date, and a duration bar that shows how long the activity will take.

Straight line activity schedule. The straight line activity schedule is the easiest schedule to construct because you just list the activities one after the other. To the right of each activity description is the duration bar showing the start and end dates. The reason it is called the straight line activity schedule is because each activity bar starts at the same point on the schedule, thus the term, straight line. It is very simple to make, easy to track, and easy to use.

In the Pat Fay Method this schedule is the schedule to be used. You will see an example of this schedule at the end of this chapter. We will use carrots and bars (see the schedule examples at the end of this chapter for an explanation of these terms) to track your progress in each activity.

Modified straight line activity schedule. This is a slight variation of the straight line activity schedule in that some of the activities will move off the straight line to show relative activity times. The best explanation is to see the example at the end of this chapter.

Common tracking elements. Tracking your schedule is just measuring how much work is accomplished in an activity and marking that level of progress on your schedule. Both kinds of schedules lend themselves to tracking (sometimes called charting) by shading or coloring in the duration bar. You can chart your progress for a particular activity by coloring in the duration bar between the carrots to show your progress in any activity. For example, if you are 50% complete with construction you color in half of the duration bar on your high level schedule.

Be careful though that you don't color in more than is accomplished. It is easy to be optimistic on your progress. However, don't worry too much if you do because you will be in good company. During my tenure with a large design build construction company, upper management would move out the construction superintendent who had built a project from start to 95% complete and then move me in to close out the project. Invariably the project would actually only be 85% complete but 95% of the money would have been spent. That was not a fun job.

What goes into your schedule? You put into your schedule all of the activities that you need to do to accomplish your project. Each activity will have a length of time allocated to it. The appropriate amount of time depends on the scope of the work needed to accomplish the task. (A scope of work is a written description that defines what is to be accomplished in a project)

The elements of a schedule. In the Pat Fay Method the elements of a schedule are the project time line, planning, preliminary design, final design, permitting, contractor selection, construction activities, inspection, lien release signature and payment. Each element will have a duration that is appropriate to your project. You will see examples of this graphically on the sample schedules at the end of this chapter.

Where does the homeowner find out how long a construction activity should take to accomplish? You will find answers at the end of this chapter. A complete list of all the activities to build Pat Fay's 3000 SF house and the time it took to do these activities is listed in the schedule of activities (SCH-3).

Is scheduling difficult? Scheduling is really not that difficult to do. The problem is that the majority of homeowners are just not sure they know all of the construction activities that need to take place to accomplish their project. Other difficulties are in which sequence the work should be done and how long each activity should reasonably take to complete.

A word of encouragement might be appropriate after mentioning that scheduling might have its difficulties. Remember that difficulties should not stop you from having fun during your project. I know that a lot of new terms and ideas are being presented to you and that alone may seem intimidating. Give yourself a few days for your mind to absorb the new information. It also helps to get enough sleep. Learning new information is tough work but in this case very rewarding.

Just think how much pride you will have in yourself once you master this information and put it to use on your own home construction project! Also, think of the bonding experience you will have with your spouse or significant other when you finish your project and you save a serious amount of money. Now that is a lot of fun!

Build in buffer times. Scheduling is the project manager's best shot at forecasting how long a project will take before it is completed. In reality I have never seen a construction schedule yet that has been completed on time. Something always happens that causes delays. Therefore, since we know this we build in buffer times between the major activities to allow for unforeseen delays. Insert one week of buffer between each major construction activity. This may seem like a lot but you will learn that it is not.

How to make your project schedule. You can copy many of the steps for your project from the schedule of activities for Pat Fay's house found at the end of this chapter. This activity schedule has all of the major activities and most of the minor activities needed to build a new house. You will find the order of activities and how long each took to accomplish. This is a very useful chart because it not only shows the duration of each activity but also in which order they should occur.

Of course, not every activity that can possibly take place on your project is listed in Pat Fay's house activity schedule. This is because every project is different. Your schedule must reflect the work that is going on in your house. For example, we had no demolition activities. If you have a remodel then you must include time for demolition. Each project is unique and part of the fun of being your own project manager is taking ownership of your unique project.

Draw your own schedules. When I first started out in construction in 1977 we did not have computers to draw our schedules for us. We drew them by hand. We printed neatly, free-hand sketched our lines and drew in our carrots defining start and end dates. These homemade schedules worked. We knew what had to be done and by writing out each of the steps and sketching in the duration bar, we became more knowledgeable about all the steps that had to occur on our projects.

In the Pat Fay Method the homeowner draws their own schedules. At the end of this chapter the example schedules are hand drawn.

Of course, if you have a computer scheduling program and you know how to use it, then use it to make your schedules. If scheduling is new to you why complicate the process by trying to learn a new program when in 5 minutes you will have mastered the art of hand drawing your own schedules. Remember the goal is to finish your construction project not get lost in unnecessary endeavors.

The use of the schedule during your project for time and cost. Scheduling is a planning tool. On a sheet of paper you can look at the schedule and tell where you are in your project, what activities are complete, and then you will be able to determine what percentage of your project is complete. The schedule will also tell you how much time is left to complete the project and what activities need to be completed.

Also, by adding up the estimated dollar values for the activities remaining, the homeowner can easily calculate how much more money will be needed to complete the project. Add this value to what you have already spent and you will have your projected project cost.

The schedule is a very valuable project management tool. However, you need to keep it up on a regular basis. Update it at least weekly. An easy way to remember to update your schedule is to set a specific time for that task. I updated my schedule on Friday afternoons.

Therefore, in the Pat Fay Method you will update your schedules on Friday afternoons too.

The biggest scheduling issue Pat Fay encountered. The biggest scheduling issue we faced in our new house construction project was that we could not schedule multiple contractors on site at one time. We found that independent contractors would not cooperate or work together on site. We were shocked by their immaturity. They just did not want to share the work space together. Some even destroyed each others work and denied that they had done it. We then had to pay extra to have it repaired.

One contractor on site at a time. To resolve this issue we decided that we would have only one contractor on site at a time. We hired a contractor to do a phase of the project, had the work inspected, paid them off and then brought the next contractor on site.

In the Pat Fay Method the rule for homeowners is to have only one contractor on site at a time.

What to do when a schedule is not being met by the contractor. When a schedule is not being met the first step is to ask the contractor what they plan to do to bring their work back on schedule. For example, the homeowner says to the contractor, "John, it is pretty obvious that with the manpower you have that you will not be able to finish the work on time (per the contract completion date). What will you do to bring this job back on schedule?"

Then wait for them to answer. Do not try to help them with any of your own words. Ask them the question and see how they respond. Let silence fill the air. If they have solutions, then fine. If they do not have solutions or will not work with you, or they get angry then you must make a decision on how tough you will be.

Let me offer a word of caution. Try to work with your contractor and be a little understanding. They have problems also. Only take the hard approach when you have a serious schedule problem. A few days to a week is not a serious problem. A few weeks or more is.

Start early in monitoring your contractor's progress. Don't wait until the last day to ask them about the schedule when you could see half way through the allocated time that only a quarter of the work was completed.

What to do when a contractor is way behind schedule. It is important that you have a contract with defined start and finish dates. If you do not, then any length of time to complete the contract is acceptable. Then you are at the mercy of your contractor.

Let's assume that you do have a contractually defined end date. What do you do when the completion date has come and gone?

What you do depends on how far the contractor is behind schedule. It also depends on the contractor's attitude.

Contractor is about a week behind schedule but on site daily. If the contractor is about a week behind schedule and they are on site and working hard every day then consider yourself successful. As long as your contractor is making a good faith effort to work every day on your project and they look to be completed in just a few more days (perhaps even in a week) then let the contractor finish. I do not recommend that the homeowner beat up the contractor for being a few days to a week late as long as they are on site and working.

Contractor is several weeks behind schedule and on site only infrequently. If the contractor is several weeks behind schedule but they only show up once in awhile then there is a problem. The problem is the lack of commitment to working on your project. It does not matter that the contractor has other projects. They committed to a contract with you with a specific end date. The attitude of the contractor is clear: disrespect for your project and the contract. The disrespect is shown by the fact that they are not working your job every day. The homeowner must bring their arbitrator in to help resolve the problem.

Contractor started the project but only worked a few days and then disappeared. This is typical disrespectful contractor behavior. They start your job, get about 10 to 20% of the project completed and then they disappear. They may or may not have any of your money. They want to lock up your project for themselves but will work other projects to earn other money leaving yours like a bank account for later. Contractors believe that the homeowner will not know what to do. In the Pat Fay Method, this is the time to call in your arbitrator and ask for their assistance.

Schedule disadvantage of the Pat Fay Method. The Pat Fay Method may have a disadvantage in that your construction will take longer than if you hired a general contractor. However, the homeowner must judge how serious this disadvantage is when compared to how much money they can save on their project cost. The homeowner who follows the Pat Fay Method has more time than they have money.

The reason that it takes longer to follow the Pat Fay Method is because the homeowner will have to arrange for contractors themselves. The general contractor will not have this problem because they have a list of contractors from previous projects. Second, the general contractor will be able to get their contractors to work together on site because they have the threat of no future work if the subcontractor does not perform. The homeowner does not.

The realities of scheduling in the homeowner construction world. The realities are that even the very best contractors can have problems meeting schedules. They have labor problems, material comes out wrong from the supplier, mistakes are made on the job and then there is rework. Sometimes nature causes problems that make it tough for the contractor to complete on time.

I have been working on construction projects in a professional capacity since 1977. I have never seen even one project actually complete on the original scheduled completion date. They always take longer than planned.

That being said your reaction to the contractor's problem of not completing on time really must be tempered by the contractor's attitude. If they are working in good faith, work with them. If they are not working with you in good faith then bring in your arbitrator.

How long will your project take? This really depends on two things: the size of your project and you.

The size of your project really matters. If you are just remodeling your bathroom you can probably get the whole project done in a couple of months including your planning, a good sketch and an over-the-counter permit. If you are remodeling your whole house then a couple of months for your planning & preliminary design, one or two months for final design, two or three months for permit, and six months for construction. That is 11 to 13 months in total. A new house project would be longer.

The other variable is you. No one can make you do anything but yourself. How quickly you get done with your project really, in the end, depends on the amount of effort and time you spend. What kind of project manager will you be? Will you be industrious or lazy, meet problems head on or procrastinate, make decisions or avoid them? Only you can answer these questions.

As I have stated before, the Pat Fay Method is not a cookbook. It is a method that gives you a fighting chance to win on your project. If you lay down in the middle of your project because it is just too much then you should expect to be trampled. However, if you face each day with action items that you will accomplish, acknowledge that you will make mistakes and move on, keep your money in your pocket rather than the contractor's, then you have an excellent chance to have a successful project.

How long did Pat Fay's new house project take? We spent about 12 months in our planning and preliminary design, final design took 6 months and permitting took 5 months. Our construction duration was 14 months for a total of 37 months.

The reason our construction took so long is because we shut our project down three times: once due to weather, once at Christmas time and once because we went on vacation.

Was it worth it? We think so because we had more time than we had money. Our cost was $227,500 for 3500 SF or $65 per SF. The lowest general contractor price we received in 1992 was $120/SF or $420,000 (before change orders). Yes, indeed, it was worth it if nothing more than to deny a general contractor $192,500 in excess profit at our expense!

Example schedules. High level straight line schedule, SCH-1
High level modified straight line schedule, SCH-2

Schedule of project activities in building Pat Fay's house. SCH-3. Please see the schedule of activities from Pat Fay's house, SCH-3 at the end of this chapter. There are five columns that make up this schedule. Column 1 is the activity description. Column 2 is the percentage that particular line item takes out of the whole project. Column 3 is the cumulative or addition of all the individual percentages in column 2. Column 4 is the number of days that activity should take with a reasonable sized crew of workers. Column 5 is the cumulative of all the individual number of days with a total of 152 days. By adding buffers and delays, the new house is a one year project for the construction phase alone in the Pat Fay Method.

Chapter 6-Working with your City; Permitting and The Building Inspector

What is a building permit?
Why you want a building permit
    Why your city wants you to have a permit
The homeowner's responsibility in regards to the permit
The homeowner's responsibility in regards to the building code
What is the building code?
    Why there is a code
    The building code is a minimum requirement only
    The code is a science and an art
    Your state has a building code
    Your city's amendments to the code
Working with your city to get your permit
    The building official's role in applying the code to your project
    The personality and attitude of your city
    The Pat Fay Method is allowed by the building code
        A word about the State of Louisiana
Pat Fay's permitting experience
Keeping notes and your cool when dealing with the city
    Questions you do not ask your city
    Questions you do ask your city
    Legal complaints against your city regarding your permit
    There are different departments in the city
What to do when your permit seems to be lost in the city
When you do not use your architect/designer in the permit process
When you do use your architect/designer in the permit process
Be wary of beginning your project with only a demolition permit
What to do while your project is in permitting
What to do when you receive your construction permit from the city
The Building Inspector
    The inspection department is not the building department
    The role of the city in the enforcement of the code
    The building inspector's right to inspect
    The work must remain accessible
    What work needs to be inspected by the city inspector?
    The homeowner's inspection duties

Chapter 6-Working with your City; Permitting and The Building Inspector

What is a building permit? A building permit is permission by your city to build your project. It is a legal requirement. Please note that I use the term "city" to mean whatever jurisdiction governs your land use. It could actually be a county, parish, state, or city.

Why you want a building permit. The most important reason that you want a building permit is because you will receive the services of a wonderful person titled the building inspector. The inspector, no matter what folklore says, is your one ally in the building process. Their services are paid for by your permit fee and their sole concern is to be sure your project is built to be safe, sanitary, and fit for habitation according to the requirements of the building code.

You also want a permit because it is a requirement by law. If you work without a permit and it is discovered you may have to remove all the improvement work done to that date. This means taking everything out that you paid good money to have installed and then paying to have it all put in again once you get a permit. You may also have to pay a fine.

Another reason you want a building permit is to be sure you realize the cost of your improvements to your home. Unpermitted work may actually decrease the value of your property because prospective buyers may not want to buy a house that has had unpermitted and, therefore, uninspected work done to it.

Why your city wants you to have a permit. There are two reasons why your city wants you to have a permit and both reasons are legitimate. The first reason is the city wants your home to be a safe and sanitary residence. The second reason is the city permitting process is a very important revenue source for the city.

The homeowner's responsibility in regards to the permit. In the Pat Fay Method the homeowner is responsible for the permit application. This means getting the permit application form, filling it out, and then submitting it with a permit-ready set of drawings from your architect or building designer to your city.

The homeowner is the first point of contact with the city, not your architect or building designer. This is because it costs money to have your architect or building designer do this clerical work. In the Pat Fay Method the homeowner does the clerical and mundane work because it makes no economic sense to pay your architect $100 an hour to stand in line.

The homeowner's responsibility in regards to the building code. The homeowner's responsibility regarding the building code is minimal. In my classes I teach that the homeowner goes to the city and picks up the requirements, glances through them but does not spend much time on them. This is because you will be hiring experts whose job it is to know the code and how to design and build according to the code.

The exception to this is if the homeowner plans to do some of the work themselves. Then they will have to know how to do the work according to the building code and have it inspected and bought off (the industry term for approved) by the building inspector.

What is the building code? The building code is a compilation of requirements that have been steadily developed over many decades to respond to issues that have caused problems in the past. These problems are usually a result of buildings either falling down, burning down, or conditions within the house that has caused illness or accidents to the occupants. Generally, the code is there to make sure that the building is structurally safe, that it is a sanitary place, and that it is fit for habitation.

The code also has evolved to encompass other aspects of modern buildings such as proper lighting, ventilation, good exits, building stability and energy conservation.

Why there is a code. The building codes were developed to address life and safety issues inherent in construction of dwelling units. There is a translation from an ancient

Egyptian building code (from the time of the Pharaohs) which required that if a building fell down and killed the son of the owner then the son of the building contractor was to meet the same fate. Thank goodness that things have progressed since those days.

The modern building code developed as a result of major and minor disasters. The code requires buildings to be constructed to protect their occupants from poor practices, which are often the case in unregulated construction. The biggest incentive to create the building code came from the results of fires, earthquakes, and hurricanes.

Our modern code has it roots mostly in the 20th Century. I know of only a few exceptions where codes were applied earlier - such as after the disastrous Chicago fire of 1871 which burned down almost all the wooden structures in the city core. The city enacted building codes that resulted in the first skyscrapers being developed. (The fact that structural steel had recently become available also helped.)

The building code gradually took into account exiting technologies so that people could escape from burning buildings, fires would not spread from house to house and so on. Important improvements are continually being made to the building code.

The building code is a minimum requirement only. Almost to a person the homeowners I teach in my classes believe that the building code is a requirement for the finest of construction materials and methods. In actuality the building code is only a minimum requirement. You can always do more than the building code requires but the city can only require you to build according to the minimum standard defined in the code.

I like to say that it is difficult to build to the requirements of the building code but it is not hard because it is difficult to understand the building code but once one has done it a few times it is not hard.

The code is a science and an art. The code is a science because if you take a particular paragraph it spells out very specifically how those particular regulations apply to your house. Those of us who have had formal training in the use of the code and how it should be applied know what an art it is to apply. This is because for any paragraph stating a rule there are several more paragraphs somewhere in the code that either contradicts it or gives an exception to it.

Your state has a building code. Each of the fifty states has either developed their own building code or adopted a standard code. The International Building Code (IBC) seems to be the standard adopted by most states in America today. This is the result of combining the former Uniform Building Code, the BOCA National Code, and the Southern Building Codes. However, it does not matter which code is adopted by your state or city because your home construction must meet the requirements found in the current building code adopted by your city.

Your city's amendments to the code. Almost every jurisdiction takes the national code or the state building code and makes modifications to it. This is called amending the code and is quite legal. In fact, it is pretty unusual to find a planning and building department that doesn't want to make their mark on how things are built in their city.

Working with your city to get your permit. It is important for the homeowner to work professionally with the employees of the city. Your goal is to get a building permit.

In the Pat Fay Method, when you go to the city, dress nicely and have a pleasant attitude. One always gets more results by asking politely and patiently than by being angry and demanding.

Dealing with the city to resolve or understand an issue is always a two step process. First you make a phone call to either the person you plan to meet with or someone in that department. Briefly state what the issue is that you are having trouble understanding or resolving and that you will be coming to the city to discuss the issue.

Always take notes on who you speak to and what is said when dealing with the city. Use the project log sheet for this. Otherwise, much of what will be told to you by the city personnel will be forgotten by you because it is new information. New information is hard to remember. One of the reasons city employees become frustrated with homeowners is because they do not remember some piece of information told to them previously. Taking notes will reduce frustration on both sides of the discussion.

The city may be sending you letters but before you respond in writing to these letters make a phone call to the person who wrote the letter and discuss the meaning of the letter and what they expect of you. This is because some of these letters will be very confusing. City officials like to quote city laws or ordinances in their letters because that is the language they are used to using. Occasionally, there will be an official who uses technical terms to intimidate the homeowner.

It is best not to reply in writing to a letter from the city until you clearly understand what the person who wrote the letter is trying to say.

The reason I say this is because I have been a part of both kinds of managed projects: management by writing letters versus discussions in person. The projects that were managed by writing letters were projects where many mistakes were made due to misunderstandings which resulted in highly adversarial relationships between the managing partners.

On the other hand, those projects that were managed by face to face discussions and telephone calls were clear in their objectives and had fewer costly misunderstandings and mistakes. They also resulted in projects where all the responsible parties maintained good working relationships throughout the project.

Therefore, the Pat Fay Method, requires the homeowner to manage their project mainly by the face to face meeting with telephone conversations to supplement those meetings.

The building official's role in applying the code to your project. It is my belief that that the building official's role in applying the code to your project is to ensure that your building is safe, sanitary and fit for habitation.

That being said you will find that all building officials have their own interpretation and understanding of the building code and areas of expertise that they feel strongly about enforcing. You, on the other hand, may not agree with some interpretation of the code that costs you additional money to construct.

I would like to be able to tell you that you can win out against some of these less than reasonable interpretations of the code but I cannot. A couple of times I felt the plans reviewer had over stepped their interpretation authority and I argued the issue. The only result was that the time to get my permit process was extended.

When I look back on the issues from hindsight I must admit that it would have been better to just accept the interpretation and pay the extra money in construction. Yes these interpretations increased the overall cost of my project but the amount was relatively small compared to the amount we saved by following the Pat Fay Method.

For example, the plans reviewer required that we install pipe from each rain leader downspout on our house to a sump in the backyard. This sump then led to an underground drain field much like a septic system drain field. The reason for this was to prevent flooding of my house by having a place for the rain to go rather than around my foundation. I fought this requirement with energy but lost and had to install it at a cost of about $10,000.

Funny thing though is that many of my neighbors have flooding problems at their houses. I must admit it is nice not to have that problem at my house.

The personality and attitude of your city. Each city seems to have a personality. I have worked with the planning and building departments in many cities mostly here in Washington State but also in Missouri and even a couple of cities in the country of Saudi Arabia. Each of the building departments had a personality in the sense that different people have different personalities. Some are more ready to help you and others are reluctant to help you. It is strange but true.

You may even find that some permitting departments do not want the homeowner to build their own house. They may even try to use the building code as a reason to deny you a building permit. Let us hope that those kinds of permitting departments are few and far between. Interestingly enough there is a provision in the International building code that allows for what the Pat Fay Method teaches.

The Pat Fay Method is allowed by the building code. The Pat Fay Method is a new method of home construction and this is allowed by the building code. In fact, the building code has always allowed for new construction methods. In the administration section (chapter one) of the 2003 International Building Code there is a paragraph on alternative methods of construction. I cannot quote from the building code because it is copyrighted, however, this paragraph of the code states that the code is not intended to prevent any design or method of construction just because it is not specified in the code. Alternative methods must be allowed and approved as long as they meet with the intent of the building code.

The reason this section is in the building code is because the code is not meant to control new ideas, new methods, and new construction materials. New ideas and new methods must be allowed otherwise the construction industry will stagnant causing construction prices to rise to unreasonable levels.

In fact, stagnation is a good way to describe home construction in America today. What new ideas have been brought to the home construction industry that have resulted in better quality and lower prices for the homeowner? Not many. There may be some out there (beside the Home Depot and Lowe's stores) but the only one I know of is the Pat Fay Method. The price of building and remodeling in all areas of America has reached absurd levels that in no way reflect the actual cost of materials and labor needed to build.

A word about the State of Louisiana. Chapter 20 has a list of all 50 states with contact information for checking on contractor licensing requirements. I found on the State of Louisiana's website a statement that homeowners are not allowed to be their own general contractor. I called and spoke to a state official who confirmed that it was against the law in Louisiana for a homeowner to act as their own general contractor. The exception to this rule is if the homeowner states they will do all the work themselves and will not hire any subcontractors.

I do not understand what the advantage is to the citizens of the State of Louisiana by having such a law. I can clearly see the advantage to the general contractors. Perhaps it is time for the citizens of Louisiana to contact their elected officials and have this law changed.

However, the people of Louisiana can still use the majority of what is taught in this book even when dealing with a general contractor. The Pat Fay Method will help you define and control such things as quality, workmanship, timeliness, defining the change order process, inspection, limiting early payment of money to the contractors and signing of a lien release before making payment.

Pat Fay's permitting experience. I did not have a very good permit experience with the City of Kirkland in 1992. It took me almost 5 months to get my building permit. General contractors were receiving their permits in two months.

I would like to place all the blame on the building officials but that would not be fair or true. Yes there was an instance or two where some building official could have been more helpful in notifying me that my permit package did not meet the requirements instead of setting it to the side and forgetting about it.

However, I think the real issue back in 1992 was that I was one of the first homeowners attempting this process by themselves. There were others, of course, and their poor track records of leaving incomplete projects to sit in nice neighborhoods as eyesores did not lend city officials to look favorably on my desire to build without a general contractor.

However, in the present time of 2006, the process has been streamlined so that one can track the progress of their permit on line. I have spoken to several persons managing their own projects and the permitting process is now not nearly as long.

Keeping notes and your cool when dealing with the city. It is easy for people at the city to sometimes forget that what they know so well is new to the homeowner. They forget that when they first started at the city the building code and the requirements of the city were difficult to understand. Over time they became experienced professionals who understand the building code very well.

So when you deal with the city be sure to take notes on the project log sheet. You will want to note the date, time, who you are speaking to, and what is said. I like to pause occasionally and review with the city employee the notes I have taken to be sure I understand what is being said. It also makes them realize that you are documenting what they are saying.

Taking notes will really change the attitude of the person on the other side of the counter. It will communicate to them that they are dealing with a professional (you). They will rarely ever see a homeowner taking notes.

The notes will also be a record of what was said and what was not said. Requirements are not always written down clearly. If you keep good records and the requirements seem to change on you then you may have to bump your conversation up to a supervisor or manager. The requirements of the city are not supposed to be a moving target. Keeping notes can prevent that from happening.

If you have notes documenting your discussions with the city you will be taken seriously. If you do not have notes you will not be taken seriously if you have a complaint about something you were previously told. What proof do you have without documentation?

Questions you do not ask your city. There seems to be a general misunderstanding by homeowners that they need to have permission on what they build on their property. That is mostly not true.

The zoning for your property governs whether you can build a single family house or an apartment building. You cannot build an apartment house in a residential zoned area. But zoning does not typically cover the aesthetics of your project.

The questions you do not want to ask are whether you are allowed to have a deck on your house or garage, or whether you are allowed to have a laundry chute, how big your kitchen can be or whether you can put an elevator in your house. The city does not govern these things except through what is allowed and not allowed in the written building code.

You can only be denied some feature in your house if the written building code specifically does not allow it. You have your architect or building designer put whatever it is you want in your house or garage. When your drawings go through the building review process at the city then that is the time for the building officials to mark in red on your drawings that, for example, the laundry chute is not allowed.

However, they can't just say you cannot have a laundry chute. This is not a subjective matter. Their exception must be because of a reason that is defined in a section of the building code. The building official is supposed to write the building code on the drawings that does not allow the laundry chute. However, they do not always do this.

I use the laundry chute as an example because at first it was not approved on our new home plans. However, our architect found an exception in the code that allows for a laundry chute if a one hour fire barrier is placed at each end. So we resubmitted with this fire barrier information and it was approved. As I have said there are exceptions and ways to comply with almost every rule in the code that at first seems to deny you some feature.

Questions you do ask your city. The kind of questions you do ask your city are such things as: what is the minimum set back from the property line, what is the maximum building height of structures, what is the percentage of building square footage versus building lot size allowed, or what material is required for driveway construction.

These are the kind of questions that the city building code governs and to which you must adhere unless you receive a variance. A variance is permission not to comply with some aspect of the code. For example, you could get a variance to build your house closer to the building lot line than the minimum distance allowed in the code.

Therefore, in the Pat Fay Method, you will not be asking your city if you are allowed to build but what are the building requirements. In America, we still are allowed to build what we want on our property unless the code specifically prohibits it.

Legal complaints against your city in regards to your permit. The Pat Fay Method uses arbitration not lawsuits as our means of resolving problems. This is also the case in dealing with your city. However, a building arbitrator will not be effective in working with your city. You will need a different kind of arbitrator.

City employees are public servants enjoined to serve the public good per the codes and regulations. It is not their responsibility to promote the general contractor profession. However, looking at it from their point of view, it is easier working with a general contractor that has been through the permit process before rather than to hold the hand of an inexperienced homeowner. This is just human nature.

Unfortunately, an unintended consequence of the personnel in the cities of America preferring to work with general contractors and discouraging homeowners from managing the building process themselves has helped to drive up the cost of building or remodeling a home in America.

If you try to get your own building permit and find yourself truly discriminated against by your city for managing your own home construction project without the services of a general contractor then there are several options.

One is to hire your architect to work the permit process for you. This will cost additional money but it is a viable option.

You can hire the services of a permit facilitator. These are individuals that know the ins and outs of the permitting process and they typically know how to assist you in working with the city. They do charge a fee.

The last option you should pursue is to consult your attorney. This should be your last option only to be used if all else fails.

A phone call or letter from your attorney to the city attorney may be all that you need to break your permit application loose. This is because if your attorney did have to file suit then all of the city's documents and records would be open to review by your attorney. It would be very easy for your attorney to determine the amount of time a typical permit application by a general contractor takes versus the time your permit application has taken. If it can be shown that your city has two sets of rules, one for general contractors and one for homeowners then the city is open for a very damaging lawsuit.

Remember, however, in the Pat Fay Method, the goal is to build your house not engage in lawsuits.

There are different departments in the city. There are many departments that will review your drawings in most cities. You submit your permit application and it typically goes to the planning, water, sanitary sewer, fire, building, and code compliance departments.

Sometimes all of these functions will be combined in one department by smaller cities. Medium and large cities will have these areas all broken up into different departments.

The point is that most of the time many eyes from many departments will review your drawings. They are all looking for things to mark up in red. There is not a person in a city that can let a set of drawings go by without making comments. It is just human nature. They want to do a good job and the only way to show they have done a good job is bleed red ink all over your drawings.

The result is that your drawings may come back with a lot of red markups. Don't worry too much. Let your architect or building designer review the comments and try to address the issues and resubmit the plans.

If, on the second time through with your drawing package, something you want is not being allowed by the city then it is time to have a face to face meeting with the city officials. Bring your architect and a copy of the code along.

What to do when your permit seems to be lost in the city. Hopefully your city has a way to track which department currently has your permit application. I learned the hard way that the homeowner should be checking in with the city to be sure the application is not stuck in some department. Mine did get stuck and no one notified me that there was a problem. The person in charge just set my application off to the side because it was 'incomplete'.

No one in the city called me or wrote me a letter to notify me that my application was considered 'incomplete' and was no longer being processed. I had to find that out for myself by calling the department after I had not received my permit. Unfortunately, it is the homeowner's responsibility to check on the progress of your submission with the city.

Therefore, using the Pat Fay Method you need to check with the city to be sure your permit package is moving through the city. Some cities have websites where you can check the progress of your package. Others require you to call. Sometimes you need to go to the city in person. Don't let a full month go by without checking on the progress of your permit. Check on your permit at least every two weeks.

When you do not use your architect/designer in the permit process. In the Pat Fay Method you will be the first point of contact with the city permit department. It will not be your architect. You do not need the architect to take on the role of a clerk. That is the homeowner's job as the project manager. Taking care of this yourself will significantly reduce the cost of your design fee.

Be sure that you are listed as the main contact on your permit application, even if you have to write your name and contact information in the margin. Your city may work with you or they may not. You need to discuss this with the management at your city not the clerk at the front desk if you encounter problems.

When you do use your architect/designer in the permit process. You will use the architect or building designer for two reasons.

First, if the city absolutely refuses to work with you. Hopefully, your city will not be the kind of place that does not believe the homeowner should manage their own home construction project. However, if they are, then for a fee, you can hire your architect or building designer to work with the city to get your building permit.

The second reason to use your architect is to revise your construction drawings after the plans reviewer has marked them up in red with comments. You will need your architect to revise the drawings to address the issues brought up by the plans reviewer.

Be wary of beginning your project with only a demolition permit. Sometimes you can receive permission to do some demolition ahead of the building permit. However, you should be careful of demolishing anything before having a permit to rebuild it. You would not want to end up in a position where you have demolished your existing structure and the city denies you permission to construct something in its place.

For example, there used to be a really nice restaurant on a pier right in the middle of Waikiki Beach on Oahu, Hawaii. It was built before the city had a permitting process. The city of Honolulu did not want the restaurant to be there because it was an eyesore on their most famous beach. The restaurant owners wanted to upgrade and modernize so they submitted their drawings for review by the city and applied for an advance demolition permit. The city issued the demolition permit and the restaurant owner tore the restaurant down. Then, however, the city would not approve the building permit application and thereby eliminated what the city considered to be an eyesore on Waikiki beach.

Therefore, in the Pat Fay Method, no demolition is to take place until the building permit is in hand.

What to do while your project is in permitting. While your permit application is in the city processing you will continue with looking for contractors, laying out your building footprint on your property (if that is appropriate for your project), and doing more planning.

What to do when you receive your construction permit from the city. Place the permit inside a plastic envelope, post it visibly at your construction site, sign a contract with your first contractor and turn them loose.

Do make a copy of your building permit for yourself in case the original gets lost. The permit is required to be posted at the building site and that is easily done if it is a remodel because you can keep it inside your house. However, a little caution would be wise at a brand new work site that is nothing but an empty lot. It might be wise to post a copy of the permit until you have the shell of the building up so the original doesn't disappear on you. Check with your building department on this issue.

The Building Inspector

The inspection department is not the building department. If you happen to have difficulty with someone in your city during the permitting process, do not allow your emotions to taint your relationship with your building inspector. The inspection department is typically made up of men and women who know how things are to be built. The people who work in the building and planning department are like engineers (including myself) and architects who sometimes forget that there is a real world out there.

So don't carry a grudge over to your building inspector.

The role of the city in the enforcement of the code. The city holds most of the cards in the interpretation and enforcement of the code but not all. The code allows them to make judgments about the interpretation of the code. However, you need to know and they need to remember that their interpretations come from the building code they have adopted. They cannot go too far away from the actual requirements stated in their adopted building code.

Since planning departments have in the past taken a pretty liberal allowance with how they interpret the code, there have been a fair number of complaints about high handedness by cities to the building code council. The 2003 IBC has been written with that complaint in mind.

The writers of this version of the code have tried to be more definitive in their requirements so that the code is less open to interpretation by building and planning departments. That is a good thing for homeowners.

The building inspector's right to inspect. The building inspector must have free access to your building site so they can inspect the work. This doesn't mean they will barge into your home but that by law they have a right to enter your premises and inspect.

This only really becomes a problem when someone is building or remodeling without a permit. Then the city can have a judge rule that the inspector needs access to the construction site, and if they have to, to get the sheriff or the police to help them get access.

This doesn't happen too often because the inspector has the ability to red card the construction site with a stop work order and demand all construction work cease and desist. This order is enforceable. If you ever receive a stop work order do stop all work. The consequences are severe.

This, however, should not be an issue for the followers of the Pat Fay Method because my method requires having a permit and recommends building to a higher quality than the code demands.

The work must remain accessible. Since you will be managing the contractors do not allow the work being inspected to be covered up before the inspector has had a chance to inspect it. If you fail to do this it can be quite expensive because you will have to have the work opened up again.

For example, if the framing is complete but not inspected and signed off, your contractor is not allowed to install the insulation and sheetrock because it would hide the framing. The inspector has the right to have the sheetrock and insulation removed so that the framing can be inspected. The homeowner would be out the cost of the labor and material to remove the sheetrock and to have it put back on a second time. The best way to manage your project is to have the inspector visit your site and inspect each phase of construction before beginning the next one.

Another example would be covering up the rebar that goes inside the concrete. Do not allow your contractor to place the concrete until the rebar and forms have been inspected. If the concrete does get poured before inspection is complete then all that concrete and rebar would have to be ripped out so that it could be put in a second time and inspected properly. Needless to say, removing and repouring concrete would be a time consuming and expensive process.

What work needs to be inspected by the city inspector? The phases of construction that need to be inspected are clearly defined on the building permit. They typically are the foundations before concrete is poured, framing, plumbing, gas piping, mechanical, electrical, sheetrock screw spacing, roofing and final inspection. You'll notice that the building inspector has no duty to inspect the finish work because it is not a requirement of the code. The city is interested in inspecting the parts of construction that affect the safety of the building.

The homeowner's inspection duties. The homeowner will want to inspect everything that gets built in their house, particularly the finishes. You look for compliance with the building plan, quality of workmanship, type of material and the lack of mistakes.

The homeowner inspects all the same things the building inspector will look at but will look for different things. The building inspector is not responsible for laying a tape measure on the length of your walls to be sure they match the plans or that the walls are even in the right place. The inspector is responsible to be sure those walls have the correct structural grade lumber and that they are nailed together properly.

In the Pat Fay Method, the homeowner is responsible for inspecting that the project is being completed to your plans and expectations. This means that the homeowner will make sure that the walls are in the correct place, of the correct length (as defined in the plans), and that the walls are straight, level, square and plumb. (The term plumb comes from using a plumb bob to determine that a wall is perpendicular to a level floor.) The framing contractor is supposed to check these things but rarely does.

One of the reasons you don't need the services of a general contractor is because they are supposed to check the framer. Inspection of their subcontractors is their responsibility but you will rarely see them out on your project with a 3 foot level or plumb bob checking the framing or anything else for that matter.

An example for checking your electrical contractor is to buy a circuit tester at your hardware store. You would use it to test each outlet to be sure it is operating and the polarity is correct. Also, turn on every light switch and every appliance to be sure they work.

The inspection of finishes is the most important inspection function the homeowner can do. If you have tile installed you will want to look at every single piece of tile to be sure they are not cracked or chipped. The lines of the tile should also be straight and level.

Ultimately, this is your project and you must make sure that it is being built to the plans you showed your contractors. The building inspector takes care of the technical issues, but you must take care of the rest.

Take the concrete foundation, for example. The building inspector will inspect the forms and the rebar placement to be sure they meet the requirements of the code which is that they have steel ties holding the forms together, that the rebar and straps are in place, and that the anchor bolts are there.

However, the homeowner needs to inspect that the forms are laid out properly per the plan. This means if the plans call for the south wall to be 30 feet long you will go out there with a tape measure and measure that the forms are actually 30 feet long. The building inspector is not responsible for that kind of check because the code does not require it. The homeowner must remember that the building code is a minimum requirement.

Here is another note about inspecting finishes because I believe it is such an important aspect of your construction project. The finishes are what make the difference between an economy grade house and a luxury grade house – which is not covered in the code, but is included in your building plan. For example, if you have counter tops installed you will want to be sure there are no chips or cracks, and that the joints are tight and clean with no extra grout or glue to be seen. The cabinets must be checked to be sure they are level, that the doors all line up so that when you step back and look at the whole installation and no flaw or mistake is noticeable. This is all the homeowner's responsibility not the inspector whether you follow the Pat Fay Method or not.

This is one of the most common complaints homeowners have is that after they pay the general contractor and they live for a time in their home they begin noticing all of the finish flaws that were not caught during a punchlist inspection. All contractors know what a punchlist is but not many homeowners. The term punchlist means to inspect everything the contractor has done and make out a list of exceptions that have either not been completed, need to be repaired, or need to be done better. This punchlist is done at the end of the contract but before the homeowner pays the contractor.

So remember, in the Pat Fay Method, the homeowner is responsible for inspection of the finishes because the building inspector will not look at the finishes because the code does not require it. The homeowner must insist upon receiving the quality of construction that was agreed to in the contract.

Chapter 7-Insurance

Speak to your personal homeowner insurance agent
    Your homeowner's insurance & the extended umbrella policy
Homeowner's construction insurance
    Coverage for liability, material theft and vandalism
    Discount available before construction starts
The contractor's insurance coverage
    Have your name listed on the contractor's insurance
State industrial insurance and workers compensation
On site construction safety and the construction safety plan
    A fence helps

Chapter 7-Insurance

Speak to your personal homeowner insurance agent. The best advice I can give the homeowner concerning insurance is to use the expertise of your own insurance agent. In fact, you should speak to your insurance agent a minimum of several times a year to be sure you are up to date on all your insurance needs - homeowner, auto, life, and health. Don't think you are covered. Know you are covered.

    Do not overlook the insurance portion of your project. Even if your contractor has good insurance coverage you will want your own liability insurance umbrella policy in case someone is injured on your project. Speak to your insurance agent and describe what you are doing and how you are contracting out the construction work. Ask for their advice and help to provide you with additional liability insurance coverage during your remodel or new construction.

    You are not looking for builders insurance or contractor's insurance because you are not a contractor. You are a homeowner hiring contractors to do construction work. Therefore, you want liability insurance.

Your homeowner's insurance & the extended liability insurance umbrella policy. When we built our new house we spoke to our home insurance agent. He recommended that we buy additional coverage to protect us from liability and loss on our construction site. Since we already had a homeowner's insurance policy he told us he could write us an umbrella insurance policy that covered us at our new house for the period of construction. It was written for a million dollars in liability and cost us about $500 in 1992.

Homeowner's construction insurance. You absolutely want to be covered by additional insurance for construction activity at your present home or the site where you are building a new home. Insurance reduces the risk of the homeowner having to pay alone for the cost for an injury due to an accident by a worker on your construction site.

    Having enough liability insurance is an essential part of the Pat Fay Method. Call your insurance agent before beginning your project. If you have already started, call your agent today.

Coverage for liability, material theft, and vandalism. Everyone I speak to about insurance coverage for their home construction project seems to know that you need liability coverage. Very few homeowners realize that they also need to insure against theft and vandalism. The homeowner will want to be sure they are covered by their own insurance provider for these potential risks.

You will find that your agent knows how to provide you with an extended coverage rider that will protect you in case someone gets hurt on your job, someone steals all of your appliances before you move in, or your house is vandalized.

Discount available before construction starts. It is very important to speak to your insurance agent before you start your project. If you do, you may receive a discount of up to 50% on the cost of the insurance. If you wait until after you start construction then your insurance agent will not be able to offer this discount.

The contractor's insurance coverage. Many states have a licensing requirement for building contractors and for specialty contractors that includes the requirement to have liability insurance. However, even if the contractor does have insurance the homeowner will want to have their own separate insurance policy as additional insurance coverage.

If you live in a state that does not have a licensing or insurance requirement for contractors then you absolutely must have your own insurance policy. You want to be covered for accidents that happen to a contractor's workers and accidents caused by a contractor's workers while working on your project or property.

Have your name listed on the contractor's insurance. If your contractor has insurance have the contractor list you on their insurance policy so that you will specifically be indemnified by his insurance while the contractor is working on your project or property. This rule also applies to specialty contractors that you hire to do a phase of your project. Have specialty contractors list you as an additional insured on their contractor's liability insurance. You should receive a certificate of insurance listing you as additional insured on the contractor's insurance and indicating the contractor's coverage.

If you decide the Pat Fay Method is not for you and you hire a general contractor do not sign a contract with them without receiving this coverage. You will be paying a lot of money for the privilege of letting the general contractor build your house. The least they can do is have you covered by their insurance. If they won't or can't, then find another general contractor who will.

It is easy for them to add the homeowner to their insurance. The contractor just calls their insurance agent and requests that the homeowner be covered by their insurance. The agent reissues the policy cover sheet with your name listed as one of those indemnified. You will want to insist on this because adding an additional insured does not cost the contractor anything.

You will want a copy of the insurance cover sheet with you listed. If you are unsure of what to do then just ask your insurance agent to help you.

What happens in the situation where the contractor is required by your state to have insurance coverage, they have proof of insurance, but the contractor fails to make the premium payments? In this case there is no insurance coverage. That is why it is so important for the homeowner to have their own insurance policy as well, to protect themselves in all cases.

State industrial insurance/workers compensation is not the homeowner's responsibility. This subject is not a homeowner responsibility. It is a business responsibility of the contractors you hire. Typically the individual state governments have set up a Department of Labor or Department of Labor and Industries. These departments manage and provide insurance for businesses in their states. Employers must provide state industrial type insurance coverage for their employees. Your contractor can buy insurance through these departments. This insurance coverage pays for medical services when a workplace injury occurs to an employee of your contractor. It also compensates individuals who are unable to work due to the injuries they have sustained. It is my understanding that one-man businesses are not required to have this insurance but it is available for them to purchase. Your insurance agent should be able to help you look into this option.

On site construction safety. Most construction insurance claims are a result of injury due to accident. Therefore, the best way to avoid claims is to prevent accidents. Your contractor and their workers should work safely.

A fence helps. A construction fence may be appropriate at your new house construction site. It will keep most people out that do not belong there. You will want to rent a chain link type fence with a gate you can lock. Even though most people who walk through houses under construction are harmless, it is still the owner who is liable for any injury that person sustains while trespassing on the owner's property. A fence is inexpensive insurance. It will keep the casual passerby out of your project.

Chapter 8-Project Safety

Why is safety important?
Who is responsible for safety?
    The homeowner's role in safety
        Safety for the homeowner's family and friends
    The contractor's role in safety
What is safety?
    Safe work environment
    Unsafe behavior
    Personal protective equipment (PPE)
Safety for the homeowner on their own construction site
Contractor safety
    The contractor's safety meeting and safety plan
Providing hardhats and safety glasses
General safety rules for the homeowner
General safety rules for the contractor

Chapter 8-Project Safety

Why is safety important? The reason safety is important is because we do not want people injured on our home construction project. No one wants to see another person get hurt, disabled or even killed due to a work site accident. The possibility of serious injury exists on all construction sites, including yours, even if you think your project is a small remodel.

Who is responsible for safety? Everyone is responsible for their own safety. That is the bottom line. However, if you, the homeowner, follow the Pat Fay Method and you hire independent contractors to do the different phases of construction then you are responsible for providing a safe work environment for the contractors. The contractors are responsible for maintaining a safe work environment once they start work and for working safely while on your project.

    The homeowner's role in safety. The homeowner is responsible for providing a safe work environment for the contractor to begin their work. Once work begins, safety is the contractor's responsibility. If the homeowner sees unsafe conditions they must point it out to the contractor. Document the infraction by writing up a Request for Information form (RFI) and give the contractor a copy and mail them another with a return receipt requested. You want to document that you pointed out safety concerns in case there is a subsequent problem.

    Safety for the homeowner's family and friends. The homeowner needs to be sure that they insist on safety for their family and friends when visiting their home construction site. It is natural to show off what you are doing to your friends but insist that if you have site tours it is after the contractor has left the site and that the site is safe. You should also have your friends wear hardhats, safety glasses, and good walking shoes.

Also, control children from entering the worksite at all times. Never allow children to tour the site while the contractor is working. Also, do not allow the work area to be a play area. Construction sites are just too dangerous.

The contractor's role in safety. Once the contractor is on site they are responsible for maintaining a safe work environment and working safely. This means the contractor must follow the safety rules established by their company, by State agencies, and by OSHA (Occupational Safety and Health Administration). It is not the homeowner's responsibility to know these rules but rather it is the contractor's responsibility.

What is safety? Safety is an attitude followed by a commitment to take the physical steps to insure that no accidents occur. In the homeowner construction world safety falls into three categories: safe work environment, unsafe behaviors, and the use of personal protective equipment.

Safe work environment. To avoid any conflicting interpretations of who is responsible for safety, include a specification in your contract that the homeowner is responsible for providing a safe work environment at the start of the project; once construction begins it is the responsibility of the contractor to maintain a safe work environment. The homeowner must provide a safe work environment each time a new contractor is brought on site.

Unsafe work sites are messy worksites. Here are some typical examples of unsafe conditions. If the work area has pieces of lumber lying all over the place as trip hazards (especially if there are nails), then it is an unsafe worksite. Walkways need to be solid with good footing, good steps that lead into the house with handrails, electrical extension cords in good condition and not allowed to be run through mud or water, railings are installed at high areas or areas where one could fall, and the contractor must be responsible for cleanup at the end of the day so the next day starts off safe.

The following example explains where the homeowner's responsibility for safety begins and ends with more than one contractor. You might have one contractor dig a ditch and a second contractor lay pipe in that ditch. The homeowner would be responsible for making sure no on falls into the open ditch during the period of time the ditch is open and the time the pipe is installed and backfilled. Either barricades must be provided or a covering of some kind so no one can fall into the open ditch.

In this case, it is a better idea to have one contractor be responsible for digging the ditch, laying the pipe, and covering the pipe back up. You do not want to break up your work into the smallest denominator but into activities that naturally go together. Putting work like this together will make your project go more smoothly, make your site safer, and your project management responsibilities easier.

Unsafe behavior. Unsafe behavior is where the workers onsite work in ways that put them at risk for injury. The main reason for this is typically lack of safety training and education. Poor attitudes about safety also contribute. These attitudes include thinking things such as: "I'm invulnerable, it won't happen to me, I've always done it this way, and no one can tell me how to work."

Examples of unsafe behavior are such things as working overhead above other workers, climbing too high on ladders, not put up railings, ignoring unsafe conditions, such as high open areas without railings, running electrical cords through water, not wearing safety glasses and hardhats, fooling around with power tools, horse play, not roping off pinch points, failing to ask for help when lifting or moving heavy objects, not taking the time needed to do a job properly and failing to follow established safety rules.

Most construction accidents (about 90%) occur because of unsafe worker behavior. When the worker is interviewed (when they survive) to determine the root cause of the accident, the most common answer is "I have worked that way for 25 years". The conclusion from the safety experts is the worker, after putting themselves at risk for many years, just ran out of luck.

Personal protective equipment (PPE). Personal protective equipment are such things as hardhats, safety glasses, boots, gloves, hearing protection, body harnesses for high work and safety vests.

Wearing personal protective equipment is mandatory on industrial construction work sites. Any worker who does not wear their PPE can be disciplined, fined and or fired. This applies to all workers on an industrial construction site; managers, superintendents, engineers, and craftsmen.

In the homeowner construction world one rarely sees the home construction workers wearing hardhats, safety glasses or gloves. PPE should be worn at every construction site, industrial or residential. These are inexpensive devices that prevent many serious injuries to the head, eyes, and hands.

Safety for the homeowner on their own construction site. The homeowner needs to pay attention to safety for themselves, their family and their friends on their own construction site. An ounce of prevention is worth a pound of cure. The first thing the homeowner needs to do is wear their personal protective devices. This is so simple and will help to eliminate the most basic risks.

Wear good boots, wear a hard hat, wear eye protection, and wear gloves. These four simple things will practically eliminate the most common causes of injury. Good boots will help to prevent injury if you step on a nail, a hard hat will protect your head from injury from falling objects or being hit by unnoticed objects, eye protection will protect you from flying objects, and gloves will protect you from splinters and scrapes. By wearing this gear you have eliminated the majority of the risk on the construction site.

The next high risk safety item you need to pay attention to is protecting yourself from falls. Maintaining the site free of clutter, debris, and garbage is important because of the trip hazard that can cause a fall. Sturdy, safe walkways with handrails, particularly at steps, on the site are essential. If you climb a ladder for any reason follow the safety rules. Falls from ladders is one of the most common causes of accidents.

Contractor safety. The contractor is responsible for their own safety while working on your construction site. This means they must maintain the site so it is a safe work environment. The contractor is also responsible for ensuring the safe behavior of their workers.

The industrial construction world has found a way to greatly reduce accidents on their worksites. The secret is to have a safety plan that is discussed at a safety meeting.

The contractor's safety meeting and safety plan. In the homeowner construction world the safety meeting is held by the contractor or their foreman and the workers. It should be held at the beginning of the work day. This meeting can be very short - sometimes five minutes is enough to review the safety plan for that day because typically there are only a few workers and a one or two activities taking place.

The safety plan defines safe behavior and identifies safety hazards on the job site. It typically identifies what activities are going to take place that day with a discussion of how to mitigate any safety issues.

For example, if there is going to be a crane on site to lift the roof trusses onto the roof then all workers would be made aware of this activity at the safety meeting. The foreman would discuss how they should not get under the lift path for the material so nothing can drop on them. They would also discuss where the material is to be lifted, who would help receive it, how they would ensure that workers do not fall in the process of releasing the material from the boom hook, and be sure the material is secured so it does not fall after being set in place.

Now that this has been discussed all the workers will be aware of the activity and the dangers inherent to that activity. This would be done for other activities being worked on that day.

As I have stated this is a contractor responsibility. However, the homeowner can easily check to see if the safety meeting has occurred by asking the contractor or the foreman. Then write the response down in your daily construction log sheet or historical log so you have a record that you followed up. If the contractor lies to you and it happens that one of his workers gets seriously hurt that day that fact will come out during the accident investigation.

Providing hard hats and safety glasses. It is the contractor's responsibility to provide these items to their workers and the workers responsibility to wear them. You might show your commitment to safety by providing extra safety glasses and hardhats. Safety glasses cost as little as $2 each and hardhats for about $10 each. Just look in the yellow pages for Safety Equipment or buy them online.

General safety rules for the homeowner.

Post a sign on site saying, SAFETY COMES FIRST! PLEASE WORK SAFELY!

When you go onto your construction site always wear boots, safety glasses, gloves, and a hardhat.

Be cautious about allowing friends and associates on your construction site. Of course, you are probably going to want to show it off but pick a time when it is safe. Don't have a tour come through when the framing is partially complete and there are fall hazards.

Never interrupt anyone using a power tool. Wait off to the side until they are finished.

Prevent fires. Keep at least two fire extinguishers on the jobsite. Don't just lay them in the corner but mount them somewhere where they are easily seen. Do not allow your contractor to store gasoline, thinner, or flammable materials in your house. Have them haul it away daily or have it stored in a separate storage shed.

Do not allow smoking cigarettes or cigars in your house. This is a fire hazard. Also, if you allow contractors to smoke in your house then that smoke will be in the wood, in the sheetrock and everything else. Insist that they smoke outside.

Have a first aid kit on site. Check it frequently to be sure it is well stocked. The most used items will be band aids. Look in the yellow pages under First Aid Supplies or contact the local Red Cross.

Know how to turn off the natural gas and the electricity.

Some homeowners may elect do some of the work on site themselves. If that is the case then be sure to follow all the safety rules for yourself. Never fall into the trap of thinking that nothing will happen because this is the last piece to cut or I just have to reach one more spot (that is too far away) while standing on a ladder. Never hurry when doing construction work. This doesn't mean that you can't be quick. However, hurrying can be deadly because with it comes a sense of panic that you must hurry or else. Never hurry!

If the homeowner is doing some work then be aware of these causes of countless accidents. Do not hold a work item in one hand and a screwdriver or some such tool in the other hand and attempt to work upon the work item. You will cut the hand that holds the work item. Place the work item in a vise or secure it to a work surface. Do not use any tool that is damaged, cracked, or shows excessive wear particularly wear on the electrical cord. If you see a frayed or bare wire on a tool or an extension cord then throw it away. Do not use a tool for other than the use intended.

Wear you safety glasses when working. There is no way for me to physically convince you to wear your PPE but if you wear nothing else then wear your safety glasses. When you injure your eye you will be blind in that eye. This truly is the ounce of prevention that the pound of cure cannot fix. Also, insist that your children, and particularly your teenagers, wear safety glasses not only when they come on your construction site but when they are mowing the yard and working in the shop. Young people believe they are invulnerable but we older folks know better.

A fence helps. A construction fence may be appropriate at your new house construction site. It will keep most people out that do not belong there. You will want to rent a chain link type fence with a gate you can lock. Even though most people who walk through houses under construction are harmless, it is still the owner who is liable for any injury that person sustains while trespassing on the owner's property. A fence is inexpensive insurance. It will keep the casual passerby out of your project.

General safety rules for the contractor.

Keep the work area clean and clear from trip hazards. Do not let clutter build up. Do not allow lumber with nails sticking up to be lying about. Remove nails or pound them flat. In the Pat Fay Method the contractor is enjoined to maintain a safe, clean and orderly job site.

Require Ground Fault Interrupter circuit breakers to be used on extension cords. They should be placed on the end of the extension cord just before the tool electrical plug.

Preventing falls is very important. Falls seriously injure more individuals then any other accident whether in the home or on the job.

-Scaffolding and ladder safety. Insist that the contractor's safety plan includes the basic safety rules on scaffolding and ladder safety. Scaffolds must be tied off to the structure to prevent movement and the brakes locked. Scaffolding must have hand rails on the top level. Scaffolding must never be moved with a person on the scaffolding. They must get off.

-Extension ladders must be secured at the base and tied off at the top to prevent movement. It takes more time but the bases of extension ladders have been known to slip and the ladder comes sliding down. It can cause serious injury or death to the worker on the ladder. You do not need that kind of headache on your job.

-There is also something called the 1 to 4 extension ladder stability rule. This means that the extension ladder's base should be only one unit away from the wall for every 4 units of height. For example, if the ladder extends up 20' on the side of your house then the base should be out 5' from the house and then tied off.

-The 6' step ladder is the most commonly used ladder and therefore this is where we find the most accidents. These result from climbing too high on the ladder, the ladder not being on a stable work surface so it shifts, and for the worker not taking the time to move the ladder close to their work but reaching too far instead. Falls from a 6' ladder have resulted in death.

-Another common source of falls is where there is a hole in the floor of the work site, such as from the 2nd to the 1st floors. Typically, a piece of wood will be thrown over the hole. At the end of the day some unfortunate worker will be cleaning up, see the piece of wood covering the hole but not know the hole is there. They will pick up an edge of the piece of wood, walk forward and fall through the hole. This accident injures hundreds and kills dozens of people every year. The pieces of wood covering a hole need to be screwed down and a note written on the wood that a hole is beneath.

-Falling due to no handrails is also quite common. No one intends to fall but fall they do. That is why high points should have handrails whether it is in a building or on a scaffold.

-Safety harnesses. Safety harnesses are devices that fit the worker like the harness of a parachute. They are tied off to a secure point of the structure with a tether. They allow for free movement while working but if the worker falls the harness senses the acceleration and the tether arrests the fall. These are used while working on roofs or areas where falls can occur.

The contractor must be sure there is plenty of ventilation whenever they are working with adhesives, pipe glue, paint or protective coatings, and/or volatile products.

All power tools should be safety checked daily for frayed electrical wires and blade guards are in place. It is a mystery why workers like to remove these guards.

Trench safety is very important because trenches are very dangerous. Hundreds of construction workers die each year because trenches collapse on them. Trenches are dug for footings, installing pipe and wire. Whenever a trench is 4' deep or more they need to either be shored with a box insert, braced, or sloped at the top to prevent collapse. Another danger is a worker will be working in a deep trench and a backhoe will come along, not see the worker in the trench, and dump dirt into the trench and bury the worker.

Protect against pinch points. A pinch point is where a piece of equipment with a rotating section, such as a crane, is set up next to a building. When the rotating section starts to rotate the clearance between itself and the house may be several feet but while it rotates through its range of motion the clearance between the house and equipment may be reduced to a foot or less making it a pinch point. Inexperienced workers have been known to walk between the house and the equipment just as the equipment starts to rotate. Every year hundreds of workers throughout the United States are crushed at these pinch points. Many die. The contractor needs to barricade off the patch between the house and the equipment to prevent this avoidable tragedy.

Chapter 9-Contract Documents

What are contract documents?
Contract law and the home construction project
What is a contract?
What is a contract versus what is a proposal?
The contract is a document for both the homeowner and the contractor
    The intent of the contract agreement
    Honoring the intent of the contract by the homeowner
    Honoring the intent of the contract by the contractor
What should not be in the contract: paying 50% of the money at the time the contract is signed
    Why the homeowner should not pay 50% of the money
    The contractor states they need the money to buy materials.
    Material can be sent to the homeowner's project on credit.
    The contractor can go to their banker.
    The contractor can pay for the materials themselves as their bond
    Exceptions to the rule of not paying 50%
What should be in the contract?
    How long and complicated should the contract be?
    When to sign the contract
    Do not follow mainstream construction management books
How to modify the contractor's contract
    What is an addendum to the contract?
    The addendum is a simple way to modify the contractor's contract
    How to attach the addendum to the contractor's contract
    Mark up the contractor's contract proposal
What is a scope of work?
What are specifications?
    How to use specifications to define materials and quality
Types of contracts to use in home construction
    Fixed price contract
    Time and material contract
    Offered price contract
Material and labor costs can be broken out
    Equipment costs
    Why the homeowner wants to see costs broken out
How to control change order costs
    Use of the No Verbal Changes form
Understanding liens
    What is a notice to lien?
    What is a lien?
    What is a lien release?
    The importance of receiving the lien release
How to resolve an impasse between the homeowner and the contractor
    When the homeowner and the contractor agree to disagree
    Arbitration

    The arbitrator agrees with the homeowner and the contractor fixes the problem
    The arbitrator agrees with the homeowner but will not allow the contractor to fix
      the problem
    Arbitrator agrees with the contractor
Contact an arbitration firm before the first contractor is hired.
    What kind of arbitrator does the homeowner hire?
Avoid lawsuits
Paying the contractor
    When to pay the contractor
    How to pay the contractor
      Use the two party check
    Getting the lien release from the contractor's material suppliers
There is no room for trust in the home construction contracting world
A word of encouragement to the homeowner that feels overwhelmed
A sample contract and a sample addendum

Chapter 9-Contract Documents

What are contract documents? Contract documents is just a term describing all the pieces of paper that make up a contract. These are such thing as the contract itself, the drawings that the architect or designer have drawn up, specifications defining the material to be used and the level of quality the homeowner wants, and an addendum if there is one.

Contract law and the home construction project. Entire libraries have been written on the subject of contracts. However, all of the knowledge and information contained in those libraries is of no use to the American homeowner. This is because all the written law does not apply to the homeowner's project unless the homeowner is willing to spend more money on attorney fees than they want to spend on their entire home construction project.

What is a contract? In the Pat Fay Method a contract is a written agreement between the homeowner and a contractor that requires both parties to perform according to both the written scope of work as well as to honor the intent of the contract.

What is a contract versus what is a proposal? The document the contractor presents to the homeowner to do construction work is only a proposal until both parties sign the document. Once it is signed then it becomes a contract.

The contract is a document for both the homeowner and the contractor. The very basis of all contracts is the fact that a contract is a document for both parties that sign the contract. Almost to a person the homeowners in my classes are aghast when I teach them to take a red pen and mark up the contractor's proposal. They believe that the homeowner must sign whatever piece of paper the contractor presents to them.
  In the Pat Fay Method, the homeowner has not only the right but also the responsibility to modify the contractor's proposal to suit their needs so that when it is signed and becomes a contract it reflects the requirements of the homeowner as well as the contractor.

The homeowner agrees to pay the contractor a set amount of money after the contractor constructs a phase of the homeowner's construction project as defined in the scope of work that is written simply and plainly in everyday English in the contract.

The intent of the contract agreement. The reason why honoring the intent of the contract agreement is so important is because the homeowner and contractor cannot put enough words into their contract to cover all possibilities. If the parties want a 40 page set of contract documents then they should go into commercial or industrial construction.

Honoring the intent of the contract by the homeowner. In the Pat Fay Method honoring the intent of the contract by the homeowner means paying the contractor in full when the work is completed. If there are exceptions or punchlist items then the homeowner may withhold payment for those items but only in the amount needed to fix or complete those items.

For example, if the contract has a value of $25,000 and there are punchlist items worth $500 remaining to be completed then it is reasonable to withhold $500 to $1,000 from the final payment. However, the remaining $24,000 should be paid to the contractor.

Honoring the intent of the contract by the contractor. In the Pat Fay Method honoring the intent of the contract by the contractor means to complete all of the construction work agreed to in the written scope of work in approximately the time frame agreed to for the price in the contract. Lien releases will be provided to the homeowner at the time payment is made.

It is not acceptable to charge the homeowner a change order for anything unless the homeowner asks for additional work that is not part of the original scope of work.

The reason the time frame is approximate is because in the Pat Fay Method the homeowner acknowledges the difficulties the contractor has in conducting business and that circumstances may require the project to extend a week or so due to circumstances beyond the contractor's control. The homeowner will work with the contractor as long as the contractor is working with the homeowner.

What should not be in the contract: paying 50% of the money at the time the contract is signed. The number one contention between the Pat Fay Method and the contractor method is the paying of 50% of the money or some other large sum of money to the contractor at the time the contract is signed. This one step is the root of the majority of problems found between the homeowners and contractors in America today.

In discussions with the homeowners who have taken my class, I have confirmed my own belief that when the homeowner pays the contractor this money homeowners all believe the contractor will then respect them, feel indebted to them and want to do a really good job for the homeowner. The opposite is actually the truth. In reality the contractor thinks one or all of the following:

- I love this business. Where else can a person receive serious money for having done no work

- now I have enough money to finish my other projects

- now I have enough money to go on vacation

- now I have enough money to tie on a real binge

- now I have enough money to pay off my truck

Then to throw salt into the wound the contractor will often be openly rude and disrespectful to the homeowner who pays the 50% down payment. The contractor will often not work the homeowners project diligently but will show up now and then, and often claims to be finished when much remains to be completed on the project.

Why the homeowner should not pay 50% of the money. The main reason the homeowner should not pay the contractor 50% of the money or some large deposit is because the contractor has done no work.

Why this practice is the standard in America today is a mystery to me. One of Pat Fay's goals is to put an end to this practice in America and to create a class of Pat Fay Method contractors who will work according to the Pat Fay Method and thereby put all other types of contractors out of business.

Another reason why the homeowner does not want to pay large sums of money at the time the contract is signed is because the contractor could easily and often does disappear with the money with no work completed on the homeowner's project.

The contractor states they need the money to buy materials. The contractors of America will tell the homeowners of America that what I teach is impractical because how else would the contractor pay for the materials needed to build the project? There are legitimate alternatives.

Material can be sent to the homeowner's project on credit. If the contractor is a legitimate businessman they will have established a relationship with material suppliers. The material supplier will recognize them as a legitimate businessman and will deliver unpaid for material to the homeowner's construction site when the contractor shows the material supplier a construction contract. The material supplier will first send out a notice to lien to the homeowner before material is delivered.

The contractor can go to their banker. The legitimate contractor can take a signed contract to their banker and get a cash advance on the power of the contract. This is how normal business in America is actually done. Only in home construction is this time tested method of signing a contract and then borrowing money against the contract from banking institutions ignored. Yes the contractor will have to pay interest but that is a cost of doing business.

The contractor can pay for the materials themselves as their bond. In the industrial construction world we require contractors to post a bond. The bond is the contractor's insurance that they will complete the project. If they do not finish the project then the bonding company has to pay another contractor to finish the project.

In the Pat Fay Method one option is to allow the contractor to pay for the materials needed to build the homeowner's project. It represents their bond to the homeowner that they will finish the homeowner's project.

Exceptions to the rule of not paying 50% at the time the contract is signed. The exception to this rule is when the homeowner receives something of real value in return for accepting the risk of paying a 50% deposit.

For example, for kitchen cabinets I use a small shop in Monroe, Washington that my wife found through word of mouth. Even though I have used this contractor a number of times over the years he will not put me on his production schedule until I pay him a deposit. However, it is worth the risk because the price for his cabinets is about 40% less expensive than I can find anywhere else. His quality is excellent and when he finishes installing the cabinets they look beautiful.

Is this a contradiction in the rules of the Pat Fay Method? It is and it is not. One must understand the reason behind the rule. In the Pat Fay Method we are looking to limit risk. By paying my cabinetmaker a deposit of about 40% I am at risk for losing that money.

However, the amount of deposit money I paid for a kitchen project in 2006 to my cabinetmaker in deposit was not large. It was $3,000. What I would never do is pay $40,000 to $100,000 to a general contractor at the time of signing a contract. That is too great a risk.

The Pat Fay Method is a new method that will take years to establish in America. In the meantime we still need to build our home construction projects and while one day I believe there will be contractors in every major city in America following the Pat Fay Method it is not the case now. It is acceptable to bend the rules but only when there is a real value to be realized by the homeowner.

What should be in the contract? In the Pat Fay Method we want the contract to describe the work to be done with a list of the work to be included, that the contractor will be responsible for building according to the requirements of the building code, what the level of quality will be, the types of material to be used, how much the work will cost, when it will be done and that the contractor will be paid when the work is completed and inspected.

A well written contract will also include a list of what is excluded in the contract. This is very important because a clear definition of what is not included clearly defines for both the homeowner and contractor what activities will not be accomplished by the contractor. The list of excluded work lets the homeowner know that they will have to pay someone else to accomplish the excluded work. This is just smart project management because the scope of work makes clear what is included in the contract and the excluded work list makes clear what work is not included.

Also, the contract will also include the name of the company or individual, their mailing address, phone number, and contractor's license number if appropriate. Please see the sample Pat Fay Method contract at the end of this chapter.

How long and complicated should the contract be? In the Pat Fay Method the contract is only one to two pages long. The contract must be simple, clear and to the point. It is not to be complicated or long winded with an excess of detail that will seem like a trap to a contractor. The homeowner is to use plain English and avoid trying to sound like an attorney.

When to sign the contract. In the Pat Fay Method, the homeowner will sign the contract about two to four weeks before the contractor is needed to come to work. The reason the contract is not signed months in advance is because the homeowner will not know exactly when they will need any particular contractor.

In the Pat Fay Method what we are trying to avoid is the situation of signing a contract months in advance and then, when the contractor comes on site, they claim the conditions are different from what they were led to believe at the time they signed the contract. Then the contractor hits the homeowner with a change order.

Another problem with scheduling a contractor too far in advance is that the homeowner may not need the contractor when they had planned. This can be a reason for some contractors to try to claim that since they were scheduled to work the homeowner's job on June 15th and now that the homeowner is not ready for the contractor then the contractor can supposedly claim they could have started on some other project. The contractor may try to claim that they are losing money and the homeowner must pay a change order for their idle time.

There are exceptions to the rule of signing a contract 2 to 4 weeks out. For example, my favorite cabinetmaker is typically about 4 to 12 weeks out on delivery. This means that if I sign a contract with him today he cannot deliver cabinets for my project from 4 to 12 weeks from the time I sign a contract. Therefore, if I want his excellent quality workmanship and reasonable pricing then I must sign a contract 4 to 12 weeks before the work is to take place.

Is this a contradiction to the Pat Fay Method? It is and it is not. It is if you just look at the rule and ignore the reason behind the rule. The reason behind the rule is the condition of the construction site.

If the homeowner is remodeling their kitchen and the project is to rip out the old cabinets and install new cherry wood cabinets then the kitchen site conditions are as they will be when the contractor brings the new cabinets on site and installs them. The time frame does not matter because the conditions are fixed. Therefore, the homeowner could sign a contract 4 to 12 weeks in advance and be confident that the measurements the cabinetmaker takes today will be the same 4 to 12 weeks from now.

What the homeowner would not want to do is sign a contract with the cabinet contractor if their kitchen remodel involved changing walls in the kitchen that affected the dimensions of the kitchen cabinets. In this case the homeowner would verbally tell the cabinet contractor they would be using them but do not want to sign a contract until the site conditions are set (they are set when the new walls are built). Then the homeowner has the cabinet contractor come to the site, take their final measurements now that the site conditions are fixed. Now the homeowner would sign a contract.

The disadvantage to this is that the homeowner may have a kitchen with new walls and no cabinets for 4 to 12 weeks. There are disadvantages to the Pat Fay Method and the inconvenience of having an inoperable kitchen for a time may be one of them. However, if this is the case there are methods of overcoming this situation.

The homeowner could set up another area as a temporary kitchen while the main kitchen is in construction, cook with hot plates, or eat out at restaurants a lot. Is this costly? Perhaps but it is cheaper than having a general contractor manage the whole project.

Do not follow mainstream construction management books. The mistake many homeowners make is to follow what is written in mainstream construction management books. These books state that to manage a project properly the owner must have all their contracts signed in advance so they have all the contractors lined up before they start their project. Homeowners that follow this method of managing their home construction project will learn the hard way that this does not work in home construction.

How to modify the contractor's contract. Some homeowners may not want to write their own contacts. If that is the case then the homeowner can modify the contractor's contract.

What is an addendum to the contract? An addendum is a document that allows the homeowner to modify a contractor's contract. The addendum is a document describing an addition, change, correction, or modification to contract documents.

In the Pat Fay Method, the homeowner uses the addendum when they decide to sign the contractor's contract. It is signed at the same time as the contractor's contract is signed. It is the primary method the homeowner will use to modify a contractor's contract so the combination of the contractor's contract and the addendum meets the homeowner's requirements.

The addendum is a simple way to modify the contractor's contract. In the Pat Fay Method the homeowner will use the addendum to modify the contractor's contract so the homeowner's issues, concerns, specific materials, construction schedule constraints, and payment schedule may be defined and made part of the contract.

The homeowner may place any reasonable requirements they want into the addendum. This may be about materials to be used and the quality of workmanship. For example, the homeowner could write that the quality of the tile work will be equivalent to the tile work shown in the attached picture. Or that only copper wire is to be used for wiring, or copper piping is to be used for all water distribution in the house. You have a right to do this.

It is not just because you are the owner and it is your money but rather it is good project management. The owner has a responsibility and the right to define what they want instead of just accepting what the contractor specifies or has stated on their preprinted forms with the word contract written at the top.

How to attach the addendum to the contractor's contract. To attach the addendum to the contractor's contract the homeowner writes the following in blue ink onto the contractor's contract, 'addendum #1 is hereby made a part of this contract'. Then both the homeowner and the contractor sign their full names (don't just put initials) in blue ink just below this statement. The homeowner keeps the ink copies of both the addendum and the contractor's contract. The homeowner makes copies of the documents for the contractor or signs two inked copies.

A sample Pat Fay Method addendum is at the end of this chapter.

Markup the contractor's contract proposal. The homeowner has the power to take the contractor's proposal and mark it up so that it meets the homeowner's requirements. This is always a shocking idea to the homeowners who take my class but this idea fits well with the rules of contracting. Namely the contract is a document for two parties.

All the homeowner need do is markup the proposal in blue ink so that it says what the homeowner wants it to say. Use blue ink because it stands out well. Both the homeowner and the contractor will want to sign by each of the markups. The homeowner should keep the inked copy and make a copy for the contractor (or make two inked copies). This is an easy way to modify the proposal before it is signed and then becomes a contract.

What is a scope of work? A scope of work is a written description of the work to be built by the contractor for the homeowner.

The homeowner must start with a broad description of the work that they want to have built. A few sentences to complete the details are all that is required. The key to a good scope of work is to be specific without getting lost in the details. The less complicated a scope of work is the better it is.

For example, let's say the homeowner wanted to add a room onto the side of their house. The first thing to have built would be the foundation. The homeowner has a set of drawings showing the whole addition that includes details showing the foundation. A scope of work to build the foundation would be something like this:

The contractor is to provide all labor, material and equipment to build the Fay house foundation as shown on drawings A1, A2, and A3 and according to the building code. Specifically, the contractor is to excavate for the footing, build all formwork, install all rebar, anchor bolts, and hold down straps, drill and place rebar to tie the new foundation into the existing foundation, arrange for the building inspector to inspect the rebar placement before concrete is placed, ensure that the foundation is square, ensure that the top of the foundation is level, coordinate the delivery of the concrete and the concrete pumping truck, place the concrete and vibrate the concrete to remove air pockets, strip the forms after the concrete has set (usually one week after placing concrete), place perimeter drain around the footing, backfill and compact soil around the foundation, and clean up all construction debris.

What are specifications? Specifications are written descriptions that describe what the homeowner wants. Specifications can be used to describe both the materials and the quality of workmanship required by the homeowner. Specifications are also known as specs.

In the Pat Fay Method we typically put the specifications on the drawings. However, if the homeowner wants to add specifications to the contract they can do so. However, the contract must remain only one to two pages long.

How to use specifications to define materials and quality. As stated previously, specifications are just words that describe the level of quality and the types of materials the homeowner wants the contractor to use on their project.

In the Pat Fay Method we write the specifications on the drawings for two reasons. One, the specifications are right there in plain sight and two because there is so much room on a drawing to write. Remember the homeowner that follows the Pat Fay Method is limited to a maximum two page contract. This constraint makes it easier to write the specs on the drawings.

The homeowner's architect or building designer will have written many of the specifications already on the drawings. However, the homeowner can write their own additional specifications on the drawings themselves.

The point I'm trying to make is that if the homeowner really wants something, such as marble, or white pine wood floors, or 1" copper pipe for branch water lines instead of the standard ½" diameter pipe then specify it in writing on the drawings!

For example, the homeowner can write in ink on the drawings that all bathroom walls are to have creamy white, 4" square ceramic tile purchased from the Tile Store at 206-555-1212. Then that is what the tile contractor must install as long as the drawings are included in the contract documents.

Types of contracts to use in home construction. In the Pat Fay Method we use only three types of contracts. These are:

- fixed price contract
- time and material contract
- offered price contract

Fixed price contract. The fixed price contract is just as it sounds. The homeowner will pay a fixed price for a fixed scope of work. The fixed price is just the amount of money that will be paid for a fixed set of construction activities.

The fixed price contract will be easy to use because this is the form that almost all contractors use when dealing with the homeowner. The contractor will specify a certain amount of money to be paid for a certain amount of work. The only problem is that to many contractors the fixed price contract is really only a starting point and their goal is to increase the contract value as they go along.

Therefore, in the Pat Fay Method we consider the fixed price contract to be just that: a fixed price contract. To accomplish this the homeowner places wording in the contract that defines how the change order process will be managed. This is because change orders are the method the contractor uses to increase the value of the contract as the project goes along. The change order is discussed only briefly in this chapter because I have dedicated an entire chapter to this subject. See chapter 10.

Time and material contract. Time and material contracts are where the homeowner pays the contractor's actual labor and material charges plus their overhead and profit. A reasonable overhead rate is 10% and a profit of 15% for a total of 25%.

In the Pat Fay Method the homeowner will only use the time and material contract for limited demolition type work. There are two reasons for this. One is because the cost of bidding out removal work is not something most contractors want to do because the real money is in the construction phase. Since no one really wants it they bid prices that are too high.

For example, let us say the homeowner has a project where they will be adding on 20 feet to the back of their house. Not knowing what the exact condition of the interior wall behind the siding could result in a change order. This condition could happen when the contractor, hired to build the new framing, removes the siding and finds something not described in the drawings. This might be dry rot in some of the studs resulting in additional work to replace them.

Therefore, in the Pat Fay Method, we remove the siding before signing the contracts for adding on the addition. Then the contractor can be shown the actual conditions before any contract is signed.

The homeowner will use the time and material contract to do the work needed to remove the siding until the interior wall is exposed and thereby be open to viewing by the contractors bidding on the construction phase of the project. There is now no legitimate reason for a change order because the building conditions are open and exposed to view.

The second reason why the homeowner does not use the time and material contract is because the contractor will never seem to complete the project. There is always something more to do, something holding them up, and the project just goes on and on costing more and more money. Also, more materials are always being purchased so the bill is always growing.

The reason why the home construction project seems to go on far too long on a time and material contract is the same reason why this kind of contact is never used in Industrial construction anymore; because it is more profitable to the contractor to spend as many hours and buy as much material as possible thereby increasing their profit.

Offered price contract. In the Pat Fay Method the offered price contract is the boldest of the methods of contracting out the phases of the project. It will take courage and strength of character because this method is the pinnacle of the true homeowner construction manager.

It is simple in its beauty. The homeowner offers a particular phase of their project to contractors at a price set by the homeowner! Take it or leave it!

The offered price contract requires the homeowner to know how much a certain scope of work should cost to build. This requires the homeowner to be able to estimate how much time, material, and equipment is required to build a particular phase of their home construction project.

At first blush this looks like a difficult undertaking. However, chapter 15 on cost estimating will allow the homeowner to accurately estimate how much a phase of their project should cost.

Once the homeowner has an accurate, reasonable price of how much a construction phase should cost then it can be offered to contractors at a fixed price. In effect the homeowner will say, I have a construction phase that I am willing to pay $8,000 to have built. I offer it to you, the contractor, do you want it or not? If you, the contractor, would like to be paid $8,000 when the work is completed and inspected then sign our Pat Fay Method contract and go to work. Otherwise, I'll look for another contractor!

For the homeowner to do this, the boldest of the Pat Fay Method forms of contracting, then the key is to know four things;

> how many labor hours a project should take
> the quantity and cost of materials needed
> what equipment will be needed
> what dollar hourly rate to pay the contractor

Chapter 15 on cost estimating will teach the homeowner how to determine these four things.

Material and labor costs can be broken out. The homeowner can specify to the contractor that they want the submitted bid price broken down into labor and material costs. Contractors typically do not do this. Why they do not, even when asked, is beyond me. I suppose they feel it would give the homeowner too much information.

      Equipment costs. Equipment charges will typically be shown as material costs. The homeowner can request the contractor to break out this cost.

      Why the homeowner wants to see costs broken out. The reason the homeowner wants to see the cost break down is so they can better compare each contractor's bid against each other. This will allow the homeowner to determine which contractor provides the best value to the homeowner.

Once the homeowner places the different contractor's price breakdown into the contractor comparison matrix (see the forms section) it is easy to see the differences between the different contractors. For the matrix to mean more than which contractor is the highest or lowest bid the labor, material and equipment costs need to be shown. Then the contractor cost comparison matrix will tell an interesting story.

The story it will tell is who is obviously trying to charge too much for a project. The labor and material breakdown will easily show if the contractor's bid is fat or not.

How to control change order costs. The homeowner will control change orders on their project by use of the Pat Fay Method No Verbal Changes form. The entire tenth chapter of this book is devoted to this subject but we must cover it here in the contracts chapter because controlling the change order must be part of the written contract.

Either the contract or the addendum must define that the homeowner's No Verbal Changes form must be used for any change order. The reason for this is because if the change order process is not defined in the contract it is not enforceable.

      Use of the No Verbal Changes form. In the Pat Fay Method we use the No Verbal Orders change order form to define all changes that occur on the homeowner's project whether they be increases to the cost, decreases to the cost, or no cost changes.

The homeowner will control change orders by requiring that all change orders must be written out on the homeowner's No Verbal Changes (NVC) form at the time of the change. Any change submitted after the fact is invalid.

The reason why the NVC form process is so important is because it will put an end to the deplorable practice of the surprise change order at the end of the job. Unethical contractors use the change order process to legally force homeowner's to pay increases to the contract price.

The Pat Fay Method is not against change orders. Many changes suggested by contractors are legitimate but the price for these changes must be defined at the time of the change. The Pat Fay Method will put an end to this con man contractor practice. At least for the homeowner who follows what I teach.

The homeowner does this by using the No Verbal Change Order form. This simple, one page form, allows the homeowner to define in writing the reason, the description, and the cost of the change at the time it is identified. It also prevents miscommunication between the homeowner and contractor by requiring all changes to be in writing.

Understanding liens. The subject of liens is an important issue for the homeowner to understand. It really is a simple process but one that has the potential of costing the homeowner a lot of money. By understanding the lien process the homeowner who follows the Pat Fay Method will eliminate this potential increase to the project cost.

What is a notice to lien? A notice to lien is a very welcome letter to the homeowner. This letter informs the homeowner of very potentially expensive situation.

The notice to lean is just a letter that informs the owner of a property that a supplier has sent material to their jobsite without having been paid. Mailing this letter is a legal requirement that establishes the supplier's right to lien the homeowner's property. This is done so the material supplier can ensure that they will be paid for the material they delivered to the homeowner's jobsite if the contractor who ordered the material does not pay them.

A notice to lien can also be a labor lien. This typically happens when the contractor you hire to do your project hires a subcontractor to do some or all of the project. Since the subcontractor to your contractor does not have a contract with the homeowner they protect themselves by sending a notice to lien.

What is a lien? A lien is the real McCoy; it is a recorded debt on the property owner's deed. It is recorded at the County or Parish. It is placed there after a legal proceeding in front of a judge or a magistrate that establishes that a material or labor debt has not been paid to the complaining party.

This situation occurs when a homeowner hires a contractor, the contractor has building material delivered to the homeowner's project on credit, the homeowner pays that contractor what was owed for material and labor on their project, and then the contractor does not pay the material supplier.

In this situation, to have the lien removed from the property title the homeowner must pay the material supplier for the cost of the material. In effect the homeowner must pay twice. This is not fair but it is the way home construction is done in America today by many contractors.

How do homeowners protect themselves? It is simple; follow the Pat Fay Method. In this situation get the lien release.

What is a lien release? The lien release is a form that you have signed by the material supplier or subcontractor that acknowledges that the homeowner has paid their bill. It is a very important document because it is releases the homeowner from further obligation or threat of lien from the parties that have supplied labor or material to the project.

Be sure to keep your lien release in case there is any future dispute about payment. The homeowner just puts it in their project 3-ring binder for future reference. A sample lien release can be found in Chapter 19.

The importance of receiving the lien release. The reason why it is important to receive the lien release is because this document is the homeowner's proof that the material supplier or contractor has been paid in full and relinquishes their right to lien your property. All processing of liens must go before a judge or a magistrate before a lien can be placed on your property title. You have your day in court or before a magistrate to show that you did pay. This is where your lien release will be worth its weight in gold. This is just good project management.

How to resolve an impasse between the homeowner and the contractor. In the Pat Fay Method we acknowledge and accept the inevitable conflict with contractors. This situation will always arise whether the homeowner follows the Pat Fay Method or the traditional method of hiring a general contractor.

How we resolve the situation is the key to finishing the project, reducing cost, and most importantly reducing stress. In the Pat Fay Method the homeowner and the contractor can agree to disagree. The resolution of the disagreement will be by arbitration. Both parties will pay equally for this service.

When the homeowner and the contractor agree to disagree. It does not matter what the reason for the disagreement because there will be many disagreements with the contractors the homeowner hires. It is just part of the home construction world.

What does matter is how the disputes will be resolved. In the Pat Fay Method the homeowner will use arbitration. This is because the goal is to complete the home construction project not to get lost in a lawsuit no matter how angry the homeowner becomes.

Arbitration. The reason arbitration must be used is because it is fast, inexpensive and final. Compared to lawsuits that is. This is how it works.

For example, the homeowner and the contractor agree to disagree on the quality of the finish on the sheetrock. The homeowner's believes that the taping job is just not good enough. The inside and outside corners are not clean and sharp, there are small gouges in the walls, and in many areas the dried mud has sandpaper marks visible. The homeowner will not allow the contractor's texture subcontractor to spray the texture because texture will not hide any imperfections. The contractor says it is good enough per industry standards and wants to get on with the job.

The homeowner and contractor cannot agree. Therefore, in the Pat Fay Method the homeowner declares that there is an impasse and calls in an arbitration firm. The arbitrator will come to the job site, interview the homeowner and look at their project log. Then the arbitrator will interview the contractor, review their notes in their notebook and look at the work.

The arbitrator will then decide how to resolve the issue. The situation will go one of three ways.

The arbitrator agrees with the homeowner and the contractor fixes the problem. If the arbitrator agrees with the homeowner that the taping and mud finish work is not acceptable per the terms of the contract then the arbitrator will make a judgment call to let the contractor fix the poor finish work on the sheetrock.

The arbitrator will be assured by the contractor that the contractor's taper will come back and finish the work properly. The arbitrator will no doubt give a short time frame within which the work is to be completed satisfactorily. If it is not then the arbitrator will bring in another firm to finish the work. The owner will then have the right to withhold payment from their contractor in the amount needed to pay the new taper's fee for completing the project properly.

The arbitrator agrees with the homeowner but will not allow the contractor to fix the problem. In this situation the arbitrator will typically know this particular contractor and inform the homeowner that this is the way this contractor works and that it would be best to terminate the contractor for failure to perform. Then the arbitrator will bring in another contractor to finish the work properly.

If the arbitrator finds in favor of the homeowner then all works well if the homeowner has followed the Pat Fay Method and has not paid the original contractor any money. Then there is money to pay both the arbitrator's contractor and then the original contractor less the amount for the rework.

Arbitrator agrees with the contractor. There will be situations where the arbitrator, after interviewing both parties, and upon inspection of the work finds it to be acceptable per the terms of the contract and to the highest construction standards. If this happens then the homeowner must accept the judgment of the arbitrator and allow the contractor to finish their work.

If the contractor is already finished with their work (forgetting the above scenario) then the homeowner must pay the contractor.

In my conversations with contractors they describe homeowners who are never satisfied no matter what the contractor does. They can repair, rework and replace and the end product is never good enough.

Another scenario is that once the contractor fixes a particular problem the homeowner has another problem that was not discovered until later. When that repair is finished then another problem arises. Sometimes this goes on endlessly until the lawyers are brought in.

The homeowner that cannot be satisfied or holds the idea that the finished product must be perfect is an unreasonable homeowner. It is true that if the contract states the work is to be done with excellent workmanship that the workmanship should be extraordinary. However, that does not mean perfect. Home construction is not perfect. One can always find something wrong.

Contact an arbitration firm before the first contractor is hired. In the Pat Fay Method the homeowner must find an arbitration firm before they hire their first contractor. The yellow pages are a good source for local arbitrators.

The reason for this is because if the homeowner is going to engage in home construction they will encounter problems with contractors. This fact will occur whether the homeowner follows the Pat Fay Method or hires a general contractor.

What kind of arbitrator does the homeowner hire? In the Pat Fay Method the homeowner wants an arbitrator or arbitration firm run by an ex-contractor. I do not recommend hiring an arbitrator who was once a judge. The reason for this is because the former judge will just not have enough construction experience.

The arbitrator who was once a contractor will know exactly the problems the homeowner is facing. They will know just how to deal with any contractor who is not working honestly and ethically or has done poor work. In fact, the former contractor turned arbitrator will probably already know most of the bad contractors in their area.

Avoid lawsuits. In the Pat Fay Method we avoid the lawsuit like we avoid the plague. The reason for this is because lawsuits are very expensive and they take years to resolve. Also, there is no guarantee that the homeowner will win a lawsuit even if they are completely in the right!

Remember the goal is to finish the construction project not engage in a lawsuit. In the Pat Fay Method the homeowner must have the maturity to move beyond a bad contractor and work toward finishing their home construction project even if the homeowner is extremely angry at a contractor.

These situations happen and that is why the fundamental premise of the Pat Fay Method must be adhered to: break the project up into small phases and only let any one contractor have a small portion of the project at a time. Then, if the contractor turns out to be a bad contractor, the homeowner is not stuck with that contractor throughout the remainder of the project.

Paying the contractor. In the Pat Fay Method we actually believe in paying the contractor when they have finished their portion of the project. The main complaint I hear from contractors is that they have to fight to get paid.

If it is unethical for the contractor to not do what they said they would do in the contract then it is equally unethical for the homeowner to not pay the contractor the amount agreed upon in the contract when the work is completed, inspected, and lien releases are in hand.

In my conversations with contractors the thing that makes life really difficult for them is to have to fight with the homeowner to be paid. This is not right!

I am principally on the side of the homeowner because they have been abused for so long by bad contractors. However, that does not mean that the Pat Fay Method condones treating contractors unethically. When a contractor completes the work satisfactorily they deserve to be paid.

When to pay the contractor. In the Pat Fay Method the homeowner will make sure of all the steps that are required by the contract are complete, the quality is as agreed to and if required signed off by the city building inspector. The contractor then provides lien releases and then the homeowner pays the contractor.

How to pay the contractor. In the Pat Fay Method we pay the contractor by a written check. We do not pay them with a stack of $100 bills. The homeowner wants the physical evidence of a written check that has to be processed by their bank so there is a record on the homeowner's bank statement that the contractor has been paid.

However, before writing out a check have the contractor sign a lien release. If a supplier or subcontractor has mailed a notice to lien then the contractor must have these parties sign a lien release also. Once this is accomplished then we actually do pay the contractor.

However, material suppliers will not usually sign a lien release until they are paid. This can be a paradox because the homeowner does not want to pay until lien releases are signed but the supplier will not sign a lien release until they are paid. How does the homeowner resolve this Catch 22?

Use the two party check. The two party check is a standard in the construction industry but unfortunately it is one of those little secrets kept from the homeowner.

The standard for the uninformed homeowner is to pay the contractor for both their labor and material for the work done on the homeowner's project. If the contractor has paid cash for the material then everything is fine because when you pay the contractor you are paying them for both labor and material. However, if the contractor bought your material on credit there can be a problem.

Here is how the two party check works: When it comes time to pay the contractor you want to be sure the material supplier also gets paid. If you know that the material has not been paid for because you have received a notice to lien, then you want to pay both the contractor and the supply company at the same time. This will satisfy the requirements of your contractor's contract because when you use the two party check you are paying the contractor.

Instead of making out a check just to John Doe contractor you make it out to John Doe contractor and the XYZ Material Supply Company. The key word is to write is the word 'and' in-between the two names. Do not put 'or' in-between the two names because then either party can cash the check. The two party check ensures that both parties are paid.

Now remember why you are using the two party check: you use the two party check to be sure the money for material actually gets to the material supply company.

Therefore, just before you hand the two party check to your contractor, call the material supply company representative who is listed on the notice to lien. Tell them you are paying the contractor with a two party check and that the contractor will be down shortly to turn over the two party check. Remind them to mail you their lien release after the check clears. Then hand the check to the contractor.

The contractor cannot cash the check but must instead go to the material supply house to get it cashed. The contractor must endorse the check and then hand it to the supply company representative who will take it, cash it, take the amount they are due for your delivered but unpaid for material and then issue a check for the balance to the contractor.

Now you know how to use a two party check to be sure the material is paid for and that you, the homeowner, do not get penalized with a lien on your property for unpaid materials.

Getting the lien release from the contractor's material suppliers. In the Pat Fay Method the most important consideration is to protect oneself. Therefore, if the homeowner has received a notice to lien from a supplier then the homeowner automatically uses the two party check to make payment to the homeowner's contractor.

Make out the two party check for the amount owed to the supplier in the manner described in the previous paragraphs. This amount will be less than what the contractor has coming to them. Then call the supplier representative listed on the notice to lien and tell them that you have made out a two party check to them and the contractor. Tell the representative that the contractor should arrive shortly to turn over the check. Tell the representative that you will want their lien release sent to you when the check clears the bank.

Then the homeowner tells the contractor that the balance of the payment will be made when the lien release is received from the supplier. The contractor may not like this but it is in your best interest. The homeowner must make sure the supplier is paid because unpaid suppliers are the main reason for a lien on the homeowner's property.

For example, a lumber supply company has supplied the lumber package for your project. They previously sent you a notice to lien because the material was sent on credit. At the bottom of the notice to lien is the name Mary Smith with her phone number. An example conversation might go like this:

"Hello. May I please speak to Mary Smith? Yes, this is Mary. Mary this is Pat Fay, you previously sent me a notice to lien before the wood package was sent to my project. Yes Mr. Fay. I remember that you called me when you received the notice to lien and we discussed the value of the wood package. I hope that you found our wood package to be superior in quality. Yes Mrs. Smith, I did as a matter of fact. My framing contractor has completed the work and I am in the process of paying him. I have made out a two party check for $32,450. Is that the correct amount that you are owed? Yes Mr. Fay it is. Good. It is check number 4572. I will be giving it to my framing contractor now. He should be delivering it to you before the day is out. Once my check clears the bank would you please send me my lien release? I will not be paying the framing contractor his balance due until I receive your lien release. So I hope you will send it quickly. Yes Mr. Fay, once your check clears the bank and we have our money we will issue you the lien release. Thank you Mr. Fay. Also, I'll be sure to call you when I receive the check. Your cell phone number is 206-555-1212 correct? Yes it is. Thank you. Goodbye.

There is no room for trust in the home construction contracting world. In the Pat Fay Method the homeowner is enjoined not to trust any contractor. Rather the homeowner's trust must be placed in a simple but well written contract.

The reason there is no trust in home construction is not because contractors are inherently untrustworthy. In fact, most homeowner contractors are good, honest, hardworking men and women.

The reason there is no trust in home construction is because the contractor who sits across the table from the homeowner is an unknown quantity. Each homeowner starts with a blank sheet of paper as far as their experience with this contractor. It does not matter the recommendations, the previous work, or how sweet they talk.

Trust is something that is built over time with shared experiences that develop a track record of trust. The typical homeowner will be using a particular contractor for the first and probably the last time. Therefore, since there has been no time for any shared common experience there can be no trust. In the Pat Fay Method we trust in the written contract and in keeping our money in our checking account until work is accomplished.

A word of encouragement to the homeowner that feels overwhelmed. After reading this chapter many homeowners may feel they are not up to the task of managing their home construction project themselves. I would like to reassure the homeowner that they really are more than capable.

In my classes, I describe how my students will feel one of two ways by the end of the class; empowered or overwhelmed. If the homeowner is feeling overwhelmed there is a simple solution. Set this book aside for one week. During that week get at least 8 hours of sleep each night. Then pick this book up again and reread it.

During the previous week your subconscious mind will have assimilated the vast majority of the new ideas found in this book. An interesting thing will happen. The homeowner will think: 'you know, this book is just good common sense. It has a lot of excellent ideas and basic project management techniques. I believe I can do this. It is my money and it is my project. Contractors will have to work for me according to the Pat Fay Method or they won't work for me at all. Let them work for someone else who doesn't know any better. Boy, I'm going to save serious money on my home construction project.'

A sample contract and a sample addendum. The example of the Pat Fay Method contract or the Pat Fay Method addendum are really the same document. They just have a different opening paragraphs.

The Fay Contract for Construction Services

Pat Fay, herein referred to as the homeowner, needing an expert in the field of house foundations, (or framing work, electrical work, tile work, fence construction, or plumbing) hires 'Name of Contractor', herein referred to as the contractor, to perform this work according to this contract.

1. SCHEDULE OF WORK. The work will start on _____ and be completed on _____.

2. SCOPE OF WORK. The contractor is to provide all labor, material and equipment to build the Fay house foundation as shown on drawings A1, A2, and A3. The contractor is required to build according to the building code, have the work inspected by the city inspector, and to rework at no additional cost any exceptions noted by the building inspector. Specifically, the contractor is to excavate for the footing, build all formwork, install all rebar, anchor bolts, and hold down straps, drill, place & glue rebar into the existing foundation to structurally tie in the new foundation, arrange for the building inspector to inspect the foundation forms and rebar spacing as well as sign off the foundation portion of the building permit before any concrete is placed, ensure that the foundation is square, ensure that the top of the foundation is level, coordinate the delivery of the concrete and the concrete pumping truck, place the concrete and vibrate the concrete to remove air pockets, strip the forms only after the concrete has set for seven days, place perimeter footing drain around the footing, remove all garbage from around the foundation, place two feet of rock over the perimeter drain, backfill and compact the excavated soil around the foundation, and clean up all construction debris.

3. PAYMENT SCHEDULE. -The owner will make payment in full upon completion of the work defined in section 2, the scope of work, receipt by the owner of a lien release from the contractor and concrete supplier, and the permit signed off by the building inspector.

4. CHANGES IN SCOPE OF WORK AND CHANGE ORDERS. All changes in scope of work and/or cost, whether an increase, decrease or no cost change, will be in writing on the owner's No Verbal Changes (NVC) form and when signed by the owner and the contractor are made a part of the contract. No payment will be made to the contractor for any change or change order that is not written on the NVC form at the time of the change. The labor rate for change orders is $35 per hour. The material cost and the number of hours to execute the change in scope will be defined on the NVC at the time of the change.

5. RESPECT. The owner and contractor, including the contractor's representatives and subcontractor's, will deal with each other in a professional manner and when speaking will use a polite, respectful tone of voice. The owner has the right to discuss all construction issues with the contractor such as, but not limited to, progress, quality of workmanship, quality of materials used on the project, safety, and site cleanup.

6. CONSTRUCTION SAFETY. The contractor is responsible for safety on this project. All construction safety rules are to be followed.

7. APPOINTMENTS AND COMMUNICATION. The contractor will keep all scheduled appointments with the owner. If the contractor is unable to keep an appointment the contractor will call the owner in a timely manner. Communication between the owner and the contractor is important. The owner's cell phone number is 206-555-6543.

8. ARBITRATION. If the homeowner and the contractor cannot come to a mutually agreed upon resolution to a problem then the homeowner and the contractor will use an arbitrator to resolve the impasse.

9. FAILURE TO PERFORM. The owner wants to have a win-win relationship with the contractor. The owner pledges to make prompt payment to the contractor upon completion of the contract. However, the contractor must work with all due diligence to complete the work per the mutually agreed upon schedule in paragraph one and to the terms of the contract and this addendum. Failure to perform is reason to terminate the contract.

_____ _____
Pat Fay   Date   Contractor   Date

_____ _____
Street Address   Street Address

_____ _____
City, State, Zip Code   City, State, Zip Code

_____ _____
Home & cell phone   Office & cell phone

                                       _____
                                       State Contractor License number

Addendum no. 1 to the Fay Contract for Construction Services

Pat Fay, herein referred to as the homeowner, needing an expert in the field of house foundations, (or framing work, electrical work, tile work, fence construction, or plumbing) hires 'Name of Contractor', herein referred to as the contractor, to perform this work according to the signed contract and according to this addendum no. 1 which is made a part of the contract. If there are any discrepancies or differences between the contract and the addendum then the addendum will be the ruling document.

1. SCHEDULE OF WORK. The work will start on _____ and be completed on _____.

2. SCOPE OF WORK. The contractor is to provide all labor, material and equipment to build the Fay house foundation as shown on drawings A1, A2, and A3. The contractor is required to build according to the building code, have the work inspected by the city inspector, and to rework at no additional cost any exceptions noted by the building inspector. Specifically, the contractor is to excavate for the footing, build all formwork, install all rebar, anchor bolts, and hold down straps, drill, place & glue rebar into the existing foundation to structurally tie in the new foundation, arrange for the building inspector to inspect the foundation forms and rebar spacing as well as sign off the foundation portion of the building permit before any concrete is placed, ensure that the foundation is square, ensure that the top of the foundation is level, coordinate the delivery of the concrete and the concrete pumping truck, place the concrete and vibrate the concrete to remove air pockets, strip the forms only after the concrete has set for seven days, place perimeter footing drain around the footing, remove all garbage from around the foundation, place two feet of rock over the perimeter drain, backfill and compact the excavated soil around the foundation, and clean up all construction debris.

3. PAYMENT SCHEDULE. -The owner will make payment in full upon completion of the work defined in section 2, the scope of work, receipt by the owner of a lien release from the contractor and concrete supplier, and the permit signed off by the building inspector.

4. CHANGES IN SCOPE OF WORK AND CHANGE ORDERS. All changes in scope of work and/or cost, whether an increase, decrease or no cost change, will be in writing on the owner's No Verbal Changes (NVC) form and when signed by the owner and the contractor are made a part of the contract. No payment will be made to the contractor for any change or change order that is not written on the NVC form at the time of the change. The labor rate for change orders is $35 per hour. The material cost and the number of hours to execute the change in scope will be defined on the NVC at the time of the change.

5. RESPECT. The owner and contractor, including the contractor's representatives and subcontractor's, will deal with each other in a professional manner and when speaking will use a polite, respectful tone of voice. The owner has the right to discuss all construction issues with the contractor such as, but not limited to, progress, quality of workmanship, quality of materials used on the project, safety, and site cleanup.

6. CONSTRUCTION SAFETY. The contractor is responsible for safety on this project. All construction safety rules are to be followed.

7. APPOINTMENTS AND COMMUNICATION. The contractor will keep all scheduled appointments with the owner. If the contractor is unable to keep an appointment the contractor will call the owner in a timely manner. Communication between the owner and the contractor is important. The owner's cell phone number is 206-555-6543.

8. ARBITRATION. If the homeowner and the contractor cannot come to a mutually agreed upon resolution to a problem then the homeowner and the contractor will use an arbitrator to resolve the impasse.

9. FAILURE TO PERFORM. The owner wants to have a win-win relationship with the contractor. The owner pledges to make prompt payment to the contractor upon completion of the contract. However, the contractor must work with all due diligence to complete the work per the mutually agreed upon schedule in paragraph one and to the terms of the contract and this addendum. Failure to perform is reason to terminate the contract.

Pat Fay Date	Contractor Date
Street Address	Street Address
City, State, Zip Code	City, State, Zip Code
Home & cell phone	Office & cell phone
	State Contractor License number

Chapter 10-The Change Order

What is a change order?
How the change order can ruin the homeowner's project
Legitimate change orders
    Example of a legitimate change order
What are not legitimate change orders
    Minor errors and omissions on the plans
    Answering questions or clarifying something in the plans
    The surprise change order at the end of the project
    The building or site conditions are different
    The building inspector's requirements have caused additional costs
    Any change that does not increase labor or material costs.
    Expensive materials that are shown on the drawings or were agreed to in writing.
    The increase in cost change order for no legitimate reason
How to respond to a change order request from the contractor
How to control change orders on your project
    Use the No Verbal Orders (NVC) change order form
    The use of the NVC form must be negotiated into the contract
    Define the hourly rate to be charged for change order work
    When to use the NVC form
        Increases to the cost change order
        Decreases to the cost change order
        No cost change order
    How to use the NVC form
    Example of how to fill out a NVC form for a new door
        If you cannot come to an agreement on the price
    Sample NVC form

Chapter 10-The Change Order

What is a change order? A change order is a method of modifying a construction contract so that there can be an addition or reduction to the scope of work and cost. Therefore, since the change order can decrease the scope as well as increase it then the cost to the homeowner can go down as well as up.

How the change order can ruin the homeowner's project. The change order can ruin the homeowner's project because unethical contractors use the change order process to add very large, unanticipated costs to the project. The homeowner may think they are merely clarifying questions about the plans while the contractor considers these clarifications to be changes.
    Unanticipated, illegitimate, change orders can increase the cost of the homeowner's project by 50% to 100%. What family can afford a $50,000 increase to a remodel that was originally to cost $75,000? It would have been better never to have done the project at all!

Legitimate change orders. In the Pat Fay Method there are only two legitimate reasons for a change order. The first is when the homeowner changes their mind about something and requests a change that results in an increase or decrease in the labor and/or material to do some activity on the project. This kind of change order changes the project that was defined in the drawings or in the contract.

The other legitimate reason for a change order is when demolition takes place during a remodel. Many times the conditions discovered behind the sheetrock do not represent what was depicted on the drawings. If the conditions are substantially different from what was promised then this is a reason for an increase in cost because the contractor will have to do additional work than had been anticipated.

For example, on one of my industrial projects we had to excavate for a foundation. When we dug down 6 feet we found an abandoned railroad line with steel rails and concrete foundations. This debris had to be removed to make way for our new project. The additional labor and cost of disposing of this discovered material was a legitimate change order because no one knew this debris was buried at the construction location.

The price I paid the contractor, however, was just the labor to remove the material and to haul it to the dump including a reasonable equipment charge, as well as the dump fees. I kept track of how many trucks were loaded, how long they took to go to the dump and back, and the actual charges from the disposal site. The point here is that the change order price is only for the cost of the labor and materials to do the change order work.

Example of a legitimate change order. Let us say the homeowner is doing a kitchen remodel. The scope of work is to remove all the cabinets, countertops, sink, garbage disposal, and appliances. To simplify this example, the new kitchen cabinets, counters, new appliances are going to go back into the exact same layout including the location of the sink. The homeowner wanted to reduce cost by not having to change any of the waste, drain and vent piping.

So a set of plans were drawn up, the cabinets were ordered and delivered, but before anything was installed the homeowner changed their mind. The homeowner decided the sink was just not going to work in its present location but it must be moved 10 feet to one side. What would be the change order scope of work?

The change order scope of work would be:
- remove kitchen wall sheetrock for piping access
- install new piping from existing sink to new sink location
- install drain line from new sink down into sanitary riser in basement
- install new vent pipe from new sink location thru roof
- change out cabinets due to revised sink location
- repair walls and sheetrock where exposed for new piping

You can see from this scope of work that the homeowner would have additional time for their plumber, carpenter, drywaller, roofer, and cabinet supplier. Appropriate charges for each craft work would be legitimate. A reasonable cost for each of these activities can be determined by using the techniques on estimating found in Chapter 15.

What are not legitimate change orders. Here are a few of the methods and reasons contractors use to charge the homeowner for illegitimate change orders.

Minor errors and omissions on the plans. Minor errors and omissions on the plans are not a reason for a change order because the contractors are expert in their fields of construction. They are supposed to know everything there is to know about their craft.

All drawings have minor errors and omissions. For example, if the architect failed to indicate a header over a window this is not a reason for the framer to charge an additional cost because all framers know there must be a header above all doors and windows.

Answering questions or clarifying something in the plans. There are innumerable questions that arise during construction that require the homeowner and contractor to have a discussion. These clarifications are not a reason for a change order.

Questions arise because sometimes there are many ways to accomplish a given construction task. Sometimes the contractor has a better way to do some part of the work. Questions also come up because many contractors do not know how to read construction drawings.

The surprise change order at the end of the project. The most common change order is the surprise change order that suddenly comes at the end of the project. A happy homeowner can be completely satisfied with the way a project has gone, thank the contractor as well as compliment them on their work, hand their final payment to the contractor, who then hands the homeowner a surprise bill for all the change orders they supposedly did on the job. This is completely illegitimate on the part of the contractor.

The building or site conditions are different. Actually, when site conditions are not as described or promised this is a legitimate reason for a change order. However, in the Pat Fay Method we eliminate this reason by not signing a contract until the contractor has visited the site and seen the actual site conditions. Therefore, the contractor knows the site conditions and cannot claim a change order.

The building inspector's requirements have caused additional costs. During the inspection stage of your project the building inspector may require rework or additional work than what has already been built. The contractors will want to charge the homeowner for this work.

In the Pat Fay Method we only hire contractors who are expert in their trade. Therefore, since they are expert in their trade, there is nothing in their trade they do not know about, particularly the minimum requirements of the building code. Remember that the building inspector can only require work to be done according to the requirements of the building code. If the inspector requires some phase of the construction to meet the code requirements then it means the contractor did not do the work up to the code specifications that they know must be met. Therefore, the contractor must do what the building inspector requires at no additional charge to the homeowner.

Any change that does not increase labor or material costs. Often a homeowner will decide they want some feature changed in their house. For example, moving an opening in a wall before the wall is built. If all the labor and material is the same then this is a no cost change.

Expensive materials that are shown on the drawings or were agreed to in writing. If the drawing shows an expensive type of material to be used whether in a note or the specification then the contractor has no basis to claim additional money for buying and installing it.

The reason I even mention this example is because this is a common complaint voiced by homeowners who have taken my class. They describe having to pay additional money to contractors for just this reason. When I ask why they would pay more money to the contractor for something that is in the drawings their answer is always one of two reasons: 1) because the contractor said I had to and 2) the contractor threatened to lien my property.

In the first case, just because a contractor says the homeowner must do something is not actually a valid reason to do what they say or demand. Since the contractor has agreed to use the specified materials per the contract they cannot charge the homeowner extra for that, regardless of the price of the materials. The homeowner needs to call their bluff. Call your arbitrator.

In the second case, if the contractor threatens to lien your property this is just plain and simple intimidation. The best course of action is to remember that Pat Fay teaches that the homeowner must have courage. Remembering this the homeowner just looks the contractor in the eye and calls their bluff. An appropriate response would be, "I would like to see you try to lien my property. I would show the magistrate the contract and how the materials in question are clearly described as part of the original price. Now either you install the materials called out on the drawings or I will call my arbitrator".

However, don't bluff. If the contractor does not state then and there to follow the terms of the contractor call your arbitrator immediately.

The increase in cost change order for no legitimate reason. What happens in this situation is the contractor will be working on your project, everything seems to be going fine, and out of the blue the contractor will say they need more money.

Often no reason will be given; the contractor just makes the statement that more money is required.

How to respond to a change order request from the contractor. The typical homeowner does not know what to say when their contractor asks for a change order or simply wants more money. What the homeowner needs at that moment is time to compose themselves and think. Therefore, the first thing the homeowner should say is, "What does the contract say about change orders?"

This statement will cause the contractor to actually think about what the contract says. This will then put the pressure on the contractor rather than you the homeowner. This will give you the moment to remember what was written in this book and determine whether the change order is legitimate or not.

How to control change orders on your project. In the Pat Fay Method we control change orders by requiring that all change orders must be written out on the owner's No Verbal Changes (NVC) form at the time of the change. Any change submitted after the fact is invalid. The homeowner negotiates the cost of the change at the time of the change or the homeowner does not allow the change order. Do this by using the No Verbal Change Order form. An example NVC form is found at the end of the chapter and in Chapter 19.

Use the No Verbal Changes (NVC) change order form. In the Pat Fay Method we use the No Verbal Orders change order form to define all changes that occur on the homeowner's project: increases to the cost, decreases to the cost, and no cost change.

This simple, one page form, allows the homeowner to define in writing the reason, the description, and the cost of the change at the time it is identified. It also prevents miscommunication between the homeowner and contractor by requiring all changes to be in writing.

The use of the NVC form must be negotiated into the contract. The use of the No Verbal Orders change order form must be in the contract the homeowner signs with the contractor or in the addendum that is attached to the contract. The reason for this is because if it is not defined in the contract it is not enforceable. We go over these details in the chapter 9 on contract documents but the NVC form must be made a part of either the contract or the addendum to the contract.

Define the hourly rate to be charged for change order work. The homeowner will want to know before a construction contract is signed with a contractor what hourly rate is to be used for any change order work.

This is something that I have found is not discussed 100% of the time by the people who have attended my class that have worked with contractors in the past. The contractors do not want to discuss the hourly rate ahead of time because they do not want it defined. If it is not defined then any rate can be charged. $250 per hour for change orders is a reasonable rate to charge an unknowledgeable homeowner by an unreasonable contractor. It is not a reasonable rate using the Pat Fay Method.

If you never discuss this issue with your contractors and particularly if you do not define it in writing then you can be charged any rate that increases the contractor's profit as much as they want.

What change order hourly rate should be used by the contractor? $25 to $35 per hour is a reasonable rate. They will want it a lot higher but it is the homeowner's job to negotiate it lower.

When to use the No Verbal Changes form. The homeowner is to fill out the NVC form at the very moment that a change or change order is being discussed for the first time with the contractor. Typically contractors will postpone giving the homeowner the cost of a change because the longer they wait the more money can be charged for the change.

This is because even if they wait even one week the contractor can double or triple the number of hours that a change actually took. Who can say how many hours were actually spent on a change when it was done a week ago. For example, moving a door opening will take about one to two hours. If the homeowner waits to see how much the contractor will charge you may get charged 8 hours for the change. I have found that contractors do not want to charge what the change actually cost; they want to charge a price that increases their profit.

The homeowner will want to use the NVC form when the following three scenarios occur:

Increases to the cost change order. The homeowner has the right to make changes on their project that increases the scope of work and therefore the cost. However, with that right comes the responsibility to pay the contractor fairly for the labor and material needed to build the change. Fairly means to pay for the actual labor and material to build the change.

Decreases to the cost change order. If there are increases to the cost then there can also be decreases to the cost. Decreases to the cost occur when the scope of work is reduced on the project.

No cost change order. There are some changes that occur on your project that do not cost any money at all. However, even these changes must be defined on the NVC form to document the change and so that the contractor cannot try to charge for it later.

How to use the NVC form. The NVC form is very easy to use because it has only seven elements to it. There is a filled out example at the end of this chapter. The seven elements are:

The number. Each change order will be numbered in numerical order starting with one.

The date and time. Look at your watch or cell phone and enter the present date and time. This is the date and time when you are actually filling out the form.

Increase, decrease, or no cost change. Circle the word that describes whether the change is an increase, a decrease or a no cost change.

Reason for the change. Explain the reason for the change. It could be as simple as the homeowner changed their mind or they just want something different. In the Pat Fay Method the homeowner has the right to make changes. On the other hand, the change could be because of new conditions discovered, as in my example of the railroad tracks that no one knew were buried at our construction site.

Description of the change. Here you will give a description which explains what the change actually is. The explanation should be simple and to the point, but should also include the important details of the change.

Cost of the Change. Here you will break out the cost of the change into material and labor.

Signature. Both the owner and the contractor need to sign the NVC form in ink. Make a copy of the form, keep the signed in ink copy for yourself, and give the contractor the copy or make out two inked copies.

Example of how to fill out a NVC form for adding a new interior door.

The number. Write in the number of the change. If it is the first change order for a particular contractor you start with the number one.

The date and time. Look at your watch or cell phone and enter the present date and time. This is the date and time when you are actually filling out the form.

Increase, decrease, or no cost change. Circle the description that describes whether the change is an increase, a decrease or a no cost change. For a new door this will be an increase.

Reason for the change. Write out the reason for the change. It is enough simply to write that the owner wants one new door leading from the master bedroom to the living room.

Description of the change. Write out that you want the contractor to add a second door leading from the master bedroom directly into the living room (in addition to the one leading to the hallway because it such a big house). You would also write something that describes the condition of the wall where the new door is being installed, such as: install the new door in the already framed wall. No sheetrock is on the wall and no wiring or plumbing is in the way.

Cost of the Change. Here you will want to break out the cost into material and labor. You will negotiate the cost of the door and the labor to install it right now with the contractor.

Put in the cost for a new door and the lumber to frame out the door opening, including the header. For example, new standard size (3'-0" x 6'8") interior solid core door with frame (pre-hung) hinges and door handle. Depending on the model, this door will cost you $150 to $250: we'll use $250. Looking at other framed openings you will see that four 2 x 4's by 8 foot long and a header are needed. Give the contractor $5 for each 2 x 4 or $20 and $40 for the header made out of a 4 x 6. The total of the material cost is $250 + $20 + $40 = $310.

Then negotiate the time needed to install the door. One carpenter will take about 30 minutes to build the door frame out from the 2x4's, including the installation of the header, lift it into place, square it up, and nail it in place. The door won't actually go in at the framing stage but you want to negotiate the total cost now. It takes one hour to install a prehung 3'-0" x 6'-8" door. Also, add one hour for the process of ordering the door, and one hour to go pick it up. The total labor cost is 30 minutes + one hour + one hour = 2.5 hours. A union carpenter earns $35 per hour in 2005. Therefore, the total labor cost is $35 per hour x 2.5 hours = $87.50. Total cost for the door is $310 + $87.50 = $397.50.

This is what you offer the contractor to install the new door. The contractor may try to negotiate for more money by saying that no labor was included for demolition of the studs that are in the way. Give the contractor an additional 5 minutes because that is all the time it will take his lowest paid worker to remove the existing studs with a sledge hammer.

The point here is that you now have a budgetary price for installing your additional door that is reasonable. It should cost about $400, not $3000.

Also, do not wait two weeks to negotiate the price because you could be charged much more than the $400 for the door. It is hard to remember what the conditions of the wall were at the time of the change. With time memory gets foggy.

In the Pat Fay Method we do not proceed with a change until we come to an agreement on the price of the change. Do not allow the contractor to cloud the issue by postponing the pricing of the change. They do this because they want to charge the homeowner too much for changes.

If you cannot come to an agreement on the price. If the contractor refuses to accept the $397.50 you offered and their price is far too high to install the one extra door then you have options. You can call your arbitrator, you can hire someone else to come in and frame the opening, or you can skip having the door installed.

     Signature. You and the contractor or their representative sign in ink on the NVC form. The homeowner then makes a copy for the contractor and the homeowner keeps the original signed in ink copy or make out two inked copies.

NVC form. The NVC form is found on the next page and in Chapter 19-Construction management forms.

No Verbal Changes Form

NVC No. _____ to Contract_____

Date & Time:_____   Increase   Decrease   No Cost Change (circle one)

Reason for Change:

_____
_____
_____

Description of Change:

_____
_____
_____
_____
_____
_____
_____

Cost of Change: (The cost must be determined before authorizing the change. Estimate all materials and their cost, labor hours and the rate of pay per hour, and list any equipment and their cost)

_____
_____
_____
_____
_____
_____
_____

This No Verbal Change, when signed by the homeowner and the contractor, is hereby made a part of the contract and authorizes the contractor to proceed with this change.

_____   _____
Contractor   Date   Homeowner   Date

Chapter 11-The Contractor

Why is a contractor called a contractor?
What is a contractor?
Definition of the terms: general contractor, builder, contractor, and subcontractor
Pat Fay's opinion of contractors
How to find contractors
    It is a myth that contractors are hard to find
    Look in the yellow pages
    Talk to your friends and associates
    Look on the Internet
    Contact local material supply houses
    Do not pass up building sites
    Look in the smaller outlying town newspapers
    Place your own advertisement in the newspaper
    Go to a freeway overpass
    Home Depot and Lowe's
        Advantages and disadvantages of Lowe's and Home Depot
        Pat Fay used Home Depot to install a roof
    Costco and other companies
    If you do have difficulty finding contractors in your area
        Move down the contractor food chain
        Pay a premium or bonus
How to screen contractors during the selection process
    Remember you are forming a business partnership
    Discuss your project and what you are planning to do
    Three questions the homeowner must ask the contractor
        Are you an expert in your field of construction?
        Why should the homeowner use your company?
        Who will do the work?
    Review the contractor's project 3-ring binder
    Look at the contractor's current project
    Look at the contractor's previous work
    Contact your State Department of Labor and Industries
Getting pricing from the contractor
    Ask the contractor if they charge for an estimate
    The detailed price breakdown will cost money
Final selection of your contractors
    Negotiating construction start date
    Negotiating price
        Comparison to the homeowner's cost estimate
        Comparison to other prices or bids
    Negotiating contract terms with the contractor
    When to sign the contract
Problems contractors have in conducting business
    Knowledge and experience
    Education

      Business issues
      Construction labor issues
      Material issues
      Quality and workmanship issues
      Mistakes
Guidelines for contractors who want to work according to the Pat Fay Method
Conversation between Pat Fay and a successful general contractor
      Homeowners need to come on site daily
      There should only be one decision maker in the construction process
      The issue of change orders and charging the homeowner additional money
      Contractors are builders first and businessmen second
The con man contractor
      There is no room for trust in home construction
      The key to the con man contractor
      The con man contractor and the law
      About the con man contractor
      What motivates the con man contractor?
      How to identify the con man contractor
      Legitimate contractors act insulted
      The Pat Fay Method is a new idea
      Pat Fay's two experiences with the con man contractor

Chapter 11-The Contractor

Why is a contractor called a contractor? A contractor is called a contractor because they work according to a contract. It is as simple as that.

If you are negotiating with a contractor that tells you that a verbal agreement and a handshake is good enough, run in the other direction. I have heard about exceptions to this rule but chances are you will not be lucky enough to find a contractor that will put your interests in front of theirs.

Without a written contract neither the homeowner nor the contractor understands what is to be done on the job. With a verbal contract the homeowner has one concept in mind and the contractor has another. These two mental concepts only touch upon agreement on the major points and they always diverge in the details. A written contract takes care of this problem.

What is a contractor? A contractor is someone who is regularly engaged in some trade or phase of the home construction industry. They may be licensed or they may not be. Some states have licensing requirements and others do not.

You will want to hire someone regularly engaged in a trade or phase of construction because in the Pat Fay Method we only hire experts in their trade.

Definition of the terms general contractor, builder, contractor, and subcontractor. To those of us in the construction industry these four terms are just understood because we have worked in the industry so long. However, during my classes my homeowner/students are always mystified by what these terms mean because they seem to be used so interchangeable. We do use them interchangeably.

A general contractor is a person or company that is engaged in building houses from the ground up. They are typically responsible for coordinating the entire home construction process. They usually have some core expertise such as framing and finish work where they have full time employees. They subcontract the remainder of the work out to specialty contractors also known as subcontractors or the sub. A general contractor is also known as a builder or a contractor.

The term 'contractors' is used to denote all people and firms involved in building construction. When we say 'the contractor' we could mean a general contractor, a builder or a subcontractor.

We use the terms interchangeably depending on the context of the conversation. To a construction person it is clear but it certainly is mystifying to the homeowner. Only subcontractor really means something different.

A subcontractor is a person or firm that specializes in some home construction specialty trade. For example, a subcontractor could be a plumber, electrician, carpenter, mason, floor installer, roofer, or any other specialty in the construction trade.

Pat Fay's opinion of contractors. Legitimate contractors are vitally needed to accomplish the construction work the homeowner needs to build their project. The negative things I say apply only to bad contractors and the con man contractor.

I believe the vast majority of contractors are legitimate, hard working, dedicated, and honest. Do not be overwhelmed by the things I say about bad contractors because by following the Pat Fay Method the homeowner can and will find good contractors to work for them.

In this book I make some pretty tough statements about contractors. I wish to emphasize that there are many legitimate contractors out there and the challenge for the homeowner, following the Pat Fay Method, is to find them. However, the bad contractor's behavior taints all contractors because the homeowner cannot easily tell the good from the bad.

The negative statements I make are about poor behavior by the contractor to the homeowner. These are things such as taking the homeowner's money and doing a poor construction job, taking the homeowner's money and making the homeowner wait months to get a one week job done, taking the homeowner's money and using it to finish someone else's job. Worst of all are things like taking the homeowner's money and spending it on a vacation, a girlfriend, alcohol, or just plain disappearing with it.

These traits are a constant problem in home construction in America today. This is because the bad contractors find so many honest but gullible homeowners willing to pay the contractor 50% of the money at the time they sign a contract.

An interesting thing will happen when the homeowner follows the Pat Fay Method; even the bad contractors will perform well for the homeowner. This is because the bad contractors need the money and if the only way to get the money is to do the work then that is what they will do.

How to find contractors. In the Pat Fay Method, the homeowner is responsible for finding the contractors they need to work on their projects. At first this looks like a daunting task but in actuality it is not.

It is a myth that contractors are hard to find. When I teach my home construction management classes the homeowners that attend usually have bought into the myth that contractors are hard to find. This is just not true because there are so many of them. Therefore, in the Pat Fay Method the goal is to find, screen and hire contractors whether they come from a big shop, work for a medium size company or have their own small company on the side.

Look in the yellow pages. I use the yellow pages a lot to find specialty contractors because they are easy to use and many contractors advertise there. The homeowner can find many of the specialty contractors they need to build the different phases of their construction project in the yellow pages. It is a low tech method of finding contractors but it works.

Talk to your friends and associates. Talking to your friends and associates about your project will give you names of contractors they have used in the past. You will definitely hear whether the contractor did a good or a bad job.

This word of mouth network is what keeps many contractors employed. The only problem with this word of mouth recommendation is that the contractor's financial situation may have changed adversely since the contractor worked for your friend.

A word of mouth recommendation is not a guarantee of a contractor's quality. Therefore, in the Pat Fay Method just because a contractor comes with a friend's recommendation does not mean we automatically use them. We still screen them.

Look on the Internet. The Internet, I understand, can be a good resource for finding contractors. However, I have not actually used the Internet to find contractors. I have used the Internet more to research the different kinds of materials to be used in my recent projects. The same rule of screening contractors before hiring them applies to any you might find with an Internet search.

Contact local material supply houses. Material supply houses have lists of contractors that buy and install their materials. These material supply houses are happy to supply the homeowner with the names of contractors who buy from them.

For example, if you want concrete foundation or sidewalk contractors call up a concrete supply company and ask them for their list of reputable contractors. They will be able to tell you which contractors can handle large jobs and who can handle smaller jobs.

Another example would be if the homeowner wanted framers they would call lumberyards. They will give you a list of framers that buy from them. They want those framers to buy the material for your house from them. It's smart business. They increase their sales by recommending the framing contractors who buy from them.

Do not pass up building sites. A good source of contractors is to go where they work: home construction sites. Before walking onto a building site be sure to have your passport with you: your hardhat. In fact, a hardhat will get you access to any construction site in America, if you are so inclined. Plus, it is essential safety equipment.

Once on site tell the workers you will be building and you want contractors that can do framing, plumbing and electrical work or whatever it is you are looking for. The workers will stop and either give you business cards or their name on a piece of paper. They would love to charge you $35 per hour rather than receive the $10 to $15 per hour they are receiving working for a builder.

For example, I went into a house under construction and told the workers there that I was building my own house and would like their business cards. One worker didn't have his own business card but took his employer's business card, crossed out his boss's name and wrote in his own name and phone number. Although, I did not end up hiring this contractor this is a good way for homeowners to meet contractors for their project.

Look in smaller outlying town newspapers. Looking in the want ads in the newspapers found in the outlying smaller towns proved to be a good method of finding contractors at a reasonable price.

My wife and I decided to take a break from our new house project planning and we took a drive to Stevens Pass on Highway 2, which is northeast of Seattle. While on our drive we stopped for lunch in one of the outlying small towns. While having lunch we read the local newspapers. In the back of these newspapers were advertisements for many different types of home construction contractors.

During the following week we called many of the contractors listed in the small newspaper and found pricing that supported our goal of building for $50 per SF (in 1992). During our conversation with these specialty contractors we discovered that these independent contractors could advertise for a whole year in the smaller newspaper for the same price that a month of advertising would cost in the larger Seattle newspapers. In fact, many of the contractors we hired were found out of the ads in the newspaper from the outlying town where we had lunch.

The reason the contractors found in the smaller outlying towns are a good source for the homeowner is because these workers are the people who the larger contractors use to build in the major cities all across America. They are the skilled craftsmen who usually work for the general contractors. If the homeowner were to watch the roads leading from these outlying towns into the city in the earlier hours of the morning they would see countless numbers of pickup trucks with construction workers heading into the city to work for the general contractors.

In the Pat Fay Method we hire these experienced, independent contractors and workers ourselves and eliminate the overpriced general contractor.

Place your own advertisement in the newspaper. The homeowner can find contractors by placing their own ad in a major local newspaper. In the Pat Fay Method we do not advertise in the smaller newspapers. The reason for this is because the contractors, big and small, always look in the larger newspapers for profitable work.

Go to a freeway overpass. An innovative method of finding contractors is to go to an overpass the crosses a busy freeway or major road. Take your notebook and perhaps your digital camera and take down the names of the contractors and suppliers you see driving by.

In Seattle we have terrible traffic during the morning and evening commute. The vehicles crawl along. During periods of slow traffic the homeowner will be able to take the names and phone numbers for the contractors driving by. Contact them and screen them as you would any other prospective contractor.

A word to small independent contractors. Place a sign on your truck with your name, phone number and business type so homeowners following the Pat Fay Method can find you.

Home Depot and Lowe's. Home Depot and Lowe's have contractors working for them who will install many of the products they sell. They are a powerful force in reducing the price of home construction in America because they have standardized, reasonable pricing. It may be on the high side but you have their guarantee. Also they only charge the homeowner a change order if it is legitimate (the issue of change orders is discussed in Chapter 10) and they stand behind their work.

If independent contractors will not work according to the Pat Fay Method then I recommend using the services of Home Depot and Lowe's whenever possible.

Advantages and disadvantages of Lowe's and Home Depot. A disadvantage of these home construction super stores is that they require full payment at the time the construction order is written up. This is against the rules of the Pat Fay Method but the reality is that we will not be changing the corporate policies of these companies.

Another disadvantage of Lowe's and Home Depot is that in some cases they turn over all responsibility to their subcontractor. This can be a problem if the subcontractor does not call the homeowner within the time frame stated by the super store. It can also be a problem if the quality of work is not as expected.

I believe Home Depot and Lowe's companies should have a project manager that works for Home Depot or Lowe's who is assigned to monitor and inspect the work their contractors do to be sure the work is done to the highest quality standards. This project manager would be available to the homeowner by telephone and in person to resolve problems.

The advantages of contracting through these super store companies, however, is that they will do what they promise to do and they will not try to charge you extra for the work at the end of the job (unless the scope of work actually changes). Also, if the quality is not to your satisfaction you have the recourse of working with Home Depot and Lowe's management to get the work done properly.

Pat Fay used Home Depot to install a roof. A few years ago I needed to have the roof replaced on my rental house. I gathered the names of 10 roofing companies and listed them on the project log. I found Home Depot listed in the yellow pages so I added them to the list.

Six out of the ten companies gave me a bid to install a new roof. The other four companies had either gone out of business or did not respond. The scope of work was to remove the old cedar shakes, install a plywood base, flashing, a roof ventilator, and then install new 3-tab composition roofing. The low bid was $5400 and the high bid was $8,400. The average price of the six bids was $7600.

I had estimated that the cost of tearing off the old roof and installing the new roof should be about $6000.

Home Depot's bid was $7,200. This was a little higher than my price but below the average price of the bids. I selected them to do the work even though they were not the low bidder. I wanted to test them so I could put this experience into my book. They did an excellent job!

They started and finished when they said they would. They installed all the plywood, flashing, trim, and roofing properly. Also, they did the best cleanup job I have ever seen.

Typically, old roofing and lots of nails are left everywhere. There was no debris left over at all.

If I had gone with one of the lower priced bids it would have saved me some money but could I trust that they would be in business ten years from now? I could trust that the Home Depot would not only be in business ten years from now but that if I had any problems with the roof they would come out and fix it.

Costco and other companies. Costco now has contractor services for carpet, flooring, garage doors & openers, and many other specialty construction phases. There are many other companies now getting into the home construction contracting business. It is the homeowner's responsibility as project manager to investigate all the local sources for construction services, evaluate them and make the decision to use them or not.

If you do have difficulty finding contractors in your area. If you find that you cannot get contractors to work for you there are two alternatives in the Pat Fay Method.

Move down the contractor food chain. If the more established contractors will not work for you then find the people who work for them and hire them to work for you after they finish their regular workday. Many construction workers moonlight. This is legitimate for these workers and it helps supplement their income. Just follow the Pat Fay Method when dealing with these as well as all contractors.

Pay a premium or bonus. The premium or bonus will convince many contractors to work your project because they want or need the extra money. The key is to not pay the premium or bonus until the work is done. However, be sure to pay them what you said you would pay. Remember, in the Pat Fay Method we are not looking to pay the lowest price. We pay a fair price for excellent work. The bonus is just an extra incentive.

How to screen contractors during the selection process. As in all business relationships, you are looking for someone with whom you can work well. If the homeowner cannot speak easily to the contractor during the screening stages of your business relationship then it is only going to get worse once construction gets underway. However, do not be scared off by the contractor who is rough around the edges because that is the way of construction men. I'd rather hire a rough and tumble kind of contractor than a silver tongued front man.

Remember you are forming a business partnership. The homeowner/contractor relationship is a business relationship first and foremost. Since money is involved this is business. The homeowner provides money and the contractors provide skill and expertise. You can be friendly and pleasant but do not forget that in business you are not making friends.

Discuss your project and what you are planning to do. The first conversation you will have with any prospective contractor is discussing what you want to do in your project.

Do not try to sound more knowledgeable than you are. There is nothing wrong with not knowing everything there is to know about the details of accomplishing your project because that is why the homeowner hires contractors. The contractors are supposed to know the details.

Three questions the homeowner must ask the contractor. There are many questions to ask the contractor and I discuss this subject in greater detail in this and other chapters. However, there are three questions that the Pat Fay Method requires the homeowner to ask. They are:
1. Are you an expert in your field of construction?
2. Why should I use your company?
3. Who will do the work?

Are you an expert in your field of construction? The homeowner must ask the contractor if they are an expert in their field of construction. The reason for this is the homeowner only wants to work with expert contractors. The expert contractor knows everything in their field and, therefore, will not encounter anything in their field of expertise that surprises them. The supposed surprise is a classic method contractors use to charge the homeowner a change order, which is the major source of cost increases and conflict between the homeowner and the contractor.

An expert will understand the building code and how it is applied to their field so that the homeowner can eliminate the possibility that the contractor will ask for additional money because the building code requires something that is not shown on the drawings.

Being an expert in their field will also eliminate the change order for minor errors and omissions in the drawings because they know that the drawings are a guide and that their expertise will take care of the project without additional charges.

Why should the homeowner use your company? The second question the homeowner must ask is "why should I use you?" You are not trying to trick the contractor or be funny with this question. You seriously want to hear their answer. This question is basically asking why should the homeowner work with this contractor when there are so many contractors out there.

Then wait for their reply. Take notes on the project log so that you can review their answers when you are comparing contractors and making your final decision.

Who will do the work? The reason the homeowner asks this question is because they want to know if the person they are negotiating with is going to do the work or will they be sending out workers. This issue is a big problem in home construction because many contractors act as if they are brokers gathering up work and then sending out others to do the work.

The best scenario is where the person you are negotiating with is actually on site doing the work themselves whether they have workers with them or they work alone.

The less desirable situation is the person you are negotiating with just sends out workers. The best case in this less desirable situation is where the workers sent out are employees and they have been trained by the contractor. The worst case is where the contractor is just a broker and sends anyone they can find to do the work.

When the homeowner determines the answer to this question they can use it as another piece of information that will be considered later when they make their decision on which contractor to hire to do a particular phase of construction.

Review the contractor's project 3-ring binder. The easiest way to review the contractor's previous work is to look at their previous jobs 3-ring binder. It will contain pictures of their previous projects. Reviewing their project manual will tell the homeowner what they need to know about the kinds of projects the contractor has worked on, the quality of the work they do, and their level of sophistication.

If the contractor has a binder of their previous work then you know you are not only getting a skilled craftsmen but a contractor who is also a businessman. This binder will show that they have a commitment to quality work because they are willing to show their previous work to their prospective clients, and that they are proud of what they do. These are the kinds of traits you want in the contractors you hire.

Look at the contractor's current project. It is also important to take the time to look at one of the projects that the contractor is currently working on. Since the homeowner may be doing their contractor research months in advance of when they actually need the contractor there should be ample time to go see where they are presently working. Be wary of a contractor who cannot or will not show you their current or previous projects.

Look at the contractor's previous work. The best way to judge a contractor's skill and expertise is to look at their previous work. The actual projects they have worked on are an excellent way to inform the homeowner of their skill level and expertise. Viewing previous work is time consuming so a little common sense should be applied in this exercise.

Contact your State Department of Labor and Industries. It is a good idea to contact your State Department of Labor and Industries to see if there have been any complaints filed against a contractor. Please see the last chapter of this book where there is a list with all the state agencies listed.

I found that in the State of Washington that the legal requirements of the complaint process inadvertently protects bad contractors. For the state to list a contractor for some poor behavior the injured homeowner has to have filed a suit against the contractor, have gone through the time and expense of a civil lawsuit, and if they won, then the state would report a judgment against a contractor.

Most homeowners do not have the time or money to do this. Therefore, the system, as it is, inadvertently protects the bad contractors. These bad contractors are able to go on doing whatever bad behavior they choose without too much fear of repercussion.

This is just another reason why the smart homeowner will protect themselves by following the Pat Fay Method.

Getting pricing from the contractor. When the homeowner asks a contractor for pricing they will typically receive simply a number with no breakdown of material and labor.

The homeowner can ask for detailed pricing from the contractor but unless they are willing to pay for the cost of a detailed estimate all the homeowner will receive is either square footage costs, lump sum costs, or price ranges. This is not a negative against the contractor because it is time consuming and expensive to do a detailed estimate.

The best way to judge whether a price received from a contractor is to compare any price against 6 to 10 other prices from different contractors for the same work. Another way is for the homeowner to build their own estimate based on the information contained in the cost estimating chapter of this book.

Remember sales tax is never included in a contractor's price. The homeowner always pays sales tax as an additional cost.

Ask the contractor if they charge for an estimate. Some contractors do not charge the homeowner to come to your house and give you a price and others do. In the Pat Fay Method we use both types of contractors to get pricing.

The reason for this is because in the Pat Fay Method we pay well for the services we receive. It is not unreasonable to pay about $50 to have a contractor take the one to two hours needed to drive to your house, look at the project, and write up a price quote. However, $200 would be too high a price. Of course, if a contractor does not charge to give a price that is even better.

The detailed price breakdown will cost money. If the homeowner does decide that they want a detailed price breakdown for the project then be prepared to pay for it. The detailed price breakdown for a small job such as installing a new power panel or installing a new window is easily done and probably would not cost anything extra.

However, a detailed estimate with a price breakdown for a house remodel or a new house will be expensive and time consuming to generate. The minimum cost for a detailed estimate is about $650.

Final selection of your contractors. At some point the homeowner must make a decision to hire their first contractor and get to work. The homeowner will select the contractor based on the work the homeowner has done in screening the contractor. The final decision will be based on the price, when the contractor can get started, the language of the contract, the language of the addendum (if one is needed), and the homeowner's assessment of the expertise and professionalism of the selected contractor.

The final step is to sign a contract and let the contractor get to work.

Negotiating construction start date. The date the contractor can get to work on your project is very important. In the Pat Fay Method we will select a contractor with a higher price if they can get started sooner than the contractor with a lower price. This is assuming the homeowner is ready for the construction to start.

If the homeowner is not ready for a contractor to start then ask the contractor how many weeks in advance they are scheduling their work. Then plan on calling them that many weeks in advance.

Negotiating price. Negotiating price is a difficult thing for most homeowners to do. Not everything in the Pat Fay Method is easy. However, it is the homeowner's money and the price must be negotiated. In the Pat Fay Method it is a requirement because the contractor's price bid is just their first offer. They are testing the homeowner. The homeowner should propose another price and negotiate with the contractor to find a price that is fair to both of them.

Comparison to the homeowner's cost estimate. Chapter 15 has a complete house cost estimating section. The homeowner can use the information in Chapter 15 to make their own estimate of what their construction phase should cost.

Once the homeowner estimates what the project costs should be they can compare the contractor's price against their own. If the contractor's price is higher than the homeowner's then you know several things. Either the contractor has too much profit in their bid or the homeowner has missed some phase of the work. Another reason may be that the contractor may think there is some risk in working the homeowner's project and has added a risk contingency cost.

If the pricing is lower than the homeowner's then we know the contractor has either a really good price, they have missed something or they are trying to buy the job. When a contractor buys a job by bidding too low they typically will try to charge the homeowner change orders to make additional money.

Whatever the reason, the homeowner must discuss the pricing with the contractor. Tell them that by using the Pat Fay Method you have estimated a cost for the work that is lower or higher than the contractor's. Then discuss the differences in your estimates and negotiate with them on the price. If they will work with you and consider your information you may want to hire them.

If they will not discuss price with you then look for another contractor.

Comparison to other prices or bids. Another way for the homeowner to compare contractor pricing without doing their own cost estimate is to get six to ten bids for the same work. Typically what the homeowner will see is a broad range of pricing. This pricing will be a reflection of two things: the relative need of the contractor for the job and reasonableness of the bidding contractors.

For example, I purchased a rental house in 2006. I needed to have the old style fuse electrical panel replaced with a modern 200 amp panel. My scope of work was to replace the panel, install required ground rods, install ground straps to the house piping, and pay for the electrical permit.

My estimate for the materials (a new panel, breakers, and wire) was $400. I estimated labor costs based on two men installing everything in one day. 2 men x 8 hours per day is 16 hours. 16 hours x $40 per hour is $640. Also, it included a permit cost of $160. Therefore, my estimate of the total cost was $1,200 ($400 + $640 + $160) without profit or sales tax. Remember, sales tax is never included in a contractor's price bid. The homeowner always pays sales tax as an additional cost.

I contacted 8 electrical contractors. One company did not respond, one had gone out of business, and six responded. The pricing received was as follows: $1,380, $1,485, $2,000, $2,307, $3,159 and $4,108.

These numbers tell a story. The companies with the two lowest figures ($1,380 and $1,485) were realistic about what the work would cost and they wanted the work. They only added a couple of hundred dollars in profit. The two companies with pricing in the mid-range ($2,000 and $2,307) were also realistic about the cost but they added $800 and $1,100 in profit. This was because they had plenty of other work and did not care whether they got this work or not.

The companies with the two highest prices ($3,159 and $4,108) price were just too high. These companies not only had plenty of work they were also hoping that I was just another uninformed homeowner who didn't know any better. These last two contractors are the type of contractor the homeowner wants to avoid no matter how highly recommended they are.

This example shows the range of construction pricing the homeowner will receive when they follow the Pat Fay Method and get 6 to 10 prices from different contractors. Incidentally, I selected the contractor with the $1,485 price because they could do the work in 2 weeks.

Negotiating contract terms with the contractor. This subject is covered more fully in Chapter 9 on contract documents. However, the homeowner must pay attention to what is said in the contractor's proposal. I liked the proposal submitted by the $1,485 contractor because they clearly defined the work that was included in the price and the work that was not included. They had a statement that any additional work would be charged as a change order. I wrote in on the proposal that no change orders were allowed unless written out on the homeowner's no verbal changes form. I also wrote in that only copper wire was to be used on my job. Copper wire is more expensive but it carries more current than aluminum. I did not attach an addendum because this was too small a job.

However, I did cross out the contractor's requirement for $500 down to start and wrote in that full payment would be made when the work was completed, even if there were any exceptions by the inspector. The reason I stated this is because the contractor verbally told me of several instances of illegal wiring existing in the house. The inspector would probably see them also and write up an exception on the project. I wanted the contractor to know I would not be holding him liable for existing conditions.

When to sign the contract. In the Pat Fay Method we sign the contract about two to four weeks before we need the contractor to come to work. This subject is covered more in chapter 10. However, the reasons not to sign a contract months in advance is because the homeowner will not know exactly when they will need any particular contractor. They also will not know what the site conditions will be like two months in the future. There are exceptions to this rule but this is a good guideline.

The mistake many homeowners make is to follow what is written in mainstream construction management books. These books state that to manage a project properly the owner must have all their contracts signed in advance so they know how much their project will cost. This method works fine in the commercial and industrial construction world but not in the home construction world! Homeowners that follow this way of managing their home construction will learn the hard way why this does not work for home construction.

In the Pat Fay Method we are trying to avoid the situation where, after signing a contract months in advance, the contractor comes on site and claims the conditions are different from what they were led to believe at the time they signed the contract. Then they hit the homeowner with change orders. This situation is very common not only in the Pacific Northwest where I live but throughout America.

I tried to warn my neighbor of this issue when he was managing his own home construction but he thought he knew best. Of course, $150,000 in surprise change orders at the end of his project forced him to sell his new home because he was unable to service the extra debt.

This situation could have been avoided simply by not signing a contract until the contractor could come on site and see the actual site conditions. Then the homeowner can ask the contractor if they see any site conditions that would alter their previous bid. If so the contractor could adjust their price. The homeowner could then reconsider whether the new price was reasonable or not. Then make a final decision whether to sign a contract with the contractor or rebid the work with new contractors.

Problems contractors have in conducting business. In the Pat Fay Method we also look at the issues confronting contractors and how they affect their ability to conduct business for the homeowner. Contractors have their own set of problems to work out each day they do business. It is not easy being a contractor. In the Pat Fay Method we recognize this and are committed to working with the contractors we hire to a win-win outcome. The following are some of the issues with which they must contend.

Knowledge and experience. The contractor that has their own business in home construction is limited in their skill by the amount of knowledge they have gathered over the time they have been building houses or practicing their specialty. Their years of experience will increase their knowledge so that they know what to do and more importantly what not to do. The only way home construction contractors and their workers learn their trade is by working on the job. There is very little formal training.

Education. Education matters in all aspects of life including home construction. The typical American homeowner has a minimum of a high school education and many have a college degree. On the other hand the typical contractor and their employees do not have even a high school diploma.

This is not stated here to denigrate the workers of the contractor world but to inform the American homeowner about the circumstances of people with whom they are dealing. The less education a person has means that person has a more limited ability to plan and execute projects, particularly multi-task, multi-phase projects common to home construction. Difference in education levels matters because homeowners often make assumptions about how contractors will behave based on the homeowner's level of education. This assumption can lead to problems with expectations on the project and communication.

Business issues. Contractors are builders first and they learn the business side second. This is almost always done through the school of hard knocks and not by any formal training or business classes.

The teachers are older and more experienced contractors who have much experience in building but not in contracts, money management or how to schedule the different activities or people needed to accomplish construction work.

Construction labor issues. Construction labor is another term used for the worker. This labor is what the contractors need to get their projects done. All contractors seem to have a difficult time holding on to their workers. The reason for this is because when times are good the grass looks greener on the other side of the fence and skilled craftsmen want to make as much money as they can. So they leave.

This means that on Thursday morning the worker who was working your project for the contractor you hired has quit. Your contractor now has to scramble to replace that person. Your project may sit idle for a week or more.

Another problem the contractor has is that their workers will just not come to work. There may be legitimate issues the worker has but the bottom line is that not enough labor is working on your project. This is a headache for your contractor. In the Pat Fay Method, we recognize these are issues affecting the contractor's ability to finish the project. Therefore, we work with the contractor as long as they are working with us.

Material issues. The reason materials can and will be a problem on your job is because sometimes the wrong material will be delivered to your job. Sometimes the material will be damaged in transit. Other times the material will be damaged after it gets to your job. Also, sometimes the contractor cannot get the material you wanted installed. To keep the project going the contractor may substitute another material. This may or may not work for the homeowner. The homeowner must be communicating on a daily basis with the contractor to be sure they are kept informed about material issues.

An example of incorrect material coming onto the jobsite occurred while the remodel of my bathroom was being done in 2005. I hired my long-time plumber to remove the old bathtub and to purchase and install a tub of my choice. I let him order it because it could be delivered to his shop and he would use his truck to deliver it. When we took the bathtub out of the box we found that the wrong tub had been delivered. It had to be sent back and replaced. This added three weeks to the job. This problem was beyond my contractor's control.

The point is that these things happen and the homeowner must be prepared for it.

Quality and workmanship issues. The individual with whom you contract a job may not be the person who actually comes to work on your job. Therefore, the quality of materials and workmanship guaranteed by the front man or salesman may not be something the individual who comes to your job knows about.

Therefore, in the Pat Fay Method when the homeowner meets with the contractor doing the work, the homeowner must review and refresh the agreed upon quality and workmanship points with the person actually doing the work.

For example, when I was young and doing one of my first jobs I had the following experience. I contracted with a company to install formica countertop in a kitchen remodel project. The person who sold the job to me stated that his workers were the finest in the business and that they would do the best job I had ever seen.

However, the young man they sent out to install the formica left glue all over the formica, threw the empty glue cans on the floor, and generally left all the construction garbage there.

I called and complained to the salesman that the quality he had promised was not delivered. I had to insist that the work be brought up to the quality agreed upon. I recall having to threaten to bring in another contractor to redo the work. This resulted in an older, more experienced craftsman coming to the project to repair the workmanship and clean up.

Mistakes. We all make mistakes and contractors are not any more immune from this problem than anyone else. However, the real question is what is done after the mistake is made. If the contractor makes a mistake then they must fix it. This can be a real headache for a contractor who is simultaneously trying to get many jobs done.

For example, let's say a cabinet door was scratched. The contractor would be responsible for repairing the scratch. Either the door or whole section of cabinets would have to be replaced. This will cost the contractor money. However, it is their responsibility and a cost of doing business. It doesn't make it any easier for the contractor though, and the homeowner should understand the contractor's perspective.

Guidelines for contractors who want to work according to the Pat Fay Method.

The homeowner comes first, second and last.
The contractor will honor the intent as well as the letter of the contract.

The contractor will follow the Pat Fay Method regarding change orders which is that there are no change orders unless written out on the no verbal changes form.

The contractor will carry current labor and industry insurance.

The contractor will keep a past projects binder with pictures of previous work and names of former clients to show to new prospective clients.

The contractor will be responsible for safety and will have a safety plan and a safety meeting everyday while on the homeowner's job.

Contractor will perform excellent quality workmanship and use the highest quality materials.

While working on the project they will clean up at the end of each day, and the contractor's workers will be considerate of the neighbors particularly concerning picking up garbage and keeping music at a reasonable volume on the construction site.

The contractor will work toward a win-win experience with the homeowner.

Conversation between Pat Fay and a successful general contractor. I have an acquaintance that is the owner of a general contracting construction company specializing in luxury home construction. He will not consider any project unless he can charge at least $250 per SF. He prefers work in the $500 per SF range.

The following are excerpts from conversations we have had. I hope these excerpts will help the homeowner understand the contractor's perspective and the Pat Fay Method counterpoint.

Point 1: Homeowners need to come on site daily.

Contractor: What contractors need is a homeowner who will come on site on a daily basis, preferably in the morning, and will be ready to make decisions. This is because a set of plans only takes the design to about 90%. This leaves issues that no one anticipates until the project is actually built.

Pat Fay Method: The Pat Fay Method agrees that drawings are really only about 90% to 95% complete. There are always things missing or not as they should be. This is just a standard in the industry. Therefore, the homeowners should come on site on a daily basis in both the morning and afternoon. In the morning the homeowner will conduct a short standup meeting to coordinate issues, answer the contractor's questions and be ready to make decisions. In the afternoon the homeowner will be checking the work that has been installed, logging the progress on the project log and noting things that need to be discussed with the contractor the next morning.

Point 2: There should only be one decision maker in the construction process.

Contractor: There is nothing worse for the job then to have two decision makers in the homeowner team. In the morning the wife will come on site and make decisions and the contractor will work according to those decisions. In the evening, the husband will come on site, see what is happening, go into a towering rage, give the contractor contradictory directions and direct the contractor to do what he says, and then leave without filling out a change order or trying in any way to capture the cost of the change.

Pat Fay Method: The Pat Fay Method again agrees: there should only be one decision maker in the homeowner team. The Pat Fay Method highly recommends that the woman in the team be the final decision maker. The husband works for the wife according to the Pat Fay Method. Regardless of who is the final decision maker, it is imperative that the homeowner team present a unified front when dealing with the contractor.

Point 3: The issue of change orders and charging the homeowner additional money.

Contractor: If I have a question that needs answering by the homeowner then I need to be paid extra for it. If the drawings are not clear then I deserve additional money for fixing the problem. I jot those changes down in my notebook, tally them up at the end of the job and hand them to the owner. This is the way home construction is done.

Pat Fay Method: The Pat Fay Method does not agree with you on the subject of change orders. A question by the contractor to the homeowner is not a reason for a changer order. The conversations the contractor has with the homeowner fall under general coordination and it helps you, the contractor, as well as the homeowner. You misunderstand the nature of the change order.

The change order is legitimate when the homeowner adds additional work not for answering clarification type questions. Since you are an expert in the field of house construction you know what has to be done to build a house and you no doubt have put enough money into your price to cover building the whole house. A change order is legitimate when the homeowner actually asks for something that was never part of the drawings, such as a new door or window, adding an additional wall, or taking a built wall, tearing it down, and then rebuilding it in a new location.

Point 4: Contractors are builders first and businessmen second.

Contractor: It is true that most builders started their construction career pounding nails, laying rebar, and building forms. Construction workers do not need a lot of formal education to do this kind of work so those that dropped out of high school can still find good paying jobs in home construction.

I will admit that most of us do not have any business training but we know how to build houses. We learn as we work and some stay in business and most do not.

Pat Fay Method: The reason that the Pat Fay Method is going to be a powerful force in home construction is because the homeowners of American are tired of having to pay for all the mistakes that are made by you while you learn your trade. There would be no reason to have even written this book if you, the contractors of America, would charge reasonable prices and do what you said you would do.

The average construction worker must start trying to educate themselves by taking classes at the local community college on how to read plans, how to write a business plan, how to write a construction schedule, and how to build a budget so they can better serve their homeowner customers.

The homeowners of America are willing to pay excellent money for excellent work but they are tired of paying excellent money for poor quality workmanship and inferior materials. (This ends the conversation excerpts with a general contractor.)

The con man contractor. Doing home construction projects is hard enough with legitimate contractors without having to contend with the con man contractor. The con man contractor's contribution to the homeowner's experience in the home construction world is similar to the moral of the story of the young man who leaves home to make his way in the world. He is young and innocent and believes what all people tell him. He has to learn that trust is something built up over time. It is not something that can be given to anyone who speaks convincingly. Learning to reserve your trust for those who have earned it is the only value the con man contractor has to offer. With the Pat Fay Method, the homeowner already has this knowledge and knows how to avoid and deal with the con man contractor.

There is no room for trust in home construction. The con man contractor is the main reason there is no room for trust in home construction. It has always been so in the industrial construction world. There we require the contractor to build 40% of the project on their own money before any payment by the owner is made to them. This often amounts to millions of dollars.

The Pat Fay Method will bring some of the rules common to industrial construction world into the homeowner construction world. The winners of this change to the home construction world will be both the homeowner and all of the legitimate contractors. This is because when most homeowners in America are following the Pat Fay Method the con man contractor will finally be put out of business. This will leave all of the home construction work available to the legitimate contractors of America.

The key to the con man contractor. The key to the con man contractor is that they want to receive money before work is accomplished. They then take the homeowner's money and disappear. That is the worst case scenario.

There are variations on the theme of stealing your money and they are infinite. For instance, taking your money and using it on anything but your project is another common con. Other common cons are: promising the highest quality workmanship and materials and delivering poor quality workmanship and inferior materials, taking the homeowner's money and making the homeowner wait months to get a one week job completed, taking the homeowner's money and using it to finish someone else's job leaving no money to work the homeowner's project, taking the homeowner's money and spending it on a vacation, a girlfriend, alcohol, or just plain disappearing with it. Sadly, the variations on these cons are infinite.

The home construction world is the perfect place for the con man contractor to work because of the unwritten rule that the homeowner must pay 50% of the money to the contractor at the time the contract is signed. The Pat Fay Method intends to end that practice.

The con man contractor and the law. State and federal law protects the homeowner from the con man contractor's illegal behavior but only after your money is gone. This means the homeowner must hire a lawyer to sue the con man contractor, wait a long time to have a civil case brought before a judge, and then endure the vagaries of a trial. Why waste the time or money on this process when you can avoid it all together? Take steps to not fall into the con man contractor's trap by following the Pat Fay Method.

About the con man contractor. The con man contractor is an interesting entity. This is because they are typically very good at whatever construction skill they perform. They are also smart but lazy. In their youth they learned they could get by on their latent intelligence without having to work hard. We remember them well from high school; they were smart kids that never seemed to find the time to do their homework and they were always getting into trouble. Whatever happened to those people? They went into the home construction contracting!

What motivates the con man contractor? Two things motivate the con man contractor. One, they need money and they can find it easily in the home construction world because there are so many homeowners inexperienced in the construction process. Most homeowners only do one or two major remodels in their lifetime and do not develop experience over time to avoid the tricks of the con man contractor.

Secondly, they have pride in their 'work'. The con man takes pride in being able to con homeowners out of their money. In their strange minds they find immense pleasure and satisfaction at having taken some homeowner to the cleaners.

How to identify the con man contractor. There is no way to identify the con man contractor by the way they look because they dress like honest contractors and they drive the same kind of trucks. They often do not have a contractor license although many do.

However, there is one particular trait common to all con man contractors. The con man contractor gives themselves away with one tell-tale trait. They all have a natural ability to know just what you need to hear to inflate your ego and to sooth away your normal sense of skepticism.

All con men have the ability to make you feel really good about yourself and they use this ability to get you to trust them. I have experienced this myself. When you are negotiating with the con man contractor you will personally experience feelings of overconfidence and almost euphoria. You will think you are speaking with the greatest contractor there is. You will instinctively trust them even though you have no basis with which to have trust. It will be their manner of concern for you and your project. You will just know that this person can do everything they say and more. You will also feel really good about yourself, very confident and strong where just an hour ago the project seemed overwhelming and almost beyond your abilities.

If you find yourself with these feelings while dealing with a contractor then be careful because you are dealing with the con man contractor.

Legitimate contractors act insulted. The contractors I have spoken to about the common traits between the legitimate contractor and the con man contractor have been very insulted. At least they acted insulted.

Pat Fay believes the contractors protest too much. Whenever anyone reacts angrily and instantly to an idea I believe it is because they know there is some underlying truth to the idea.

It is unfortunate to lump all homeowner contractors in a common category titled untrustworthy. However, in the Pat Fay Method there is no room for trust on a personal level. The trust on both sides is in the contract and the homeowner and contractor following it to a successful end of the project. There is nothing wrong with requiring the contractor to do the work, do it well, have it inspected, and then pay the contractor. In the Pat Fay Method we are not saying that all contractors are untrustworthy but rather that because some contractors are untrustworthy the homeowner must act cautiously. How is the homeowner to know which kind of contractor they are dealing with if legitimate and con man contractors appear the same? That is why in the Pat Fay Method do not rely on trust because the homeowner must rely upon the power of the contract, a well written scope of work and keeping their money in their own pocket until the work is complete.

The Pat Fay Method is a new idea. The problem with the Pat Fay Method is that what I teach is new to the homeowner construction world. You will hear that what I teach is not done in construction or in contracting. Also, the legitimate contractors will act insulted. You will need courage and self-discipline to break the unwritten standard of paying 50% of the money at the time the contract is signed. It is your money and your project. Be in charge. Just know that if one contractor will not accept your reasonable terms then there is always another who will.

Pat Fay's two experiences with the con man contractor. The first time I was taken by a con man contractor was in late 1979 when I was managing the remodel of an apartment building for the owner. The owner had found this contractor and recommended I use him to replace the siding on the apartment building.

The contractor and I negotiated the terms of the contract and when it was finalized he insisted I pay 50% of the contract amount. I hesitated but was convinced by the con man contactor that it was the standard in home construction. So I did. He took off with the money and I never saw him again. I did speak to him on the telephone and he always promised to start the project next week. He never did.

The second time I was taken by the con man contractor was in 1994 during the construction of our new home. This con man contractor did concrete flat work. I hired him to install the red concrete in our entryway. I told him up front that I only paid after the work was complete. He agreed to that.

When the concrete work was complete I tried to pay him but he refused to accept the check. He stated that he wanted me to be completely happy with the way the concrete work turned out. I was surprised but inwardly please to have such an honest contractor.

When it came time to place all the exterior flat concrete (sidewalk and driveway) I called this con man contractor back. Everything went fine. He did some final grading, placed the forms and made one pour, which was about one third of the project scope. Once that was done he took me aside and asked if I could help him out by paying him the money for the work even though it wasn't done.

He had a sob story about losing the house and his children and he being out on the street and other pitiful details. Regrettably, I bought it, hook, line and sinker.

I went inside, discussed paying him with my wife, and she said, "are you sure? I thought your rule was not to pay the contractors until they are completed with the work?" I told her that was true but we could trust this contractor because remember what a good job he did before. I reminded her that he didn't want payment the time before.

Well, you know what happened. He took the check, cashed it and I never saw him again. How could this have happened? Particularly, how could this have happened to an experienced person like me?

It happened because of two things. One, I had a false sense of trust in this con man contractor because he had done a previous job for me. He planted a seed of trust with me by the con of refusing to accept my money on the smaller job knowing the bigger outside flatwork project was coming up. Two, I broke my own rule of not paying the contractor until the work was completed. Why did I do this? I did this because I liked the con man contractor before I realized he was a thief. That is why I teach you are not making friends with the contractor. You have a professional, business relationship with them based on the written contract.

      These two examples and the countless stories told to me by my students are why in the Pat Fay Method there is no room for trust in home construction. The homeowner must trust only in the power of the contract and the power of keeping one's money in their own pocket rather than in the contractor's.

Chapter 12-Managing and Using Competition to Drive Down the Cost of the Home Construction Project

The pure Pat Fay Method for managing the home construction project
    Hire a different contractor for each phase of the project
    Who are the different contractors the homeowner needs to hire?
Acceptable modification from the pure Pat Fay Method
Two methods of driving down the project cost
    Competition drives down the project cost
    Bidding out project work packages
        The pre-bid walk through
        Contractors see the actual work site
        Contractors see each other. Therefore, they compete
        An interesting thing happens at the pre-bid walk through
        How to conduct the pre-bid walk through
            A simple example: replace kitchen cabinets
            A more complex example: concrete foundation
        Other details for the pre-bid walk through
Request for proposal (RFP)
    How to issue the request for proposal
    A sample RFP letter

Chapter 12-Managing and Using Competition to Drive Down the Cost of the Home Construction Project

The pure Pat Fay Method for managing the home construction project. The ideal or pure Pat Fay Method is to hire a different contractor for each separate phase of construction. When my wife and I built our house we hired about 30 different contractors.

    Hire a different contractor for each phase of the project. The homeowner that follows the Pat Fay Method to build a new house will also hire from 20 to 30 different contractors. A remodel can require from 5 to 10 separate contractors. This is a time consuming process that takes planning, organization and courage. However, this is the only way I know to drive the cost of the homeowner's home construction project down to the $100 per square foot cost or less.

    Since the Pat Fay Method eliminates the general contractor the hiring and managing of all the different contractors will be the homeowner's responsibility. However, by following the Pat Fay Method the homeowner is more than capable of managing the home construction project to a successful completion.

    Who are the different contractors the homeowner needs to hire? The scheduling chapter has a complete list of all the activities that went into the construction of Pat Fay's house.

    However, to recap, the following are a list of the activities where a different contractor was hired to build the different phases of our house. The list is of 35 construction activities. We hired only 30 contractors because we hired some contractors to do more than one activity and we did our own landscaping.

> Surveyor: to establish the property lines
> Excavator: to dig the hole need to place the concrete footings and concrete walls
> Foundation: to install forms, rebar, anchors, straps, place and vibrate concrete
> Waterproof basement concrete walls
> Install underground plumbing: this is the drain piping under any slab on grade
> Place basement concrete slab or slab on grade: this is the concrete floor
> All wood framing: this is exterior & interior walls, stairs, closets including exterior doors and windows
> Install rough plumbing: this is the drain, waste, vent, hot & cold water to point of use
> Roofer: to install roofing and flashing (flashing is used to prevent water infiltration)
> Install natural gas piping
> Install rough electrical wiring and main panel
> Install telephone, cable, and communication wiring
> Furnace and air conditioning units and supply & return sheetmetal ductwork
> Fireplace and vents to outside for exhaust fumes
> Install outside vapor barrier and siding
> Stain siding
> Install wall and attic insulation
> Install drywall, tape, mud, PVA coating and texture
> Paint interior walls
> Install hardwood floors
> Install tile and vinyl work
> Install cabinets
> Install countertops
> Install finish plumbing
> Install finish electrical work
> Install interior doors and trim
> Paint interior doors and trim
> Finish hardwood floors
> Install carpets
> Install appliances
> Install mirrors, shower doors, and bathroom accessories
> Install garage door and opener
> Install outside concrete flatwork; sidewalks, driveway, patios
> Perform outside final grading
> Install landscaping

Acceptable modification from the pure Pat Fay Method. Based on the feedback I receive from homeowners in my home construction management classes, I realize that not all homeowners will follow the pure Pat Fay Method and hire 30 different contractors. If you find yourself in that category then there is an acceptable alternative.

The hardest part of the home construction project is getting the project out of the ground with the basic structure built. By this I mean the construction and installation of all of the underground utilities needed, an excavation crew to dig the hole for the foundation, the foundation poured, backfill around the foundation, the house wood framing built, and all the exterior doors and windows installed.

Once the basic structure is built then the rest of the finishing of the project will seem easy by comparison. If you are going to hire one contractor to do multiple parts of your project, let them do the early stages. Once the project is out of the ground then the homeowner can easily manage all the finish work by hiring specialty contractors to do the remainder of the finish work.

Two methods of driving down the project cost. The Pat Fay Method has two methods of using competition to drive down the project cost: by bidding out the projects and through the request for proposal. The standard method of calling contractors one by one is not included here because it does not include competition.

Competition drives down the project cost. Competition between contractors is a very good thing for the homeowner. Competition is the only thing that will reduce the price of a work package. Bidding out work packages is a standard practice in the industrial construction world. It is Pat Fay's goal to teach homeowner's how to use industrial construction project management methods to better manage the home construction process and reap the same benefits as industrial and commercial owners.

Bidding out project work packages (aka bidding out the job). Bidding out a project is a relatively easy thing to do. The process is as follows: define a set scope of work (preferably with a set of drawings or at least a sketch with dimensions), invite interested contractors to do a pre-bid walk through, hand each contractor a copy of the scope of work, a set of drawings, show them the work site, and ask them for their best price.

The pre-bid walk through. The pre-bid walk through is the most important part of the bidding out the job process. There are two reasons for this. First, the contractors see the actual work site and second, the contractors see each other.

Contractors see the actual work site. In the Pat Fay Method it is very important that the contractor visit the actual work site. This is because they then can give a price that reflects the actual site conditions. As discussed in the change order chapter, having the contractor visit the site eliminates any reason for a surprise change order. The contractor has inspected the actual site and can't claim he didn't know the conditions. Therefore there are no legitimate reasons for a surprise change order.

Contractors see each other. Therefore, they compete. The only way competition works in the home construction process is for the bidding contractors to know that they are competing against other contractors. Having a pre-bid walk through where all the contractors gather at the same time accomplishes this. The homeowner sets a date and a time for the pre-bid walk through, invites all the contractors, those that are interested in the work show up, and they all see each other. This is a good thing because now they know they have competition and will have to offer a competitive price if they want the job.

An interesting thing happens at the pre-bid walk through. When the contractors show up for the pre-bid walk through an interesting thing happens. The contractors all know each other! They have either worked together previously, have competed against each other for other projects, or they just know each other. They will greet each other by name, perhaps chat for a few moments but then stand by themselves.

Also, they do not like each other. They consider each other to be the competition and they generally don't have a good opinion of each other. They think the other doesn't do very good work and that they cut corners.

However, once they see each other their natural desire to beat out their competition comes into play. Those that need the work will measure the area carefully so they know exactly how much material will be needed. Then they will add just the exact amount of labor to do the work and then add on their minimum amount of profit acceptable to themselves. Those that really want the work will not inflate the numbers because they know that Bill or Jack is going to try to undercut them on the job and take the work from them.

How to conduct the pre-bid walk through. The key to the pre-bid walk through is to have a written scope of work with a set of construction drawings. Each bidder gets one set of the documents. The homeowner is there to hand out the information and show the contractors the site.

The homeowner is not to go into great verbal detail about the job because this will actually confuse the contractors. It could even result in higher prices. When there is confusion, there is risk, and the only thing that mitigates construction risk is a higher price.

The homeowner does not have to go into a lot of verbal detail because the scope of work and the drawings do most of the talking. The pre-bid walk through is an occasion for the bidding contractors to meet the homeowner, get the scope of work and the construction drawings, visit the construction site, and to get a feel for the job and the homeowner.

A simple example: replace kitchen cabinets. Let us say the scope of work is to install new kitchen cabinets. The homeowner can make a general statement about the project to the contractors. The homeowner could say, "Thank you for coming to our pre-bid walk through. The project is to install new maple wood kitchen cabinets in the same layout as what you can see now. The old cabinets are to be removed and new kitchen cabinets installed. Included in the work is the removal and reinstallation of the existing kitchen appliances as well as the sink. The sink will remain where it is. As you can see our microwave sits on the counter and we want a new microwave to be installed above the stove. Therefore, you will also be responsible for a new electrical circuit for the microwave. The drawings and the written scope of work describe in better detail the work required. You are to bid based on the information contained in the drawings, the written scope of work, the requirements of the building code and the existing site conditions. I will look forward to receiving your bid a week from today. Are there any questions?"

A more complex example: install the concrete foundation: Let us say the scope of work is to install the concrete foundation. For example, the homeowner could say, "Thank you for coming to our pre-bid walk through. The project is to install the foundation for our new house. As you can see the excavation work is complete. I would like to receive your bid to provide all labor and material to install the foundation for our house. I will read the scope of work that I have written. The scope of work is to install all forms, rebar, hold down straps, anchor bolts, 3000 psi concrete, concrete pumper truck, and any other equipment needed to install the foundation as described in detail on the drawings provided to you. We do require that you vibrate the concrete to remove any air pockets. You must build according to the requirements of the building code and have all work inspected by the city building inspector. You will responsible for calling the inspector for inspection of the rebar and forms before you place the concrete. The drawings and the scope of work describe in better detail the work required. You are to bid based on the information contained in the drawings, the written scope of work, and the existing site conditions. I will look forward to receiving your bid a week from today. Are there any questions?"

Other details for the pre-bid walk through. Be sure to specify that you want the contractor to include a list of what is included in their price and a list of what is not included. Then the homeowner will be able to analyze each bid to determine which is the best value.

The homeowner can and should answer questions but the answers should not be an off the cuff remark but a referral to the scope of work which defines the job. This is a reasonable answer because you are not trying to define the scope of work verbally. Referring to the drawings prevents any miscommunication.

Sometimes a legitimate question will be asked that you do not know how to answer. Simply state that you do not know but that you will find out the answer and will fax or email an answer within two days to all the bidders.

Request for proposal (RFP). The request for proposal is a more formal way to solicit bids from contractors. It is typically for projects on the larger side. It is the ideal method to solicit proposals from contractors to get the project out of the ground per the acceptable modification from the pure Pat Fay Method.

I have only used the RFP at the industrial construction level. I did not use the RFP process on our home construction project because we hired different contractors for each construction phase. There is no reason that the homeowner cannot use the RFP technique if they do not want to use the pure Pat Fay Method.

The homeowner can place in the RFP letter specifications as to the types of special materials wanted as well as any other unique requirements. The homeowner will also want to set a date for the pre-proposal walkthrough so the contractors can see the construction site and see each other. The pre-RFP walkthrough is exactly the same as the pre-bid walkthrough. Just because it is an RFP doesn't mean the homeowner wants to eliminate the element of competition.

How to issue the request for proposal. The first thing the homeowner would do would be to phone as many contractors as would be required to get a list of ten that would be interested in doing your project.

The homeowner then writes a request for proposal letter that has a scope of work, a set of drawing included, and requests the contractors' proposals on how they would build the project.

Then put a two week deadline on the proposal request and mail the RFP to each contractor who expressed an interest. Of course, the homeowner will want to screen them per the guidelines in Chapter 11 on contractors.

A sample RFP letter

Re: Request for Proposal to build the Fay house construction project

Dear Sir,

I enjoyed speaking to you on the telephone on [date]. Thank you for your interest in submitting a proposal to build my house construction project through the building framing phase. The following is the specific scope of work.

The scope of work is to provide all labor and material to accomplish the following:
- install all underground utilities to the house. These utilities are water, sanitary sewer, electrical power, natural gas, cable, and telephone. They will be brought just inside the foundation wall in the locations marked on the attached drawings.
- all excavation required to install the above utilities, as well as excavating for the footing and foundation work. Backfill and compaction of all trenching and around the completed foundation is to be included.
- install the concrete footing and foundation walls with all required rebar, hold down bolts and straps.
- install foundation drain piping per the details on the drawings.
- install and construct all framing, walls, floors, roof joists with all exterior wall and roof sheathing in place. All fascia boards are to be included. A complete framing job is required. Framing is to be plumb, level, square, and straight.
- install all exterior doors and windows
- this work is to be built according to the Fay house construction drawings A1, A2, A3, and A4. One copy is included in this RFP.
- all work is to meet the requirements of the building code and to be inspected by the building inspector.

Work not included is:
- no roofing
- no gutters
- no siding or insulation
- no interior distribution of installed utilities except to the point inside the foundation
- no finish work, no cabinets

Please provide your price in two weeks from the date of this letter. Please provide a breakdown showing material and labor costs.

Sincerely,

Pat Fay, homeowner
Address
Telephone number

Chapter 13-Construction Materials

Material quality is important.
    Strength and grade type materials
    Finish materials
Methods of acquiring the materials needed to build your project
    The homeowner buys the materials
        Getting good pricing for materials
    Having the contractor supply the materials
        The contractor discount
        Does the homeowner share in the contractor discount?
    Where to buy the materials
        The advantage of Lowe's and Home Depot warehouses
        Home Depot and Lowe's install the materials they sell
        Disadvantage of Lowe's and Home Depot
        Pat Fay used Home Depot to install a roof
Paying for materials
    When the homeowner buys the material
    When the contractor buys the material
        The two party check
        What if you never received a notice to lien from a supplier?
        Get your material lien release
        Review of notice to lien, liens and lien release
Inspection and counting of delivered material
    Incorrect or damaged material

Chapter 13-Construction Materials

Material quality is important. The quality of the construction materials that are purchased and used to build your home construction project are very important because they ensure the strength and beauty of your home. Most of the materials that have strength requirements are defined in the building code and really are not a concern for the homeowner. However, there is a wide range of price and quality for finish materials.

    Strength and grade type materials. For example, the strength and grade of the materials that make up the foundation and framing are defined in the building code. The typical minimum strength requirement of concrete is 2500 psi. This means the concrete when 28 days old must be able to withstand a force of 2500 pounds per square inch of compression and not fail.

    The grade of the 2x4 studs must be a minimum number 3 standard when supporting a load bearing wall. If the wall is not load bearing the studs can be utility grade lumber. This is pretty meaningless to anyone except engineers, architects, contractors, and inspectors. As I have stated this is not a homeowner concern because we hire experts to do this kind of work.

    Finish materials. The materials that really matter to the homeowner are the finishes because they are what the homeowner will see. If the finish materials are not excellent then every day the homeowner will look at a less than desirable finish and be continually dissatisfied. Therefore, the homeowner must be sure to know what quality of material they want for their finishes. They must also be sure to specify their desires in writing in the scope of work to be sure those materials are used by the contractor who installs the finish work.

Methods of acquiring the materials needed to build your project. There are two ways to acquire the material needed to build or remodel your house. You can buy the material yourself and have the contractors install them; or you can have the contractors supply the material and install them.

    The homeowner buys the materials. There is no rule that says the homeowner cannot buy material themselves and then have a contractor install it. I have done it both ways. The advantages of buying the material yourself are that you may find a material that you want at a good price and to ensure that the material you want installed is on hand and exactly what you want. A disadvantage to ordering materials yourself is that it takes time and effort.

    For example, during my planning phase I found a cedar siding supplier that was going out of business. Since they had the type of cedar siding that I wanted at a discount I bought enough to side our house. Later I hired a carpenter to install it.

    For our foundation I contracted directly with the concrete supply company to deliver the concrete for our foundation. I then hired a foundation contractor to provide all other materials (rebar, forms, anchor bolts) and the labor to install the foundation per the drawings and the code. The bill for the concrete arrived in the mail about a week later from the concrete supply company. I mailed them a check.

    I used my framer's lumber supplier to provide the wood package needed to frame our house. I wrote up our contract so that I paid for all materials directly to the supplier and the framer for labor. Even with this agreement the lumber supply house sent me a notice to lien to protect themselves. A notice to lien is a document sent to the homeowner by a supply company notifying the homeowner that materials are being delivered to your project without having been paid for. The notice to lien protects the supply company in case they are not paid. Please see the end of this chapter for further explanation of liens. This subject is also covered in Chapter 10 on contract documents.

    Getting good pricing for materials. When the homeowner is buying the materials themselves they want to get the best price possible. However, in the Pat Fay Method finding the lowest price is not the goal. We are looking for the highest value at the best price. We are willing to pay top dollar for excellent quality material.

    One way to get good pricing from contractors is to bid a project out to contractors so they must compete against each other. The homeowner has all the contractors come to the construction site for a pre-bid walk-through. This is where the contractors see the condition of the site as well as the competition.

    However, this will not work for material suppliers. In the Pat Fay Method, the homeowner defines the type and quality of material they want clearly on the project log. Then the homeowner begins calling suppliers for pricing, going to their places of business, and generally looking for and speaking to all suppliers that can supply the particular material wanted.

    Talk to many suppliers but the goal is to get a list of 6 to 10 suppliers. This is the minimum (but still manageable) number of companies. Be sure to understand the pricing each can offer so it is clear in your mind. Then call each supplier a final time, review with them the material you want, and the pricing they have quoted. Then it is time to negotiate.

What we negotiate is the quality of the material, the pricing and their ability to deliver the material. At this point the homeowner can say to the suppliers, "I would like to buy my material from you but I really need you to come down on the price. What kind of discount can you offer me?" Then stop speaking and listen to what they have to say. Write down their offer on the project log. Some will offer you a discount and others will not. Now you know their best offer.

This approach will typically not work with the Home Depot or Lowe's. They set their prices and you either take them or leave them.

Having the contractor supply the materials. The contractor will often prefer to supply the materials because they know what needs to be ordered. Also, they have their favorite supply houses with which they do business. There is nothing wrong with having the contractor supply the materials as long as they charge you what the materials cost and do not charge a handling fee.

Some contractors will order the material and then charge the homeowner a markup fee. This fee could be from 5% to 40% or more. There is no reason the homeowner should have to pay this because it is not a legitimate charge. It also can be very expensive on larger orders. However, the contractor should be paid something. That something would be their actual time to order, go pick the material up and deliver it. About 4 hours of their time is appropriate. A reasonable hourly rate would be $25 to $35 per hour for one person.

Unless, of course, you write up a lump sum contract that states the contractor will supply all material and labor to build your remodel at a given price. This kind of contract typically requires the contractor to buy everything, install it all, have the work inspected, and then get paid the agreed upon price. In the Pat Fay Method this is one of the contracting forms to use. Please see the chapter 10 on contract documents for more on this subject.

The contractor discount. Most homeowners do not know that the contractors get a discount from their material supply house that actually is a bonus. It is like a finder's fee. The way it works is the material supply houses reward the contractors who order from them by giving them a percentage of the cost of the materials ordered.

I'm not sure of the exact amount but I have been told by various sources that this finder's fee is about 10%. So if you pay $30,000 for your wood package to frame your house then your framing contractor is receiving a $3000 finder's fee for bringing your work to his wood supply company.

Does the homeowner share in the contractor discount? No. Contractors do not usually tell the homeowners of America this bit of information. With this information, you should be able to negotiate a better price from your contractor if you have them buy the materials.

Where to buy the materials. The yellow pages of your local phone book are full of material suppliers. That is a good first place to look. The advantage of the yellow pages is that the supply companies found there are local companies where you can actually go look at the product and speak to someone who is expert in that material.

The internet can also help you research the purchase of materials. However, I have found that many finish suppliers use their websites to display their materials and if you want to buy them then they list retailers. The phone book is often a faster way to find retailers in your area.

There are also the home construction super stores such as Home Depot and Lowe's.

The advantage of Lowe's and Home Depot warehouses. The Home Depot and Lowe's have really changed the face of home construction for the better. These companies are providing materials at reasonable prices directly to the homeowner.

In the old days, before Lowe's and Home Depot, one had to try to get a friend's contractor number so you could buy at contractor pricing from supply houses. There was this built in price increase for homeowners as second class citizens who were charged a premium for the honor of buying material from contractor supply houses. Contractors were given the discount price so they could add on a material handling fee to their homeowner customers.

When we built our house in 1994 I went through a major plumbing supply house using a friend's contractor number to get the discounted contractor pricing for all our plumbing fixtures. During installation one toilet was broken and we needed to replace it. Instead of going back to the supply house I went to Lowe's and bought the exact same model toilet for less than what we paid at the contractor discount price!

Home Depot and Lowe's install the materials they sell. Also, both Home Depot and Lowe's now have contractors working for them who will install many of the products they sell. I write more about this in the contractor section. However, Lowe's and Home Depot are now a potent force in reducing the price of home construction in America. If independent contractors will not work according to the Pat Fay Method then I recommend using the services of Home Depot and Lowe's whenever possible.

Disadvantage of Lowe's and Home Depot. One disadvantage of these home construction super stores is that they require full payment at the time the contractor order is written up. This is against the rules of the Pat Fay Method but the reality is that we will not be changing the corporate policies of these companies. The advantages of contracting through these companies, however, is that they will do what they promise to do and they will not try to charge the homeowner extra for the work at the end of the job (unless the scope of work actually changes). Also, if the quality is not to your satisfaction you have the recourse of working with Home Depot and Lowe's management to get the work done properly.

Another disadvantage to Lowe's and Home Depot is in some cases they turn over all responsibility to their subcontractor. I believe they should have a project manager assigned to monitor and inspect the work their contractors do to be sure the work is done to the highest quality standards. This project manager would be available to the homeowner by telephone and in person to resolve problems.

Pat Fay used Home Depot to install a roof. A few years ago I needed to have the roof replaced on one of my houses in Kirkland, WA. I gathered the names of 10 companies doing that work and listed them on the project log. I found that Home Depot was listed in the yellow pages so I added them to the list.

Six companies gave me a bid to install a new roof. The other four companies had either gone out of business or did not respond. The scope of work was to remove the old cedar shakes, install a plywood base and the flashing and trim, and then install new 3-tab composition roofing. The low bid was $5400 and the high bid was $8,400.

I had estimated that the cost of tearing off the old roof and installing the new roof should be $6000.

Home Depot's bid was $7,200. This was a little higher than my price but not too much above the median prices of the bids. I selected them to do the work even though they were not the low bidder and to test them so I could put this experience into this book. They did an excellent job!

They started and finished when they said they would. They installed all the plywood, flashing, trim, and roofing properly. Also, they did the best cleanup job I have ever seen. Typically, old roofing and lots of nails are left everywhere. There was no debris left over at all.

I did not use the companies with the lower bids because I could not trust that they would be in business ten years from now. I could trust that the Home Depot would not only be in business ten years from now but that if I had any problems with the roof they would come out and fix it.

Paying for materials. Materials cost money and, therefore, the homeowner must pay for them. Or do they? There are alternatives.

When the homeowner buys the material. When the homeowner buys the material they naturally pay for them at the time they receive them. Buying construction materials is not much different than buying groceries. You either gather them up or order them to be delivered and you pay for them.

When the contractor buys the material. When the contractor buys the material they can either buy on the homeowner's credit or use their own money to buy the material. The homeowner will eventually pay the contractor for the material.

The standard in today's home construction world, however, is that the contractor receives the homeowner's money and then uses it to buy the materials. In the Pat Fay Method we do not want to do this because of the potential for misuse of the money.

If the contractor buys on the homeowner's credit then the material supply company will always send the homeowner a notice to lien before the material is delivered. This is so they have a legal recourse to lien the homeowner's property if they are not paid. See chapter 10 for the subject of liens.

In a perfect world, when the homeowner makes a payment to the contractor the contractor pays the supply company. Unfortunately, this does not always happen. If the contractor is paid by the homeowner but the contractor does not pay the supplier then the homeowner must pay the supply company effectively a second time.

The problem that sometimes occurs is that the contractor orders, receives and installs materials they ordered on your credit. This is a standard in the construction industry because of the large expense of the material. The material supply houses are setup to work with contractors who can have material delivered to your project on your credit if the contractor has a contract with the homeowner. The contract is like a letter of credit.

(I realize that I am repeating myself in this section but it is because this is such an important homeowner issue.) The problem that occurs is when the homeowner pays the contractor and if the contractor does not pay the supplier they are left unpaid. The way the material supply house protects themselves against this situation is to mail a notice to lien to the homeowner. Once it is delivered then the supply house is legally protected so that if they are not paid for the material they can lien the homeowner's property even if the homeowner pays the contractor. This lien is placed on the property title and cannot be removed until the debt is paid. That is why in the Pat Fay Method we use the two party check.

The two party check. The two party check is a standard in the construction industry but unfortunately it is one of those little secrets kept from the homeowner.

The standard for the uninformed homeowner is to pay the contractor for both their labor and material for the work done on the homeowner's project. If the contractor has paid cash for the material then everything is fine because when you pay the contractor you are paying them for both labor and material. However, if the contractor bought your material on credit there can be a problem.

Here is how the two party check works: When it comes time to pay the contractor you want to be sure the material supplier also gets paid. If you know that the material has not been paid for because you have received a notice to lien, then you want to pay both the contractor and the supply company at the same time. This will satisfy the requirements of your contractor's contract because when you use the two party check you are paying the contractor.

Instead of making out a check just to John Doe contractor you make it out to John Doe contractor and the XYZ Material Supply Company. The key word is to write is the word 'and' in-between the two names. Do not put 'or' in-between the two names because then either party can cash the check. The two party check ensures that both parties are paid.

Now remember why you are using the two party check: you use the two party check to be sure the money for material actually gets to the material supply company.

Therefore, just before you hand the two party check to your contractor, call the material supply company representative who is listed on the notice to lien. Tell them you are paying the contractor with a two party check and that the contractor will be down shortly to turn over the two party check. Remind them to mail you their lien release after the check clears. Then hand the check to the contractor.

The contractor cannot cash the check but must instead go to the material supply house to get it cashed. The contractor must endorse the check and then hand it to the supply company representative who will take it, cash it, take the amount they are due for your delivered but unpaid for material and then issue a check for the balance to the contractor.

Now you know how to use a two party check to be sure the material is paid for and that you, the homeowner, do not get penalized with a lien on your property.

What if you never received a notice to lien from a supplier? Simply ask your contractor to show you the receipt for the material that was installed on your project. If it was paid for they will have it. If they do not have a receipt then you need to find out who supplied the material and determine if they have been paid before you pay your contractor.

The reason I mention this is because one of the students in my class went on vacation about the time the notice to lien was sent to her. The contractor continued to work on her project while she was gone. She had arranged for a friend to pick up her mail and put it on the kitchen table. When she returned she went through her mail but never saw a notice to lien. The supply company had proof of mailing so she knew it had been sent. It had somehow disappeared.

Time passed and the contractor finished her remodel, she paid her contractor, and then a few weeks later the notices began to arrive asking for payment for the materials delivered to her project. She called her contractor but he refused to accept or return her calls. In the end, she had had to pay the material supplier herself again even though her contractor was supposed to have paid them.

The point here is that you need to be sure the material is paid for. Another point is to have the post office hold your mail if you go on vacation.

Get your material lien release. I mentioned the lien release from the material supply house in the above scenario. You will also want to get a lien release from the contractor at the time you make the payment to them.

Review of the terms notice to lien, liens and lien releases.

Notice to lien. A notice to lean is just a letter that informs the owner of a property that a supplier has sent material to their jobsite without having been paid. This is a legal requirement that establishes a suppliers right to lien your property so that they can get paid for the material they have delivered.

A lien. A lien is the real McCoy; it is a recorded debt on the property owner's deed to their property. It is recorded at the County or Parish. It is placed there after a legal proceeding that establishes that a material or labor debt has not been paid to the complaining party even if the homeowner paid a contractor for the material or labor.

This situation occurs when a homeowner hires a contractor, the contractor has unpaid for material delivered to the project, the homeowner pays that contractor what was owed for material and labor on their project, and then the contractor does not pay the material supplier.

In this situation, to have the lien removed from the property title the homeowner must pay the material supplier for the cost of the material. In effect the homeowner must pay twice. This is not fair but it is the way home construction is done in America today by many contractors.

Lien Release. The lien release is a form that you have signed by the contractor or material supply house that proves that you have paid your bill. It is a pretty important document because it is releases you from further obligation or threat of lien from the parties that have supplied labor or material for your project. Be sure to keep your lien release in case there is any future dispute about payment. You do not file it with the county but keep it in your project 3-ring binder for future reference in case you are notified of a lien judgment process being filed against you. All processing of liens must go before a judge or a magistrate before a lien can be placed on your property title. You have your day in court or before a magistrate to show that you did pay. This is where your lien release will be worth its weight in gold.

Inspection and counting of delivered material. When material is delivered to your job site someone must inspect and count the material. Most homeowners rely on their contractor to do this. In the Pat Fay Method, it is the homeowner's responsibility to double check that what is on the delivery bill is what is actually delivered.

I learned early in my career as a field engineer in the construction of hundreds of houses in Saudi Arabia that supply companies can be sloppy or even deceitful with their deliveries. Fortunately, I had superintendents who taught me the importance of verifying the contents of every delivery. The average American homeowner is not so lucky. The only way you can be sure you get what you ordered and only pay for what is actually delivered is to double check the delivery bill and delivery.

Incorrect or damaged material. You must also check the material to be sure it is what you ordered and to be sure it is not damaged. This is a constant problem with any delivered material. Has the correct product been delivered? Is the product undamaged? How will you know unless you look at it and inspect it?

It is easy to have the problem noted and corrected at the time the material is delivered but difficult to fix a few weeks later, particularly if a product had been damaged during shipping.

Chapter 14-The Construction Phase: Monitoring and Inspection

What is the construction phase?
Being prepared for the construction phase
A few steps to get started
    Step 1: Build the construction phase 3-ring binder
    Step 2: Take pictures before, during and after
    Step 3: Have an arbitrator lined up
    Step 4: Have insurance coverage updated
    Step 5: Call before digging underground
    Step 6: The homeowner hires their first contractor and turns them loose
A review of construction safety
    What to do if the contractor is not following their safety plan
Managing relationship with the contractor during the construction process
    The homeowner visits the site daily.
    Working and negotiating with the contractor on site
    Have a single point of contact
    This is a business relationship
    Short construction coordination meetings when the homeowner comes on site
        Leaving notes for the contractor
    Maintain communication
        Allow the contractor to vent
        Do not embarrass the contractor in front of their workers
        The homeowner's behavior
        When to call the police
Managing the quality of the work by monitoring and inspecting the work
    Why should the homeowner inspect daily?
    An example of what can happen if the homeowner does not inspect
    Carry the construction 3-ring binder
    Use the daily construction log
    Use of the request for information form (RFI)
    What to do if the contractor will not sign the RFI form?
    When the homeowner does not feel qualified to inspect a phase of construction
Monitoring and inspecting the materials used on site
Managing the inspections by the city building inspector
    Post the building permit on site
    Call for inspection per the city's requirements
    Working with the building inspector
    The building inspector only inspects per the requirements of the code
    Exceptions to the completed work by the inspector
    Contractor's responsibility to fix or repair
    Inspector signs off on a phase of construction
Monitoring and tracking the construction schedule
    Measuring or determining the amount of completed work
Controlling change orders in the construction phase
    The homeowner has a right to make changes
    With this right comes the responsibility to pay

      Use the no verbal changes form (NVC)
      What to do when the contractor suggests a change
      Changes the homeowner wants
      Changes the homeowner does not want
      What to do when the contractor asks for more money for no reason
      Are there changes driven by the building inspector? This is a trick question
Paying the contractor
Project money management
      How to use the cost control form
      Project money management must be kept up daily

Chapter 14-The Construction Phase: Monitoring and Inspection

What is the construction phase? The construction phase is where the homeowner actually hires contractors and lets them get to work. All the time spent on planning, preliminary design, and final design is only done so that the construction work can be accomplished.

The homeowner's role in the construction phase is one of monitoring, inspection, and negotiation. This means the homeowner will spend their time making sure that the work is being done according to the drawings, the correct materials are being used, the quality of the construction is acceptable and negotiating with the contractors hired to complete each stage of the construction process. The homeowner visits the site regularly in order to accomplish each of these tasks. Remember, however, that the homeowner who follows the Pat Fay Method hires only contractors who are experts in their field. This means that the homeowner is not there to babysit the contractor. Turn them loose and let them do what they know how to do.

      Being prepared for the construction phase. To be prepared for the construction phase the homeowner must know what it is they plan to do, have a schedule of construction activities that need to be accomplished and in the correct sequence, a realistic cost estimate, and, last but not least, the courage to follow the Pat Fay Method. The homeowner must have faith in their own abilities to manage the project themselves without a general contractor.

      A few steps to get started. The Pat Fay Method is not a step-by-step cookbook process. This is because the construction process can vary so much depending on the type and size of the home construction project. However, the listing of a few steps common to all projects will help the homeowner to get started in their construction phase.

      Step 1: Build the construction phase 3-ring binder. The homeowner should never start a project without having created a construction phase 3-ring binder for him or herself. The construction 3-ring binder is similar to the design binder but it will actually be more concise. The tabs will be of the actual construction activities, construction forms, contracts, and project money management.

      Step 2: Take pictures before, during and after. The homeowner must get their camera out and take pictures. Start with the project as it is before any work is done. Take pictures during the construction so they can have a record of how the job has progressed and what it looked like during the project. Don't forget to take the final as is pictures so the completed project is recorded.

It is not just nice to have the pictures of how your project looks before the construction is started: it is needed for the management of the project. Pictures give the homeowner a pictorial record of what the original conditions of the construction site looked like before work started. The sad reality is that they may be needed in a dispute.

Keep the pictures in the 3-ring binder with dates and descriptions. If the homeowner has a digital camera then the master pictures can be stored in the computer.

Step 3: Have an arbitrator lined up. The homeowner must hire an arbitration firm before hiring any contractors. Problems are an unfortunate part of home construction. What does the homeowner do when they and their contractor agree to disagree? They call the arbitrator. This is a direct and professional way to resolve a serious problem with your contractor.

Step 4: Have insurance coverage updated. The homeowner must protect themselves from liability and loss by ensuring that they have adequate insurance. Please see chapter 7 on insurance coverage for more details. The homeowner wants to be covered for liability, theft, and damage.

Step 5: Call before digging underground. The Pat Fay Method prescribes to the old adage that an ounce of prevention is worth a pound of cure. Therefore, this rule really applies to any excavation that takes place for the homeowner's project. Many utilities are buried underground where they belong: out of sight. You and your contractor will probably not know exactly where they are. If an underground utility is hit it is very costly to repair and it could be dangerous. In many states it is against the law to dig or excavate before calling to locate the buried utilities. This applies both on and off the homeowner's property.

Therefore, in the Pat Fay Method, the homeowner is enjoined to call two business days before any contractor digs. The number to call can be found by calling the city or county where the homeowner lives. Also, many cell phone companies have designated #DIG as a toll free call to connect the homeowner with the local utility location service.

When the homeowner calls the location service just tell them you are going to excavate and need to have all utilities located and marked at your location. A location service will then come to your construction site, find the underground utilities, and mark them with paint. Then the contractor will know where the utilities are located before they dig. This service is usually free to the homeowner because it paid for by the local utility companies.

Step 6: The homeowner hires their first contractor and turns them loose. All your planning, screening and organizing have been preparation for this moment. Once you have completed that, hire the first contractor. It is then up to the homeowner to continue to manage the project by visiting regularly, communicating with the contractor and staying organized.

A review of construction safety. Since the homeowner will go on site while the project is under construction, the homeowner must take steps to protect their personal safety when on site. Chapter 8 covers safety in detail but the issue is so important it deserves a review.

1. Protect the homeowner's personal safety by wearing safety equipment.

2. Discuss the contractor's safety plan – then hold them to it.

3. Do not allow the project site to become cluttered or messy.

4. Take measures to prevent falls, some of the worst construction accidents.

5. Ensure electrical safety on the site and in the construction process.

What to do if the contractor is not following their safety plan. If the contractor is not following their safety plan then the homeowner must write them a letter describing how safety is being ignored on the project. State in writing that during the negotiation stage the contractor assured the homeowner that all safety rules would be followed. Then send it to their business address by certified mail or with return receipt requested so that the homeowner has proof that they tried to get the contractor to work safely.

Then if an accident happens the homeowner will have proof that they did not ignore safety but the contractor did. Documentation like this may help a homeowner if the contractor's poor safety practices result in serious injury and a lawsuit by an injured worker.

Managing relationship with the contractor during the construction process

The homeowner visits the site daily. The homeowner should be visiting the construction site daily. Get out of the car, walk around the site and talk with the contractor. When our new home project was under construction I would drive by our new house on the way to work. If a contractor was there we would speak together and have a coordination meeting.

On the way home from work I would stop at the construction site before going home. Of course, for me it was pretty easy to do this because I was living only 8 blocks from the new house construction site.

If the homeowner's construction site is a long way from where they live then this presents a coordination issue to the homeowner. However, the site must be visited often. If it is impractical to visit the construction site daily then the homeowner should visit as often as possible (at least twice a week).

Working and negotiating with the contractor on site. The homeowner and contractor will be working together, therefore, the two parties must be able to communicate and coordinate with each other effectively.

Have a single point of contact. Having a single point of contact will make communication easier and will help prevent misunderstandings. If the contractor's crew is large, deal with the foreman of the crew on site. The homeowner should not talk to just any construction worker because they take their orders from the foreman and not the homeowner. If the contractor is a one person shop or a handyman then of course the homeowner will be dealing with that person directly.

This is a business relationship. The homeowner must remember that the relationship with the contractor is a business relationship. The homeowner provides money and the contractor provides expertise. Both parties must use respect.

Keep the conversations to the project. The homeowner must be ready to speak to the contractor about the schedule, the materials, the quality of the workmanship, and many other subjects that come up on the project. The homeowner must remember though that the contractor wants to get the job done. Therefore, the homeowner is not there to talk at length about the weather or the latest news but about the job. Developing rapport with the contractor is important to having a good working relationship. However, the homeowner is not trying to make friends or be a buddy. Coordinate what has to be coordinated, say what has to be said, make your concerns known and then let the contractor get to work.

Likewise, the contractor must allow the homeowner time to discuss the project and coordinate. The contractor is not working in a void: he is working for the homeowner. Ten minutes of coordination is not going to break the bank. It is the right of the homeowner to discuss the schedule, the materials, the quality of the workmanship, and the other issues as they come up (and they will). In fact, it is to the contractor's advantage to coordinate with the homeowner so they have a project that runs smoothly instead of an adversarial relationship.

Short construction coordination meetings when the homeowner comes on site. The way the homeowner and the contractor coordinate is by holding a short 5 to 15 minute coordination meeting when the homeowner comes on site. This is something that must be negotiated before hand, but often the contractor needs to be reminded of once construction is underway.

However, the fact of the matter is that a short, standup, coordination meeting is as necessary for the contractor as it is for the homeowner!

Leaving notes for the contractor. It may happen that the homeowner is unable to meet regularly with the contractor on site due to the homeowner's work schedule. In cases such as this the homeowner can coordinate with the contractor via written notes.

For example, if the contractor leaves the job at 4 PM and the homeowner does not arrive home from work until 6 PM then the homeowner would still visit the jobsite in the evening. If there are coordination items or questions then the homeowner can use the request for information form (RFI) as a note to the contractor.

If the homeowner has a question or concern, they should notify the contractor by filling out the RFI form. Then tape or nail it to the area in question or have a clipboard set up for this purpose.

The next workday the contractor can read the RFI and be aware of the homeowner's concern. The best situation would be for the homeowner to visit the jobsite the next morning and coordinate face to face with the contractor. If that is not possible then a phone call will have to suffice.

Maintain communication. Construction does not always go smoothly. Even so the homeowner and the contractor must maintain open lines of communication. Respect and consideration on the part of the homeowner and the contractor are required during all conversations, especially tense ones.

Allow the contractor to vent. In the Pat Fay Method we allow the contractor to vent. The type of venting allowed is when the contractor just needs a sympathetic ear. Yelling at the homeowner is not allowed. Venting is a component of the rapport between the homeowner and contractor.

This is a necessary thing for the homeowner to allow to happen. Knowing how to react and how to guide the contractor's venting is easily done, but only if the homeowner is aware of the phenomena ahead of time.

Here is a sample situation the homeowner can use as a guide when a contractor vents their frustration. The homeowner walks on site and greets the contractor who answers in a tone that tells the homeowner something is wrong. The homeowner would just say, "is there anything wrong, Bill?" Then the contractor has an opening to vent. It might go something like this. "Yeah, I'm having a few problems today, John and Mike haven't showed up and I need their help in lifting these walls into place. I'm not sure what I'm going to do. And you know, my wife and kids are sick with the flu and I'm not feeling that well myself."

Now the contractor is not looking for the homeowner to try to help resolve these problems. They just need someone to listen to them for a moment. All the homeowner has to do is nod their head, say a few things such as, "I'm sorry to hear that, Bill" or "I hope you and your family feel better." The role of the homeowner is to just be there to listen.

After a few minutes of this the contractor will typically say something like, "Well, I'd better get back to work or let me show you what we did yesterday". Then it is over.

Managing the contractor/homeowner relationship by allowing the contractor to vent briefly will improve the working relationship. Not to allow the contractor a moment to vent now and then could quickly become the reason why the contractor becomes difficult to work with for the remainder of the project. For a moment the contractor is just another human being who needs someone to lend a sympathetic ear.

Do not embarrass the contractor in front of their workers. When there are differences of any kind concerning the construction project the homeowner must be very careful about how they display their frustration.

One thing that absolutely must not be done is to embarrass the contractor or the foreman in front of their workers. If the homeowner does this the only thing the contractor can do is to become adversarial and belligerent.

The homeowner will never win a shouting match with a contractor. The homeowner who does yell at the contractor in front of the contractor's workers will then learn the hard way that the contractor must yell back at the homeowner. If the contractor does not he will soon be without a crew of workers. He will have lost face.

Therefore, in the Pat Fay Method, when the homeowner has some tough words to say, will ask the contractor to go for a cup of coffee or at a minimum a walk to the other side of the street out of hearing distance and sight from the work site. Then the homeowner can say what needs to be said to the contractor (maintaining professionalism, of course). The contractor will not like it but they will react less belligerently than if they are seen to lose face in front of their employees or coworkers.

The homeowner's behavior. The homeowner must be reasonable. Be aware of the problems that contractors face in conducting business. To a point. In the Pat Fay Method we work with the contractor as long as there are working with us.

The homeowner must also not behave in such a manner as to not embarrass themselves in front of the contractor or their workers. The most common way homeowners embarrass themselves is when a couple has a fight about construction issues. The stress of the project and making many decisions can lead to couples having large, personal arguments. However, if this happens the contractors will take every short cut they can think of to get the work done as quickly as possible – and to get away from those people. Quality goes out the window.

When to call the police. The majority of home construction contractors are good people. However, there are some out there that are not. The homeowner never has to put up with theft or physical threat.

The homeowner should call the police if the contractor is stealing construction material, threatens the homeowner or tries to intimidate the homeowner.

Of course, communications with the contractor will be strained after the police are called but the homeowner must never put up with abusive or illegal behavior. If, after calling the police, the contractor does not complete the work in the time allotted the homeowner must use their arbitrator to resolve the issue and/or terminate the contract with the offending contractor.

Managing the quality of the work by monitoring and inspecting the work. The homeowner must monitor and inspect the construction from the beginning to the end of construction. The contractor's understanding and interpretation of the plans may be quite different from the homeowner's desire for how the project should be built.

Monitoring the construction work is a very easy thing to do. It is very similar to managing the relationship with the contractor. The most important thing to do is show up and walk around your construction site. The second thing to do is to take notes on the daily construction log detailing how many workers are there and what construction work they are doing. The mere act of taking notes on the daily construction log changes the homeowner from a tourist into an inspector.

However, in the Pat Fay Method the homeowner does a lot more than just look and take notes. They bring their carpenters level along and they lay it on the floor, the walls, the door and the window frames. The homeowner has a tape measure and uses it to measure the distance between walls and compare the distance measured to what is shown on the drawings. This is your project, your home and your money: you have the right to make sure it is being completed properly.

Why should the homeowner inspect daily? The homeowner should inspect daily because they may discover something is being built incorrectly and if they catch the mistake on the day it is made it will be easy for the contractor to fix the problem. Wait two days and the contractor will have built on top of the mistake and then it will be a difficult and costly problem to fix. For example, for foundation work the homeowner will measure to be sure the width, length, and depth of the forms (before the concrete is poured) matches the foundation drawings. A few minutes with the tape measure can prevent having to break up a poured concrete wall because it is the wrong size.

Another reason for inspecting daily will be that the contractor should be building the project exactly as the plans describe, but the homeowner just did not realize it would look the way it does. This is because many homeowners are not able to visualize the three dimensional project from a set of two dimensional drawings. In this case the homeowner may change their mind and direct the contractor to change the construction (by using the NVC form). If there are no drawings (if the project is very small) then the homeowner should look to be sure that the contractor is following the homeowner's written scope of work with the verbal explanations that always go along with scopes of work in home construction.

The most important reason to inspect is that it will cause the quality of construction to rise. When the homeowner walks around with a level, a square and a tape measure the contractor and their workers take notice. This is a rare thing for any contractor or their construction workers to witness. The fact that the homeowner is inspecting hits a chord with the construction workers. It makes them do a better job because they take pride in their skills and they will respect that the homeowner is showing the same care for the project.

If the homeowner is seen to be checking the work the construction worker is going to increase the quality of their work. This is just human nature. If the contractor knows the homeowner is inspecting, not just looking around casually, then the quality of workmanship will automatically go up.

An example of what can happen if the homeowner does not inspect. When many homeowners walk through their construction sites they are no better than tourists. They just take in the view and do not bother to look at the detail. Without paying attention to detail and checking the contractor's work carefully, you might end up with a situation that happened to a couple that attended one of my classes.

This couple's project was to remove the small windows on one side of their house and install a large picture window. They wanted to improve their view from their dining room table.

They hired a window replacement contractor, signed the contractor's contract, and let the contractor go to work. The contractor did everything that he was supposed to do: removed the old windows, framed out the studs and installed a header for the larger window, installed the window, repaired the interior and exterior walls and painted. They were happy that the project had gone so well so they paid the contractor. The homeowners did no inspections.

A week later they were eating dinner, enjoying the view out the large, newly installed window when the wife asked the husband if the window looked a little crooked. They got a level and checked the window. Indeed it was crooked. After discovering the problem they could not understand how they had not noticed it before.

They called up the contractor and told him about the problem. They asked the contractor to please come out and fix the window by making it level. The contractor told the homeowner that they would have to pay additional money for that. The homeowner's protested that the work should have been done correctly the first time and besides it should be covered under their warranty. The contractor told them, "I'm sorry but I will not come out and fix the window without additional payment because you only paid for average quality not excellent quality."

This story is a pretty good testament why the homeowner who follows the Pat Fay Method inspects daily.

Carry the construction 3-ring binder. To inspect and monitor professionally the homeowner must carry their 3-ring binder with them so they have all the forms needed to log what is inspected. The 3-ring binder also has all of the homeowner's critical design information. If the binder is with the homeowner it is a resource to them. If it is left elsewhere it is of no use.

Use the daily construction log. In the Pat Fay Method the homeowner will fill out a new daily construction log each day. They will keep blank copies in their 3-ring binder. The homeowner will record what they see, what they measure, and all points of activity on the daily construction log form.

Record the date and time of the inspection, the weather, what contractor is working on that day, how many workers are on site, what they are doing and how much progress has been made since the previous day or last time the homeowner inspected. Keep the completed log in the construction 3-ring binder.

Why does the homeowner fill out the report daily? They fill it out daily because it turns the homeowner from a tourist into a project manager and it makes a daily record. If there is a dispute and the arbitrator comes on site the homeowner needs to have written documentation of the problem. All contractors have a little notebook that they keep their notes in which constitutes a log. The homeowner should as well.

Use of the request for information form (RFI). The request for information form is a very, very useful tool to the homeowner. The RFI is a method of communication. There must be open and clear communication on the jobsite. Most of the time just talking to the contractor is sufficient. However, when there is a problem then clear communication means in writing. The homeowner must put into writing anything that needs to be recorded and given as a communication to the contractor. A sample RFI form can be found in the Chapter 19.

To use the RFI form the homeowner just fills it out with the question or issue then dates, signs it themselves, and has the contractor or the contractor's representative sign it also.

The contractor should sign it so that there is acknowledgment that they have seen the RFI and are aware of the homeowner's issue. Otherwise it is just another piece of paper.

Then the homeowner makes a copy of the RFI and gives the copy to the contractor. The homeowner always keeps the original inked copy or make two inked copies.

What to do if the contractor will not sign the RFI form? If the contractor will not sign the RFI form the first thing for the homeowner to do is ask them why. Try to understand their issue or concern and if there is some problem with how the homeowner has written the RFI try to resolve it.

If it turns out the contractor just does not want to acknowledge the problem then there is a problem with this contractor. For example if incorrect material has been delivered there is no legitimate reason for the contractor not to sign the RFI. Could it be that they do not want to acknowledge that the wrong material has been delivered to the job site?

If the contractor refuses to sign the RFI then the homeowner knows they have a problem with this contractor. The best course of action is to call your arbitrator and have them come to the jobsite. Tell the arbitrator about the situation of how the contractor will not sign the RFI and you are afraid the contractor is going to try to install the wrong material on your job (in this example).

Also, the homeowner will now know that they will not use this contractor on any other phases of their project. For that matter, the homeowner would never use that contractor again or recommend them to anyone!

When the homeowner does not feel qualified to inspect a phase of construction. The situation may arise when a homeowner does not understand a particular phase of construction and does not feel they can inspect it. If the phase in question is inspected by the city building inspector then rely on them. If it is not then call your arbitrator and ask them to come out and inspect that phase of the construction work. They are more than qualified to inspect anything in home construction because the best arbitrators are former contractors. The arbitrator will charge the homeowner a fee to do this service, but it can be worth it to have the work properly inspected.

Monitoring and inspecting the materials used on site. In the Pat Fay Method one of the homeowner's responsibilities is to monitor and inspect the materials when they come on site. This is not as difficult as it may sound because not that much material comes on site for any one of the many construction phases (except for perhaps the framing phase). Even so the homeowner wants to inspect the material to be sure it is what they wanted, that the right amount is delivered and that it is undamaged. By inspecting the materials, the homeowner can make sure that only the material they ordered and new, high quality material will be used on their project. They can also make sure they are getting the quantity and quality they paid for.

If the homeowner is not on site when material is delivered then check it as soon as you get to the jobsite. Even if the contractor has checked the material the homeowner must also check it.

Managing the inspections by the city building inspector. The building inspector must inspect many phases of the home construction process. The homeowner will know which phases are to be inspected because they will be listed on the building permit. The building inspector works for the permitting agency where the homeowner purchased and received their building permit.

Post the building permit on site. When the homeowner receives their building permit they will want to post it at their building site. The permit itself is just a piece of paper about the size of a regular sheet of paper (sometimes even smaller). It is easy to post the permit at the homeowner's remodel because one can just tack it to a wall. However, for new construction there is usually nothing but an empty building lot. Therefore, until a structure is built the homeowner will want to keep the permit in their construction 3-ring binder.

Call for inspection per the city's requirements. The city will have instructions, usually written on the permit itself, on how to call for an inspection. Typically the homeowner can call the day before to schedule a permit. Most agencies have voice mail requiring the homeowner to dictate their request. The city will typically ask for the permit number, name of permit holder, address, and time preferred for the inspection. The homeowner must confirm the actual requirements with their local permitting agency.

Many permitting agencies will allow the homeowner to call the morning of the inspection to speak with the inspector to confirm the time of the inspection. This will save the homeowner from having to wait all day long for the inspector. The homeowner will find that the inspection department tries to make the process flow smoothly.

Working with the building inspector. When the building inspector comes on site the homeowner's responsibility is to greet the inspector and show them the building site. Then it is the building inspector's job to do their inspection of the particular phase of construction they are at the site to inspect. The homeowner really only needs to be there to let the inspector into the building site.

The homeowner is not to treat the inspector as if they are a contractor. They can be more relaxed and easier to talk to than one would be with their contractor. The inspector doesn't want more of your money. Besides the arbitrator, the building inspector is the one ally the homeowner has in the construction process. The building inspector only wants to make sure your house is built per the requirements of the building code and that it is safe, sanitary and fit for habitation.

The building inspector only inspects per the requirements of the code. The building inspector will inspect the work completed to be sure it meets the minimum requirements of the building code. They are limited in what they can or will inspect because their authority is based only on what is written in the current building code. They are not there to make sure the construction is being built per the homeowner's specifications and drawings.

Many homeowners mistakenly think they will receive assistance from the building inspector on issues of quality or compliance with the construction drawings if there is a dispute with the contractor. This is not the role of the building inspector. It is not their role to take any side between the homeowner and the contractor. That is the role of the arbitrator.

Exceptions to the completed work by the inspector. If the inspector does find something that does not meet the requirements of the code it is known as an exception. If the inspector finds one they will write the exception on the building permit. I have found that their explanations are quite short and to the point, sometimes even so short as to be cryptic. I believe they should have a reference to the building code section that is not being met but this is often not included.

However, if there is an exception it is the contractor's responsibility to fix the exception at no additional cost to the homeowner in order to satisfy the inspector. This is because in the Pat Fay Method the contractor is required to build according to the minimum requirements of the building code. This should be spelled out in any construction contract.

Contractor's responsibility to fix or repair. If the inspector finds a problem the homeowner will then call the contractor and tell them there is an exception that must be fixed before the inspector will sign off on the building permit. This also means the homeowner will not pay the contractor until he takes care of the exception. Having not paid the contractor is the only leverage the homeowner has to get the contractor to come back and fix the work per the requirements of the building code.

Inspector signs off on a phase of construction. Once the contractor fixes the work then the homeowner will call for a re-inspection of that phase of the construction work.

Hopefully the contractor will have done the repair properly so the inspector will be satisfied and then will sign off that phase of the construction work.

If the inspector is not satisfied that the rework has been done properly they will not sign the permit off until the work is redone up to code.

Monitoring and tracking the construction schedule. The homeowner will want to monitor and track the progress of the contractor so they will know how far along the contractor is on their project. This is because the homeowner will want to know during the project if the contractor is on schedule or not.

Measuring or determining the amount of completed work. The only way to determine how complete the project is to compare the amount of work installed versus the amount of work remaining to be built. Often the comparison is simple. For example, 50% completion of the framing for a two story house to be built on a slab on grade would be when the entire main floor is framed and then about one third of the exterior walls of the second floor are in place. This is because 50% would be a bit more than the main floor framing because there is also the roof framing to do.

If the plumber is responsible for the rough-in plumbing work and it is supposed to be done in six days. The homeowner can count the number of areas to be plumbed. Let us say there are 3 bathrooms, a kitchen and a laundry room for a total of 5 areas. If after 4 days of work the plumber only has the waste and vent run for 3 of the areas and no hot and cold water copper piping then the homeowner knows the contractor is not at 4/6ths or 66% of the work.

If the project is falling behind schedule the homeowner needs to have a private discussion with the contractor to determine what the contractor will do to bring the project back on schedule. Typically, the contractor needs to either spend more hours on the project or bring in more workers.

Controlling change orders in the construction phase. In the Pat Fay Method the homeowner will want to be sure to control the change order process so that changes are not the reason for their project going seriously over budget. A review of this subject is appropriate here but the homeowner must review chapter 10 for a complete discussion of change orders.

The homeowner has a right to make changes. The homeowner has a right to make changes on their project. The fact of the matter is that there is not a construction project on the planet that does not have changes. It is just the nature of construction.

With this right comes the responsibility to pay. With this right to make changes comes the responsibility to pay an appropriate amount for the changes. The homeowner must pay for increases to the scope of work. Likewise, the contractor must give a credit for decreases to the scope of work.

Use the no verbal changes form (NVC). In the Pat Fay Method the homeowner will use the no verbal changes form. This is the only way for the homeowner to control changes to the project. It is a clear and consistent way to communicate changes. The NVC form must be established as the method of handling all changes in the contract. The key is to fill out the NVC form at the time of the change. This process must be followed.

What to do when the contractor suggests a change. When a contractor suggests a change the homeowner must ask questions to determine whether they want the change or not. Contractors sometimes come up with many suggestions that improve the project, so don't dismiss the suggestion immediately. However, the homeowner must ask questions to determine whether a particular change is to their advantage or to the contractor's advantage and what the cost will be.

Changes the homeowner wants. The homeowner wants changes that improve the project. The homeowner must be the judge of what constitutes an improvement but a good definition is one that adds value, convenience or beauty.

Changes the homeowner does not want. The changes the homeowner does not want are those changes that do not improve the project or are simply a convenience to the contractor that will save them money. If the change is just easier for the contractor (saving them time and material) but the homeowner receives no benefit then the best answer is no. Just tell them to build it the way they agreed to when they signed the contract.

What to do when the contractor asks for more money for no reason. I have encountered many contractors who simply state that they need more money. They will not even give a reason. This is a change the homeowner definitely does not want.

The request for more money will usually catch the homeowner off guard. Therefore, the best response to this statement is, "what does the contract have to say about that?" This puts the ball back in the contractor's court and allows the homeowner a moment to gather their thoughts.

All changes must have a reason. If there is no reason for a change there is no reason the contractor needs more money. If the contractor pushes the issue then the homeowner just simply states that they will call their arbitrator to resolve the issue.

Are there changes driven by the building inspector? This is a trick question. This is actually a trick question because the rulebook that governs home construction is the building code. All contractors must build according to the code. The building inspector can only require work to be done according to the minimum requirements of the building code.

If the homeowner uses the Pat Fay Method sample contract or addendum there will be a sentence stating that the contractor must build according to the building code. This means that if the building inspector finds exception to work performed by the contractor then the contractor must fix the work to satisfy the inspector at no additional cost to the homeowner. Even if you don't use the sample contract here, make sure this statement is included in your contract.

Paying the contractor. This subject is covered in detail in chapter 11 on contractors. However, the best way to pay the contractor is after the work is complete, the inspector has inspected the work and signed off that portion of the permit.

In the Pat Fay Method we have the contractor sign a lien release and then hand or mail them a personal check for the contracted amount. Do not pay the contractor with cash. The reason for this is because the homeowner wants a cashed check as proof of payment.

Project money management. In the Pat Fay Method part of the homeowner's duties is to track the money spent on the project. This is one of the easier things to do on the home construction project as long as the expenditures are recorded as the money is disbursed.

To do this the homeowner must use the cost control form and the Pat Fay Method of double entry accounting. This means that for every expenditure the homeowner will write that one expenditure on two separate copies of the cost control form. One entry will be on the particular construction phase cost control form and one entry on the total cost control form.

This way the homeowner will know both the total amount of money spent and how much each phase costs.

How to use the cost control form This cost control form is simple and easy to use. Each activity, contract, or phase of construction will have its own cost control form. Plus there will be another cost control form that records all project expenditures so there is one sheet with the total amount of money spent on the entire project.

For example, when the homeowner is setting up their 3-ring construction book they will have a tab with total construction cost. In it will be a cost control form which the homeowner will have written 'total project cost' in the title. Then when any materials are purchased or a contractor is paid to do work on any portion of the project the homeowner will immediately write in the amount paid on the construction phase cost control sheet. They will also enter the exact line item on the total project cost sheet.

All receipts and copies of contracts will be kept in the folder in the particular tab for each phase of construction.

Project money management must be kept up daily. The reason the recording and tracking of the money spent must be done daily is because once the homeowner gets behind in the tracking and managing of the money the whole project is in jeopardy.

Therefore, in the Pat Fay Method the homeowner must write down and record when and for what reason the money was spent as it is spent. Ignore money management at your own peril.

Chapter 15-Home Construction Pricing & Cost Estimating

Pat Fay's goal in the home construction pricing and estimating chapter
What is home construction pricing?
Three methods of arriving at construction pricing
    Gathering home construction pricing from contactors
        Contact 6 to 10 contractors
            An example in pricing a new 200 amp electrical panel
    Use Home Depot, Lowe's and Costco for comparative pricing
        Contractors must beat Costco, Lowe's and Home Depot pricing by 20%
What is cost estimating?
    Cost estimating for the homeowner
        Budgetary estimating
            Residential SF costs from RS Means Company
        Detailed takeoff from drawings
        What does square foot costs mean?
        Determining square footage
        Square foot cost by activity
        Square foot costs go down for larger jobs, up for smaller jobs
        Cost by lineal foot
The Pat Fay Method of how to think about estimating
    Think in terms of labor, material, equipment, contractor profit
        Estimating labor according to crew size
            What hourly rate to pay for labor
        Estimating material cost for an activity
        Estimating equipment cost for an activity
Adding contingency or risk to the estimate
Overtime will destroy a homeowner's budget
Contractor profit
    What is a reasonable profit for the contractor?
Detailed cost estimating sections

    1. Design, structural engineering, civil engineering, surveying, permit fees, scaffolding, portable toilets

    2. Utility trench by trencher, utility trench by backhoe, excavation for a basement, exterior grading.

    3. Underground Utilities; water, sewer, electrical power, natural gas, telephone

    4. Concrete foundations; spread footings & concrete walls

    5. Framing & insulation.

    6. Drywall/sheetrock; tape & mud, PVA coating, texture

    7. Roofing & flashing, gutters & downspouts.

8. Exterior siding.

9. Finishes; doors & hardware, windows, flooring, kitchen cabinets, counters

10. Appliances

11. Plumbing; underground plumbing, above ground rough-in plumbing, finish plumbing: kitchen sink with garbage disposal, all other sinks, kitchen appliances, toilets, showers, bathtubs, laundry room, hot water tank, and hot water recirculation system.

12. Heating Ventilating and Air Conditioning (HVAC)

13. Electrical and Communications. Detailed costs; electrical panel, dedicated 120V outlet for a microwave or furnace, 6 outlets on one circuit, light switch, light, stove, electric clothes dryer, air conditioning compressor, hot water heater, telephone/data outlet.

14. Concrete flatwork; sidewalks, driveways, patios.

15. Decks

Chapter 15-Home Construction Pricing & Cost Estimating

Pat Fay's goal in the home construction pricing and estimating chapter. My goal for this chapter is to teach the homeowner how to determine what a reasonable price should be for a phase of construction.

The price the homeowner comes up with just needs to be in the ballpark. This means they are reasonably close to what a construction phase or activity should cost. After all the homeowner is not trying to bid and win profitable work rather they are trying to understand what they should pay to a reasonable contractor to have work accomplished.

Once the homeowner knows what a reasonable price is for a construction activity they will then know which contractors are low, high or reasonable in their pricing. Knowing how much an activity should cost is just like knowing what cards everyone else is holding at bridge or poker. This information allows the homeowner to distinguish the contractors who are dealing fairly with them regarding cost from those that are not.

What is home construction pricing? Home construction pricing is just the process of having potential contractors give the homeowner pricing for a phase of construction. In the Pat Fay Method, construction pricing means getting bids (or pricing) from 6 to 10 contractors.

A problem I have discovered about homeowners is that when they are gathering pricing from contractors they will rely on one or two estimates and think they have found a good price for a phase of construction.

The homeowner cannot know whether a price proposal or bid is good if they only get one or two. This is because the two contractors contacted may not need the homeowner's work. The way contractors price construction work depends on whether they have lots of work lined up or whether they need the work.

If the contractor has lots of work lined up they will increase their price for the homeowner's project so that if they get the work it will be really profitable work. If the contractor has a large backlog of work they will not care if they get the new work or not.

On the other hand, if the contractor does not have a lot of work lined up they will give a reasonable price hoping to get the work. This is the way construction pricing is done in the real world of home construction contracting.

The key to knowing if pricing from contractors is good or bad is to have 6 to 10 contractors give a price for the same work. A sampling of this size makes it pretty likely that at least some of the contractors will give you a reasonable price, without inflated profits. Then the homeowner can see where the numbers fall. Some contractors will be high, some low, but many will be in a fairly close price range telling the homeowner what a fair price for the work is.

Three methods of arriving at construction pricing. In the Pat Fay Method there are three methods of determining a reasonable price for a phase of construction:

1. Gathering home construction pricing from contractors

2. Use Home Depot and Lowe's for comparative pricing

3. Cost estimating

Gathering home construction pricing from contractors. The only way to get construction pricing is to ask contractors for it. Therefore, the homeowner who follows the Pat Fay Method must sharpen their pencils and do some construction price planning work. The first step is to gather the names of 6 to 10 contractors that perform the type of work in question. See chapter 11 on contractors for a good discussion on how to find and screen contractors.

Contact 6 to 10 contractors. The process the homeowner will want to follow is to take a blank project log sheet and use it to list the names and phone numbers of 6 to 10 contractors. Try to keep this process to one sheet (a maximum of two). One sheet is ideal so that the homeowner can see all the contractors and their prices at a glance.

The homeowner then begins calling and speaking to each of the contractors. Some contractors will have voice mail but this should not discourage the homeowner because most of these contractors will return the call in the next day or so.

The homeowner makes sure they have a written scope of work to refer to when speaking to each contractor to ensure the same scope of work is conveyed to each contractor. The homeowner needs to describe the job accurately and consistently in order to be able to compare the bids that come back from the contractors.

Typically the contractors will give the homeowner a price in square feet or lump sum over the phone with the final price based on a site visit. Write the price from each contractor on the project log for later evaluation.

An example in pricing a new 200 amp electrical panel. For example, I purchased a rental house in 2006. I decided to have the old style fuse electrical panel replaced with a modern 200 amp panel. My scope of work was to replace the panel, install two ground rods, install ground straps to the house piping, and pay for the electrical permit.

My estimate for the materials (a new panel, breakers, and wire) was $400. I estimated labor costs based on two men installing everything in one day. 2 men x 8 hours per day is 16 hours. 16 hours x $40 per hour is $640. Also, it included a permit cost of $160. Therefore, my estimate of the total cost was $1,200 ($400 + $640 + $160) without profit or sales tax. Remember, sales tax is never included in a contractor's price bid. The homeowner always pays sales tax as an additional cost.

I contacted 8 electrical contractors. One company did not respond, one had gone out of business, and six responded. The pricing received was as follows: $1,380, $1,485, $2,000, $2,307, $3,159 and $4,108.

These numbers tell a story. The companies with the two lowest figures ($1,380 and $1,485) were realistic about what the work would cost and they wanted the work. They only added a couple of hundred dollars in profit. The two companies with pricing in the mid-range ($2,000 and $2,307) were also realistic about the cost but they added $800 and $1,100 in profit. This was because they had plenty of other work and did not care whether they got this work or not.

The companies with the two highest prices ($3,159 and $4,108) price were just too high. These companies not only had plenty of work they were also hoping that I was just another uninformed homeowner who didn't know any better. These last two contractors are the type of contractor the homeowner wants to avoid no matter how highly recommended they are.

This example shows the range of construction pricing the homeowner will receive when they follow the Pat Fay Method and get 6 to 10 prices from different contractors. Incidentally, I selected the contractor with the $1,485 price because they could do the work in 2 weeks.

Use Home Depot, Lowe's and Costco for comparative pricing. Another tool available to the homeowner is the fact that Lowe's and Home Depot super stores also install many of the products they sell. Costco is just starting to get into the home installation business with products such as carpet, closets, window coverings, garage doors, and counter tops.

Contact their installation service to find out how much an activity will cost and use it as a benchmark to grade independent contractors. I have found the prices at these super stores to be a little bit high but it is in the right ballpark. As mentioned in Chapter 11 on Contractors, there are other benefits to using Home Depot, Lowe's and Costco instead of an independent contractor.

Contractors must beat Costco, Lowe's and Home Depot pricing by 20%. When the homeowner uses the Home Depot, Lowe's and Costco for pricing then the independent contractors must beat their price by at least 20%. This is because 20% will cover all the added expense that a large corporation has to carry just to operate a large company. Smaller independent contractors do not have this added overhead.

If the independent contractors cannot beat the superstores by at least 20% then the homeowner should just use Lowe's, Costco or Home Depot to do the phase of construction under consideration!

What is cost estimating? In the Pat Fay Method, cost estimating is the process of establishing a reasonable cost for a construction activity. All home construction activities are made up of four things:

1. Labor hours to perform the work
2. A certain quantity of construction materials
3. Equipment costs, if any, to assist the workers in their construction activities
4. Contractor profit

Cost estimating is not too difficult for the homeowner if their goal is to determine what a reasonable and fair cost is for a particular phase of construction. This is because the homeowner need only be in the ballpark of what a construction activity should cost to be able to make sure they are paying a fair price for quality work.

Cost estimating for the homeowner

Budgetary estimating. Budgetary estimating is used in the early planning stages of a project to get a feel for how much a project could cost. The square footage of a project is multiplied by the approximate cost in dollars per square foot to determine a budgetary project cost.

For the homeowner who follows the Pat Fay Method the budgetary dollar number to use is $100 per square foot for all your projects; a custom 3,000 SF house or a 700 SF new addition. Kitchens remodels are the exception to this rule because of the high cost of cabinets and the relatively small square footage footprint common to kitchens. For the homeowner who is going to hire a general contractor then the budgetary number to use is $200 per square foot. This is because $200 per SF is what the project will cost the homeowner by the time the general contractor is through with the homeowner.

Residential SF costs from RS Means Company. Any data titled from RS Means comes *"from Means Square Foot Cost Data, 2005. Copyright Reed Construction Data, Kingston, MA 781-585-7880; All rights reserved."* Their website is www.rsmeans.com.

First, however, a review (and a repeat from the introduction section) of what general contractors are charging for home construction in the Seattle area is useful. I believe these costs are indicative of what is being charged in most of the major cities in America today: too much!

A custom, two story, 3200 SF house with wood siding built by a general contractor in Seattle will be a minimum of $150 to $200 per SF (not including land prices). The homeowner may get quotes for less than this but by the time the house is completed the cost will be in the $150 to $200 per SF range due to change orders and increases to the scope of work that the general contractor says was not included in their original price.

Means Estimating states that this custom, two story, 3200 SF house with wood siding should cost $79.15 per SF in 2005. What is more startling about this number is that it also includes the general contractor's overhead and profit.

A luxury house built by a general contractor in Seattle will be a minimum of $250 to $300 per SF (not including land prices). Once again the homeowner may get quotes for less than this but by the time the house is complete the cost will be in the $250 to $300 per SF range due to change orders and increases to the scope of work that the general contractor says was not included in their original price.

Means Estimating states that this luxury, two story, 3200 SF house, with wood siding should cost $91.05 per SF in 2005. Once again this number includes the general contractor's overhead and profit.

Where does the extra money go? It goes into the general contractor's pocket as pure profit. Who pays for all that profit? The homeowner does.

The following charts show what Means has determined a house should cost versus what general contractors are charging for building houses. I added the far right column to show how much extra profit the general contractors of America are receiving per house. These charts show how much a house should cost based on RS Means cost estimating data compared to what general contractors charge.

Custom House			Low Cost Range-$150/SF		
Square Footage (SF)	RS Means Cost per SF	Final Cost by RS Means	Contractor Cost per SF	Final Cost from the Contractor	Difference (Pure Profit)
2400 SF	$88.30/ SF	$211,920	$150/ SF	$360,000	$148,080
3200 SF	$79.15/ SF	$253,280	$150/ SF	$480,000	$226,720
4400 SF	$72.80/ SF	$320,320	$150/ SF	$660,000	$339,680

Luxury House			Low Cost Range-$250/SF		
Square Footage (SF)	RS Means Cost per SF	Final Cost by RS Means	Contractor Cost per SF	Final Cost from the Contractor	Difference (Pure Profit)
2400 SF	$101.80/ SF	$244,320	$250/ SF	$600,000	$355,680
3200 SF	$91.05/ SF	$291,360	$250/ SF	$800,000	$508,640
4400 SF	$83.55/ SF	$367,620	$250/ SF	$1,100,000	$732,380

Custom House			High Cost Range-$200/SF		
Square Footage (SF)	RS Means Cost per SF	Final Cost by RS Means	Contractor Cost per SF	Final Cost from the Contractor	Difference (Pure Profit)
2400 SF	$88.30/ SF	$211,920	$200/ SF	$480,000	$268,080
3200 SF	$79.15/ SF	$253,280	$200/ SF	$640,000	$386,720
4400 SF	$72.80/ SF	$320,320	$200/ SF	$880,000	$559,680

Luxury House			High Cost Range-$300/SF		
Square Footage (SF)	RS Means Cost per SF	Final Cost by RS Means	Contractor Cost per SF	Final Cost from the Contractor	Difference (Pure Profit)
2400 SF	$101.80/ SF	$244,320	$300/ SF	$720,000	$475,680
3200 SF	$91.05/ SF	$291,360	$300/ SF	$960,000	$668,640
4400 SF	$83.55/ SF	$367,620	$300/ SF	$1,320,000	$952,380

Note: The difference between the custom and luxury houses is in the quality of the materials and workmanship. The custom house will have materials and workmanship above average. The luxury house will have extraordinary materials and workmanship as well as many special features.

As you can see the dollar incentive to manage your own project without a general contractor is high. The homeowner can save serious money by managing their home construction project without a general contractor.

Detailed takeoff from drawings. When construction drawings are complete then a detailed takeoff estimate can be done. The detailed estimate will count or measure everything that goes into building the house. This includes all the material and labor required to build the project.

This is expensive to have done if the homeowner hires someone to do this. The homeowner can do this themselves by using the techniques described in this chapter and using the detailed estimate examples at the end of the chapter.

What does square foot costs mean? Square foot cost is the way construction people communicate a price to homeowners. Therefore, homeowners need to understand the term.

A square foot cost can be determined for any construction project. One just need take the cost of the project and divide it by the square footage of the building (or space, if your project is a remodel) and one has the square foot cost. Therefore if a contractor says a project will cost $90,000 and it is a 450 SF addition then the project costs $200/SF ($90,000/450 SF). Square foot costs is just an easy means of establishing a standard method of speaking about construction costs.

Determining square footage. To determine the square footage of a one story building the homeowner just multiplies the width times the length of the building. If it were a two story building then the total square footage would be both floors added together. Just remember your junior high math that the area of a rectangle is the width times the length. It is the same principle.

For example, if the addition is 25 feet wide and 30 feet long then 20 feet times 30 feet is 600 square feet.

Square foot cost by activity. Each construction phase can be broken down into a square foot cost. In fact the homeowner will see the different sections of the detailed cost estimate at the end of this chapter broken down into a square foot cost.

To do this the homeowner just needs to determine the cost of a phase of construction and divide it by the total square footage of the house or project to determine the square foot cost for that activity.

Square foot costs go down for larger jobs and up for smaller jobs. For example, if a homeowner is building an 8,000 SF house then the square footage cost will go down compared to a 3,000 SF house. A reasonable price for an 8,000 SF house is in the $70 to $90/SF range or $560,000 to $720,000 respectively.

The reason the cost goes down is because the amount of labor and material required to build a larger house goes down per unit square foot. In other words, when a larger house is built there are economies of scale realized.

I have an associate who paid $350/SF for an 8,000 SF house. He paid way too much. It is not his fault though because he didn't know any better and he took the contractor's word that $350/SF was what it should cost. The homeowner should not be surprised if the pricing is high if the price comes from a general contractor. The contractor is there to do make a profit. It is up to the homeowner to make sure that profit is reasonable, not a fleecing.

Cost by lineal foot. Sometimes the homeowner will hear costs spoken in term of lineal foot. As a matter of fact, most kitchen cabinets and counter tops are quoted in the cost per lineal foot. You will see a number of costs at the end of the chapter listed as per lineal foot.

The Pat Fay Method of how to think about estimating. In the Pat Fay Method estimating is based around the question 'what is a reasonable and fair price to pay for a construction activity?'

Think in terms of labor, material, equipment, and contractor profit. As I stated earlier, estimating what a project should cost is made up of labor, construction material, the cost of equipment, and a reasonable contractor profit.

Estimating labor according to crew size. The main question that the homeowner needs to answer is how many hours of labor are reasonable for a phase of construction. The way to mentally think about this is to ask yourself how many hours of labor are required to do an activity. The next step in the thought process is to then think in terms of crew size.

The way to think about crew size is to first start with a crew of one or two men. Ask yourself, for example, would two men be able to do the work in one day (or 16 man-hours of labor)? Would two men be able to do the work in two days (or 32 man-hours of labor)? Perhaps it is a bigger job and would require a larger crew of say 5 men: a foreman and 4 workers. Would five men be able to accomplish the work in 2 days (or 80 man-hours)?

Would it take a week for the 5 men (or 200 hours)? This is the thought process that field engineers are taught when they first start working in construction. It will also help a homeowner come to a reasonable number of labor hours to do any kind of work.

What hourly rate to pay for labor? In the Pat Fay Method we want the contractors working for the homeowner to make a good but reasonable hourly wage.

Union construction wages are a good benchmark for understanding what the maximum hourly rate is for construction workers. In 2006 union wages per hour (without benefits) are approximately:

-carpenter: $35
-cement finisher: $34
-electrician: $40
-equipment operators: $35
-painters: $32
-plumbers: $40
-tile layers: $35
-laborer: $20

These wages are what experienced construction workers are making working for large union construction companies. This is not what the home construction worker is making. The home construction worker is making an average of about $10 to $15 per hour. If they are really lucky they will be making $20 per hour. The typical home construction worker will not be receiving any insurance benefits, vacation or sick time. They only get paid if they work.

The home construction general contractors and well established subcontractors will tell the homeowner that the hourly rate they must charge is anywhere from $40 to $90 per hour. That is what they will charge the homeowner but they will still only pay their employees $15 per hour.

Then what rate should the homeowner pay independent contractors for construction work? A reasonable rate is from a low of $20 to a high of $40 per hour. To put this in perspective consider that there are 2,080 hours in a working year. Multiplying this out means that a worker making $20 per hour (times 2,080 hours) is making an equivalent of $41,600. At $40 per hour they are making an equivalent of $83,200. These are respectable incomes.

Estimating material cost for an activity. Determining the material cost for a project requires some thought and planning. This is because the only way to determine how much material to use is to count or measure it.

This is easily done if the subject is windows or doors because then the homeowner just counts how many of each there are. It is also fairly easy to determine how many feet of flooring is needed because the room where it is to be place can be measured.

The hardest material costs to measure are the parts the homeowner will not see directly, such as how much lumber goes into framing a whole house or how much pipe is needed for plumbing systems.

However, in many cases the homeowner can either count or measure how much material is needed. Then the homeowner just needs to call material suppliers to find out how much material costs or go to Home Depot and Lowe's to get pricing.

Estimating equipment cost for an activity. Many projects will not need any special equipment that needs to be listed as a separate line item. The small tools and small equipment that a contractor needs to do a job are not listed separately. For example, if you are having hard wood floors installed then the floor sander would not be listed as a separate cost because it is a piece of equipment that is relatively small and that the contractor should already have. The kind of equipment that I mean are large pieces of equipment that the home construction contractor cannot afford to own but rents. These are things such as a backhoe, dump truck, a front end loader, or a concrete pumping truck.

To get a cost for renting this type of equipment look in the yellow pages under equipment and call companies that rent this kind of equipment and get the daily and weekly rates.

Adding contingency or risk to the estimate. The contingency allowance added for a project is one of the most misunderstood principals in all of construction. It would be better if the word 'contingency' were thrown out of construction vocabulary and replaced with 'risk allowance'.

The term contingency is misunderstood because people in and out of construction believe that contingency is there to cover the cost of new scopes of work. It is not! Contingency is to be used for those activities that were unanticipated in building the existing scope of work.

The reason contingency (risk) is added to a budget is to anticipate the unknown. The homeowner will want to add a risk allowance when some phase of construction is not well defined or represents some kind of risk. For example, if a house is built on a slope it would be wise to add a risk allowance for anything that might go wrong when placing the foundation on the slope. This is because more things could go wrong in placing the foundation on a slope than on level ground.

The homeowner who follows the Pat Fay Method will want to have between 10 to 30% in reserve as a contingency or risk allowance for those phases of construction that are not well defined or present a risk on the homeowner's project.

Overtime will destroy a homeowner's budget. The homeowner who follows the Pat Fay Method will not want to pay the contractor overtime. Overtime is usually time and a half or double the hourly rate. Pat Fay knows of no better way to destroy the homeowner's budget than to pay a contractor overtime.

The situation may occur where a contractor will suggest to the homeowner that if they paid for overtime the contractor could be finished sooner than planned. The homeowner must think long and hard about this subject because it is very expensive.

Hopefully this will not be an issue because the homeowner who follows the Pat Fay Method will be using the fixed price contract. Overtime is not a part of this contract. If the contractor falls behind schedule they must pay overtime out of their own money to complete the project on time.

Contractor profit. In the Pat Fay Method we want the contractors that work for the homeowner to make a reasonable profit. However, the homeowner does not want to be part of a scenario where the contractor makes too much profit at the homeowner's expense. The transaction has to be fair both to the homeowner and the contractor.

What is a reasonable profit for the contractor? In the Pat Fay Method, 25% is a reasonable profit for the homeowner to pay the contractor. This is typically broken down into 10% overhead and 15% profit for a total of 25%.

Contractors, on the other had will state that 25% is not enough. However, the homeowner must remember though that the contractor is also making an hourly wage that will no doubt be in the $25 to $45 per hour range for fixed price work. The 25% added on for profit is on top of the hourly wages.

On a fixed price contract, however, the contractor will not list their profit margin. It is just built into the fixed price given to the homeowner. It could be 25% or it could be 200%. A good estimate allows the homeowner to look at a contractor's price proposal and determine what the contractor is adding for profit. Then the homeowner can decide whether the contractor is building in a reasonable or an inflated profit margin.

Detailed Cost Estimating Sections

The costs found here are cost estimating sections needed to determine a reasonable cost for most home construction activities in 2006. As the Pat Fay Method teaches once the homeowner has a reasonable price for a construction activity then the homeowner can look at any contractor's bid and know how much extra profit is being added. Then the homeowner can make their contractor selection based on knowledge not just on feelings.

I show a dollar cost and a unit cost per an appropriate unit such as square foot or lineal foot. The homeowner can use these estimating sections along with the estimating methods presented earlier in this chapter to determine what a reasonable price should be for a construction activity. Do this for each step of your construction project, add them up and the homeowner then knows what their construction project cost should actually cost.

Often you will see a summary at the end of section that displays the following pricing information:

$20,971 or $6.99/SF for installing clear cedar siding on a 3000 SF house.

This means I determined that for my 3000 SF house the unit cost to install cedar siding was $6.99/SF. The homeowner would use $6.99/SF in budgeting their project even when their house has a different floor area. The 3000 SF is my house which is the basis for this calculation. I need to use some SF to determine a dollar per unit SF number. If your house is a different square footage you can still use the $6.99/SF to budget your project.

Some of these estimating sections get a little long and technical. The explanations of how I arrive at the cost basis number may be of interest to some homeowners and not to others. However, these sections can be scanned and the real information is in the summary costs with a unit cost basis in square feet, lineal foot or whatever unit is appropriate at the end of each section.

My estimates all have a lot of detail and therefore the prices are all on the high side. I use retail rates for materials often found by going into local Home Depot and Lowe's super stores to see what they are charging for materials. Contractors will often be paying 20 to 40% less at wholesale rates from their suppliers.

The reason I have as much detail in my estimates as I do is so that my estimates will be high. I don't want to low ball the pricing. By being high then when the homeowner compares the prices found herein with the prices given by a contractor and the contractor is higher than my numbers then you will know they are really adding a lot of extra profit. By the way the slang term for a high estimate or a high bid is that it is 'fat'.

Also, by using the techniques in chapter 12 on managing competition it is very possible to competitively bid many of the construction phases to get a lower price than what I show in the following sections. However, the homeowner must be careful to be sure they are not paying an unreasonably low price because without profit a contractor cannot stay in business.

The hourly labor rates I use for contractors are those listed earlier in this chapter.

The homeowner will not find sketches associated with these estimating sections rather I paint a word picture with descriptions of activities and their costs. I believe what I have produced gives the homeowner a reasonable cost basis for construction activities.

If the homeowner would like estimates with sketches then I recommend the homeowner go to the RS Means website (rsmeans.com) and buy their excellent home construction cost estimating manuals.

Please note that all costs are without sales tax. Sales tax is not a construction cost. The homeowner will find this to be true in the pricing they receive from contractors.

1. Design, structural engineering, civil engineering, surveying, permit fees, scaffolding, portable toilets

2. Utility trench by trencher, utility trench by backhoe, excavation for a basement, exterior grading.

3. Underground Utilities; water, sewer, electrical power, natural gas, telephone

4. Concrete foundations; spread footings & concrete walls

5. Framing & insulation.

6. Drywall/sheetrock; tape & mud, PVA coating, texture

7. Roofing & flashing, gutters & downspouts.

8. Exterior siding.

9. Finishes; doors & hardware, windows, flooring, kitchen cabinets, counters

10. Appliances

11. Plumbing; underground plumbing, above ground rough-in plumbing, finish plumbing: kitchen sink with garbage disposal, all other sinks, kitchen appliances, toilets, showers, bathtubs, laundry room, hot water tank, and hot water recirculation system.

12. Heating Ventilating and Air Conditioning (HVAC)

13. Electrical and Communications. Detailed costs; electrical panel, dedicated 120V outlet for a microwave or furnace, 6 outlets on one circuit, light switch, light, stove, electric clothes dryer, air conditioning compressor, hot water heater, telephone/data outlet.

14. Concrete flatwork; sidewalks, driveways, patios.

15. Decks

1. Design, structural engineering, civil engineering, surveying, permit fees, scaffolding, portable toilets

1. Design. Design is the cost of having the homeowner's construction plans drawn up by an architect or building designer. The price will vary based on the size of the project. However, I can establish reasonable costs for this work. The following costs are based on the homeowner having completed their planning and preliminary design according to the Pat Fay Method so the architect or building designer can get right to work with design instead of having to drag requirements out of the unprepared homeowner.

$5,000 or $1.67/SF for a new 3000 SF house. This consists of 40 hours at $100/hour or $4,000 for producing the construction documents including all meetings between the homeowner and the architect/designer. Two site visits of 4 hours each at $100/hour for another $800. Phone calls to coordinate with the city to discuss design issues for $200.

$3,000 or $2/SF for up to a 1500 SF second floor or new room addition to an existing house. The SF cost is higher for a smaller project compared to a larger project.

1. Structural engineering. Structural engineering consists of the time a structural engineer needs to take to review the architect/designers drawings to calculate loads, stresses and shear forces. Once these forces are determined the sizes of columns, posts, and beams can be defined. A set of structural calculations will also be produced that will need to be submitted with the construction drawings given to the city for permitting.

$2,000 or $1.50/SF for a 3000 SF house. $1,000 or $0.67 to $2/SF for a 500 to 1500 SF second floor or new room addition to an existing house.

1. Civil engineering. Civil engineering for a house would be for a septic system or a drain field. Septic systems are used where there is no municipal sanitary sewer system available. Drain field systems are used when there is no storm drain system in the street and the city requires the homeowner to drain all house gutter downspouts to a drain field. The septic field and the drain field are basically the same thing. They take water from the house to a vault or manhole that collects it in one place and then allows the water to flow into a below grade drain field away from the house.

$4,000 or $1.33/SF for a 3000 SF house.

1. Surveying. The services of a surveyor would be used to establish property corners and boundaries. Most lots in America today have already been surveyed and are recorded at the county or parish. The issue is typically that the stakes defining the property corners have been lost or removed. I paid $1200 to re-establish our 4 property corners in 1992. In 2006 the cost will naturally be higher.

$1,800 or $0.60/SF for a survey to establish 4 property corners on a lot to build a 3,000 SF house.

1. Permits fees. Permit fees cover the cost for permitting and inspection fees. The city must pay the plan reviewers and inspectors. These fees are also a source of revenue profit for the city. Permit fees are the fees the city requires to be paid for the right to build on your property. This cost varies quite a bit even in the greater Seattle area depending upon which city or county your project is located. Some cities base the permit cost on a percentage of the cost of the building and some have a fixed fee based on square footage. However, a reasonable cost for the homeowner to budget for permit and inspection fees is $3,000 to $6,000. Of course, a simple phone call to your city will answer this question.

$3,000 to $6,000 or a maximum of $2/SF for a permit for a 3,000 SF house.

1. Scaffolding. Scaffolding is used to allow the carpenters to install the outside sheathing and siding on the exterior of the house. This cost is typically born by the contractor but it is here so when I do the cost for sheathing and siding I know what the cost of equipment is to accomplish that work.

Scaffolding comes in frames. The homeowner will have or will now see scaffolding set up on a construction site and then this will make sense. A scaffold frame is typically 6' tall x 10' long x 4' wide. The widest part of my house is 40' and the height is 25'. This means 4 frames would make up the base and 8 more frames for two more levels to get up high enough for the workers to reach the peak. This is a total of 12 frames.

A frame costs $8/month to rent. Each frame requires two crossbars at $2/month each or $4/month. The base frames require two jacks which cost an additional $8/month. Once the frames are set up the carpenters need something to stand on which I call decks. They typically are aluminum and are about 19" wide with hooks on either end so they can rest on a frame. They cost $32/month per frame. However, to save money only enough decks are rented to go over one level of the frame. This is because as a level of work is completed the decks are moved to the next level where they are needed.

The cost summary per month for scaffolding would be the cost of the base jacks at $8/frame x 4 frames is $32, frames with crossbars at $12 each x 12 frames is $144. Four decks x $32/deck is $128. The total cost for scaffolding would be $32 + $144 + $128 = $304 per month. There is also a delivery and pickup charge that is typically charged by the hour. I was quoted $50/hour recently for this service. Guesstimate 2 hours to drop off and 2 hours to pickup for a total of 4 hours x $50/hour or $200. Therefore the total cost for scaffolding for one month would be $304 + $200 = $504 for one month.

A little thought into planning construction tells the homeowner that there will be two separate times when scaffolding will be needed; once for sheathing and once for siding. (Windows may require scaffolding but ladders work just fine.) Each of these activities does not take one month but for budgeting purposes I will assume the one month cost for renting scaffolding for each activity. Therefore, the scaffolding cost is 2 months x $504/month = $1,080.

$1,080 or $0.36/SF for scaffolding rental for a 3000 SF house.

1. Portable toilets. The homeowner will want to rent a portable toilet for the workers to use. The cost of a portable toilet is for the rental of the toilet per month with a certain frequency of cleaning. A typical monthly rental rate with a weekly cleaning is $100/month. There is also a pickup and delivery charge of about $50. I will assume that the portable toilet would be needed for 12 months. Cost is 12 months x $100/month = $1,200. Add the $50 pickup and delivery charge and the total is $1,250.

$1,250 or $0.42/SF for a one year rental of a portable toilet for a 3000 SF house.

2. Utility trench by trencher, utility trench by backhoe, excavation for a basement, exterior grading.

Note: all underground work requires the homeowner or contractor to call the 'call before you dig' phone number 48 hours before digging underground. This applies to digging on or off your property! Contact your city for this number. Save yourself a lot of grief by calling first. Do not dig without calling! They will come out and mark the locations of the major underground utilities.

2. Utility trench by trencher.

Trenching is where a narrow excavation is made into the ground so that utilities can be placed into the trench. I will assume the trench is to be 6" wide x 2' deep x 100' long for this estimate. Trenchers are limited in how wide a trench they dig but it is ideal for wire and small pipe.

This scope of work will assume the trench runs down your side of the street to a utility source 100 feet away. Also assume that there is no asphalt or concrete to contend with just gravel and dirt. The location of the underground utilities will be marked since the homeowner will have called the 'call before you dig number'. Be safe though and double check with the city utility department because often side sewers are not marked by the utility location service.

A trencher can be rented for $100/day. One man working with a trencher should almost be able to excavate 100' in a day with a trencher. However, let us assume it takes two days. That is 2 days x $100/day or $200 for the trencher rental.

One laborer at $20 per hour x 2 days or 16 hours is $320. In those 2 days one man can operate the trencher to dig the trench, lay the wire, use a shovel to backfill the trench, stamp on the dirt to compact it every so often, and cleanup. Add an allowance of $300 for miscellaneous materials and barricading. Total cost is $200 + $320 + $300 or $820.

$820 or $8.20 per foot for a 6" wide x 2' deep x 100 foot long trench dug with a trencher.

2. Utility trench by backhoe.
If the trench has to be dug by equipment then the backhoe is the machine to do it. The front end has a bucket that can be used for earth moving and grading. The backhoe has an arm on the other end that allows for digging and excavating with a bucket attached. There are other attachments such as a hydraulic ram for demolition and even a plate compactor for compacting. It is a very versatile piece of equipment.

It is also relatively inexpensive to rent. If the homeowner were to open up the yellow pages and look under equipment rentals they would find many companies willing to rent a Case 580 backhoe, 2 wheel drive for $200 per day and a 4 wheel drive for $240 per day. Add a delivery and pickup charge of about $70, fuel and oil consumption costs of about $150 per day, and the homeowner now knows the equipment cost for one day for a backhoe is $200 (backhoe)+ $70 (delivery) + $150 (fuel & oil) = $420. Equipment operators earn $35/hour so for an 8 hour day the labor cost would be $280. Therefore, the total cost to rent and operate a backhoe is $420 + $280 = $700 for one day.

The scope of work is to dig a 2' wide x 3' deep x 100 foot long trench. Assume the trench runs down your side of the street to a utility source 100 feet away. Assume that there is no asphalt or concrete to contend with just gravel and dirt.

Backhoes come with a number of different width buckets and since the trench is to be 2' wide I would rent a backhoe with a 2' wide bucket. The equipment rental company will have a number of different width buckets laying about the yard and they can easily be interchanged.

How long must the backhoe be on the job? In reality 100' is not a very long trench. I have been on backhoes when I was a field engineer in Saudi Arabia and I had no formal training on operating a backhoe other than a coworker showing me the basics. I could operate the backhoe and dig a 2' wide by 3' deep x 20' long trench in about 30 minutes. A trained equipment operator would take much less time. However, I will assume the backhoe must be on the job for one week so I have a high equipment rental cost.

The rental rate for a backhoe for a week is typically only 4 times the daily rate, therefore, the weekly rate is 4 x $200/day or $800 week. The delivery and pickup charge remains about $70 but I increase the fuel and oil consumption costs to $300 for the week. The equipment operator labor cost would be $280/day x 5 days = $1,400. Therefore the total cost for a backhoe with operator for one week is $800 + $70 + $300 + $1,400 = $2,570.

Once the trench is dug the public must be prevented from falling into the trench while it is open. A contractor doing trenching work will have barricades and they will charge the homeowner some fee for the use of the barricades. $300 for one week is a reasonable charge. High but reasonable. If the homeowner is managing this activity themselves then they can rent barricades from a construction rental company just as a contractor would. However, the homeowner should remember that they are trying to prevent pedestrians from falling into the open trench. So the homeowner could buy 2x4's, cut the bases to a point and drive them into the ground every 10' and run rope and safety tape around both sides of the trench. A good allowance for the material and labor for this activity is $300.

When the trench is dug then the utility wire or pipe can be installed. These costs are in section 3-underground utilities. Once the utility is placed the trench must be backfilled.

Often the dirt dug out of the trench is full of rocks and is not suitable for backfill around the utility pipe/wire or it may be a requirement of the city that bedding is placed below and over the utility. Bedding is typically sand, gravel, or clean fill (dirt with no rocks). A call to a local sand and gravel company reveals that 10 cubic yards (CY) of sand, gravel (5/8 crushed or 5/8 minus) or clean fill delivered to a site within 10 miles ranges in price from $365 to $390 for 10 CY yards delivered. I will use the $390 because it is the highest so one cubic yard of fill costs $39. Delivered cost means trucking charges are included.

Some sand and gravel companies will quote in tons of material. Sand, gravel, and clean fill weighs about 100 pounds per cubic foot. There are 27 cubic feet in one cubic yard and there are 2,000 pounds per ton. Therefore, 10 CY of gravel x 27 cubic feet per CY x 100 pounds per cubic foot all divided by 2000 pounds per ton is equal to 13.5 tons. If 10 CY of gravel costs $390 or $39 per CY delivered this is also equal to $28.89 per ton delivered. They mean the same thing but different units.

How much bedding and clean fill is needed? Typically 6" to 12" below the utility and 6" to 12" above. The maximum then is 2' of fill. The volume of fill is the length of the trench x the width x the depth. Therefore, 100' long x 2' wide x 3' deep is 600 cubic feet. Divide 600 cubic feet by 27 cubic feet per cubic yard and the volume of bedding and fill is 22.22 CY. Round up to 23 CY. 23 CY x $39 per CY delivered and the cost for bedding and fill is $897.

The fill will be delivered in a pile on your property and will have to be placed into the trench. Since the backhoe and the operator are on site for one week this equipment and the operator are there to be employed. It would take just a few hours to put 6" to 12" of fill in a 100' long trench. Lay the utility and another few hours to place 6" to 12" of fill for cover.

The fill usually has to be compacted so a 21" wide plate compactor could be rented for one week for about $150. It could be operated by the now idle backhoe operator but to make this estimate high add another laborer for 2 days or 16 hours to run the plate compactor and use a shovel to help with the trench work. 16 hours x $20/hour is $320. Therefore, the plate compactor and a laborer for 16 hours add $150 + $320 or $470 to the cost.

The last foot of the trench could be backfilled with the dirt removed from the trench. The volume of dirt removed from the trench excavation is 100' long x 2' wide x 3' deep or 600 cubic feet or 22.22 CY. In actuality dirt fluffs when pulled from the ground by 30%. This means the dirt removed from the trench is in a pile with a volume of 22.22 CY x 1.3 or 28.89 CY. I only need 7.41 CY (100' long x 2' wide x 1' deep) of backfill now. That means 28.89-7.41 or 21.48 CY must be disposed of. If the dirt is relatively clean fill it can actually be sold. However, to make this estimate high I will dump it. Dump fees are approximately $25/ton. (Please note that dump fees at the county dump are about $90/ton. No one dumps dirt there because it would be so expensive. Remember dirt has value and yards where it is dumped reuse it.) 21.48 CY x 27 cubic feet/CY x 100 pounds/cubic foot divided by 2000 pounds per ton means there are 29 tons to dispose of. 29 tons x $25/ton is $725 in dump fees. One 10 CY dump truck will cost about $650 for a day with an operator. This one dump truck will need 3 trips to a dump. This can be done in one day. Therefore, the cost of dumping the excess dirt is $725 + $650 = $1,375.

Summarizing the costs of this trench estimate is:

Equipment	$2,670
Barricades	$300
Bedding/sand	$897
Plate compactor	$470
Dump fees/truck cost	$1,375
Total	$5,712

$5,712 or $57.12 per foot to dig a 2' wide x 3' deep x 100 foot long trench with a backhoe.

2. Excavation for a basement. At my house the basement excavation had dimensions of 40' wide x 9' deep x 45' long. This is a volume of 16,200 cubic feet or 600 CY of excavation. The dimension or our house foundation was 35' wide x 9' deep x 40' long or 12,600 cubic feet. 16,200 minus 12,600 gives a volume of 3,600 cubic feet or 134 CY of fill to dispose of.

The trucking company I hired only charged me for the trucks and operators but nothing to dump the dirt. I thought that was a good deal. In hindsight I could have sold the dirt for at least $10/CY or $1,340. In 2006, clean fill costs about $25/CY + trucking charges. This company put my clean fill to use on some fill job and made a little more profit for themselves.

If you, the homeowner, have a large excavation then advertise in the newspaper or place a sign on your site to sell clean fill at a 20 or 30% discount. You'll earn money on your excavation.

How long did it take to excavate the pit for my foundation? 2 days. There were 2 dump trucks, one large excavator with a one cubic yard bucket. A call to an equipment rental company will reveal that an excavator with a one yard bucket can excavate from 50 to 60 CY of dirt in an hour. So by doing a little math my 600 CY excavation could take place in about one 10 hour day. For this estimate I will say it will take 3 days to excavate.

To summarize, the equipment and labor costs are as follows. Two 10 CY dump trucks at $650/day each (includes operator) x 3 days is $1,950. A large excavator will cost $450 to $500 per day or $1,500 for 3 days without an operator. An operator for 3 days is 24 hours x $35/hour or $840 for a total of $1,950 (dump trucks) + $1,500 (excavator) + $840 (operator labor) equals $4,290.

$4,410 or $1.47/SF for a 3000 SF house basement excavation with dimensions of 40' wide x 9' deep x 45' long. There were 600 CY excavated so the CY cost to excavate is $4,410 divided by 600 CY or $7.35 per CY.

2. Exterior grading. Exterior grading is where a piece of equipment is used to cut, fill and grade a lot so that the contours of the land are as the homeowner wants them. Once this work is complete then such final work as landscaping and concrete flatwork can be installed.

Exterior grading can be done with a backhoe but the expert equipment and earthmoving person I discussed this section with says a mini-track-hoe would be better. This machine can dig and grade because it has a blade on one end and a digging bucket on the other end.

The homeowner will have to make a judgment of how many days are needed to accomplish this work. Our lot was 10,000 SF with not too much needing to be done other than taking some of the excess dirt from our excavation and spreading it out so our yard was at a level grade.

This work took two days. A mini-track hoe costs a little less than a backhoe at $150 per day + $70 (delivery) + $150 (fuel & oil) + $280 (operator) equals $650 per day. 2 days x $650/day is $1,300.

$1,300 or $.43/SF for a 3000 SF house to grade a 10,000 SF lot.

3. Underground Utilities; water, sewer, electrical power, natural gas, telephone. This section has the cost of the pipe, wire, or cable needed to provide the subject utilities. Underground utilities also require cost for trenching to run the utility to your house. Costs from the trenching section will be added to these prices. These sections of work assume that the city or utility has the respective service in the street outside the house.

Water pipe. The scope of work is to install a trench and water pipe from the city meter to just inside the house with an adjustable pressure regulating valve. Length of pipe is assumed to be 100'. Most of the time 20 or 30 feet is all that is needed. The pipe to use is 1" diameter plastic poly pipe rated for potable water. The cost of 100' of this pipe at your local super store is $40. A good adjustable pressure regulating valve will cost less than $200. Add $20 for miscellaneous material. Therefore, the material cost is $40 + $200 + $20 = $260.

The trench only needs to be just wide enough for the 1 inch diameter pipe and it will be on your property from the city water meter to the house. From the trenching section I know that a trench dug by a trencher costs $8.20 per foot.

Labor to install the pipe is only one plumber for one hour because this is plastic 1" pipe rolled up in a coil. To install it the plumber just needs to make the connection at the city meter, unroll the plastic pipe, occasionally kick some dirt over the pipe to hold it in place until it is installed. This one hour includes the connection at the city water meter. Another hour is reasonable for the installation of the pressure valve just inside the house including caulking the penetration where the plastic pipe penetrates the concrete foundation. Allow 2 hours to drive to the super store to pick up the pipe and the valve. Therefore total labor for the plumber is 4 hours. 4 hours x $40/hour is $160. Total material and labor is $260 + $160 is $420. Add the trench cost of 100 feet x $8.20 per foot or $820. Total cost is $420 (labor) + $820 (trench) = $1,240.

$1,240 for 100 feet or $12.40 per foot for installing a 1" diameter water line with pressure regulating valve and trench.

Sewer pipe. The sewer pipe is known as sanitary sewer. From a house to the city sewer a 4" diameter ABS pipe could be used. This cost assumes that a connection will be made to an existing sanitary sewer main in the street.

The pipe would be run from the sewer main to the house. Assume 100' of 4" diameter pipe. 4" diameter ABS pipe at a super store costs $17 for a 10' section of pipe. 11 sections of pipe costs 11 x $17 = $187. Add $150 for fittings and glue and the material cost is $187 + 150 or $337.

The trench only needs to be wide enough for the 4" pipe. The pipe will be made up on the ground adjacent to the trench and then lowered down into the trench. The trench will be wider at the point of connection at the city sewer line because the workers need room to work. From the trenching section I know that a trench dug by a backhoe is $5,712.

Labor to install the pipe is 4 hours x $40/hour or $160 to make up the pipe which consists of gluing the pipe joints together and installing it into the trench. The connection at the city main is more difficult and time consuming. Making a connection to the city sewer main requires a hefty allowance. Add 4 men one day for labor to do this work. 4 men x 8 hours/day x $40/hour = $1,280. Total labor is $160 + $1,280 or $1,440.

Total cost is $337 (material) + $5,712 (trench) + $1,440 (labor) for a total of $7,489.

$7,489 or $74.89 per foot to install 100' of 4" ABS sanitary sewer pipe and make a connection to the city main in the street.

Electrical power. The local power utility will be bringing the power to your lot but the homeowner must pay for it. They will set a power box in the ground to bring their hot wires. I have researched the cost to do this in the Seattle area and an allowance of $3,500 to pay your power utility company is reasonable for running power to your property from 100' down the street. Add trenching cost of $7,285 if you want the power line underground. Total allowance is $3,500 + $7,285 or $10,785.

The homeowner is typically responsible for installing power cable from the utility manhole on public property into their house. However, the rules vary so check with your local power utility company. In my case, they set a box in the ground adjacent to the power pole and ran power into the box. I had the responsibility to run power cable from their power box into my house. A 3' deep trench was dug for placing the power. When I was ready for power to be turned on the power company made the connection from their hot wires to my wires in the power box.

The homeowner should check with their local utility company or rely on their electrical contractor to confirm the correct size and type of power cable to be used. However, aluminum power cable is the way to go for long exterior runs because it is so much cheaper than copper. The cost of a 4-0/4-0/2-0 aluminum power cable at a superstore is $2.53/LF. A 100' run from the box to the house electrical panel x $2.53/LF is $253. Add the trench cost of 100 feet x $8.20 per foot or $820 for a trencher to go from their power box to your house. Labor to install the power cable in the trench would be 2 men 2 hours each or 4 hours x $40/hour or $160 for labor. The final power connection would more than likely be done at a separate time so add another $160 in labor for the second site visit. Total labor is $320. Total cost to run power from the power box into the house is $253 (material) + $820 (trench) + $320 (labor) or $1,393.

Total electrical power to the house cost is $10,785 for getting the power from 100' down the street plus from the power box 100' to your house of $1,393. Total is $10,785 + $1,393 = $12,178.

$12,178 or $4.06/SF for a 3000 SF house for the power company to run power 100' to a box in front of your house and the cost to run power cable 100' from the box into your house.

Natural gas. I recently had the natural gas supplier in Seattle install gas service to one of my rental houses. There was no cost to me because I signed a contract with them that I would have a gas furnace and gas hot water tank in the house. The homeowner will want to check with their local gas company to see if this is the case in your area.

However, let us assume that this is not the case in all parts of the country. Assume the work conditions are such that the gas main is across the street from your house. The way the gas company installed the gas line from the main to my rental house was to drill a path under the street so the gas pipe (actually high pressure hose) could be installed without excavating. They then did the same thing from the house side of the street for the 35 feet to the gas meter location adjacent to the house.

The scope of work to install a gas line to your house from a main on the other side of the street would be to excavate at the main, excavate a hole on your side of the street, and excavate a hole adjacent to the house where the gas meter is to be set. Install the gas line underground, make a connection at the gas main, set the gas meter at the house, backfill, and place an asphalt/concrete patch if needed.

I know the labor to do this was 3 men one day because I watched them do the work. 3 men x 8 hours/day x $35/hour is $840. Equipment used by the gas company was a dump truck with a load of crushed gravel/sand mix. They had a trailer with a backhoe for the excavation and backfill work. We know from section 2 that the cost for a dump truck is $650 for the day, a backhoe is $420 (equipment cost only because labor is captured in the value for the labor for the 3 men), the backfill used was just a few cubic yards or say 5 CY x $39/CY is $195. One asphalt/concrete patch was all that was needed and there is always a minimum charge for an asphalt patch and $500 is a good allowance. Natural gas hose/pipe and connection cost is in the $400 to $800 range so we will use $800.

The total cost is $840 for labor, $650 for the dump truck and trailer, $420 for the backhoe, $195 for backfill, $500 for the asphalt patch, and $800 for material for a total of $3,405.

$3,405 or $1.14/SF for a 3000 SF house for the natural gas company to install a gas line to your house from a location across the street.

Telephone. The best way to get pricing for telephone installation is to call you local telephone provider. Many telephone companies do not have a charge to hook up your house but do require a one or two year contract. However, a budgetary cost can be determined through the labor and material cost to run telephone wire from the street telephone pole to your house.

The scope of work is to install telephone wire/cable from the telephone pole to your house in a trench. We will assume there is a telephone wire overhead as that is usually the case. The telephone wire used most today is Category 5 (aka Cat 5) cable and it is made up of four to eight #24 twisted wire. A trip to a super store shows this material costs from 18 cents per foot to 40 cents per foot. 100' x $0.40/foot is $40 for material. Add $100 for the telephone terminal block attached to the outside of your house and the total material cost is $140.

The trench only needs to be just wide enough for the cable so the cost for a trench dug by a trencher is what is required. From the trenching section a trench dug by a trencher costs $8.20 per foot or $820 for a 100' trench.

Add labor for the wire man to come out with his truck with a lift built on it for access to telephone wires hanging about 15' off the ground. Give an allowance of $400 for the truck (equipment cost). Once the trench is opened the labor to install wire to the house and make the connections is about 4 hours. 4 hours x $35/hour is $140.

Total cost to install Cat 5 telephone wire from the telephone pole to your house is $140 for material, $820 for the trench, $400 for the truck, and $140 for labor for a total cost of $1,500.

$1,500 or $0.50/SF for a 3000 SF house to install telephone wire from a telephone pole on the street through a trench to your house.

4. Concrete foundations; spread footings & concrete walls. Concrete will take almost any kind of force in compression (pushing together) but very little in tension (pulling apart). Tension forces are always the cause of concrete cracking and concrete always cracks. We add reinforcing bar (rebar) and wire mesh not to hold concrete together but to carry the load where the concrete cracks.

Foundations are made up of spread footings and concrete walls. The spread footing is formed and placed first and then the concrete wall is formed and placed second. Both footings and walls require rebar. The top of the concrete walls have always required anchor bolts to hold the framing to the foundation. Recent changes in the code now require sheetmetal straps to be embedded into the concrete so that it can be nailed to the exterior walls.

A spread footing looks like an inverted T. It will be 2' tall with the base about 3' wide and the narrow portion at 8" wide on top. A one foot long section of a spread footing would require 0.14 cubic yards of concrete per foot. An 8' tall wall x 8" thick x 1' long would take 0.20 cubic yards of concrete per foot. The calculation is: 8' tall x 8"/12" wide x 1' long is 5.33 cubic feet. 5.33 cubic feet divided by 27 cubic feet per cubic yard is 0.20 CY. The total would be .14 + .2 is equal to 0.34 CY per foot of footing and 8' wall.

The foundation of my house is 160' long. 160' x .34 CY per foot is 54.40 CY of concrete. Round this up to 60 CY for waste and column pads. Concrete will cost from $100 per CY to $150 per CY depending on your location and the number of concrete suppliers in your area. The high side cost of concrete would be 60 CY x $150/CY or $9,000. Note: the homeowner may be able to negotiate a lower cost for concrete if there are several concrete supply companies in your area. Large jobs do negotiate the price of concrete down to the $65/CY price range for projects with thousands of yards of concrete to be placed.

#4 rebar is what is commonly used in house foundations and walls and it weighs about .7 pounds per foot. The rebar is run both horizontally and vertically in the foundations. A good estimate for rebar is about 30' per foot of footing and 8' wall. That is 30' x .7 pounds per foot or 21 pounds per foot. For my 160 feet of foundation that is 1,260 pounds of rebar. Round that up to 2,000 pounds for corners and waste. Rebar costs about $1 per pound to buy, deliver and install. Therefore, 2,000 pounds x $1/pound is $2,000.

I do not carry any money in this estimate for the cost of the form boards because a company regularly engaged in foundation work will have their own form boards. If they really want the job they will not add anything for forms just the labor to install and take them down. If, however, a form has to be cut for your foundation pay them $50 per board.

A pumper truck will cost $900 for a day. Figure on 2 days because of two pours and the pump truck rental cost will be $1,800.

The labor to install forms, install steel rods and shoes to hold the forms together against the force of the concrete and to take them down is normally calculated through the method of square foot of contact surface area. That is too hard to teach. A better way is by crew size.

I watched a house foundation (for a 4,000 SF two story house) being placed recently by a foundation crew of 5 men for 4 days. Not all 5 men were there every day and the crew never actually worked any full 8 hour days except for the pour day for the walls when they were all there about 12 hours. A good estimate of the hours to place forms, rebar, concrete, and remove forms is 5 men x 8 hours per day x 4 days or 160 hours. 160 hours x $34/hour is $2,040 in labor. The labor for the foundation on my house was closer to 120 hours but I like these numbers to be fat. Total labor, material and equipment costs are $2,040 (labor) + $9,000 (concrete) + $2,000 (rebar) + $1,800 (pumper truck) is $14,840. For 160 feet of 8' tall foundation wall and footing is $93 per foot.

$14,840 or $4.95 per SF for the concrete footings and foundation walls for a 3,000 SF house.

5. Framing & insulation. Framing for homes in America is almost always wood and the pricing shown below is for wood. The reason I state this is because there are also steel studs but they are more common in commercial buildings than houses. Also, steel costs more than wood. The costs listed below are for all wood, nails, and seismic straps to frame an entire 3,000 SF house. More specifically, the cost covers, beams, columns, headers, floor joists, walls, roof trusses and exterior sheathing and roof sheathing and all fascia boards. Roof sheathing is ½" plywood, exterior walls are 2" x 6", interior walls are 2" x 4", sub-floor is ¾" plywood and joists are prefabricated I-beam type joists.

Framing costs. I have an associate who is a builder. He can make good money by charging homeowners $5 per SF for labor to frame a house. That mean for a 3,000 SF house the labor charge would be $15,000. $5 per SF for labor would work on projects that have floor areas down to about 500 SF. For projects smaller than 500 SF the labor cost would go up to about $7/SF.

In 1993 I paid $22,500 for the wood package for my 3,000 SF house. That is $7.50 per SF for material. I have a friend who just built (in 2006) a 3,200 SF house and he paid

$38,400 or $12/SF for his wood package. The range for material for framing, therefore, is in the $8 to $14/SF. Total labor and material cost would be $13/SF to $19/SF.

$39,000 or $13/SF to $57,000 or $19/SF to buy wood and frame a 3000 SF house.

Insulation. The energy portion of the building code requires that our houses have insulation. The reason we have insulation is to reduce the amount of heat loss through the walls and roof. The thicker the insulation is the better barrier to heat transfer it is.

Luckily for the homeowner fiberglass is a very good insulation material and it is cheap. The code requires a minimum of R19 insulation in the walls and R38 in the attic. R19 is 6.5" thick and costs 46 cents per SF. R38 is 13" thick and it costs 90 cents per SF at your superstore. These prices are for batts of insulation with one side with paper facing and the other open fiberglass insulation. Sometimes it is cheaper to have insulation blown into an attic.

I had insulation blown into a 900 SF attic space at one of my rental houses and it cost $780 or $0.87 per SF. Two men came in a truck with insulation and a blower with a long hose on it. One man went into the attic through the crawl space and one fed insulation into the blower hopper. They were done in less than 4 hours each or 8 hours total labor for the job. The only disadvantage to blown in insulation is that if I have to go into the attic for any reason the insulation gets flattened down and it is hard to find anything in it.

If I have an 8' tall wall by 30' long wall this is 240 SF of R19 insulation required. It will actually be less than this because of windows. 240 SF x $.46/SF is $110 in material. To install batts of insulation the laborer just staples it into the space in-between the exterior studs. It is easy to do because the paper facing on the insulation has little paper tabs that fold out and are stapled to the stud. That is it. Labor to install insulation in this 240 SF wall is about two hours for one man or 2 hours x $20/hour or $40. Total labor and material is $40 + $110 or $150. This is $0.63 per SF of wall surface area. This converts to $0.67/SF of floor area to install batt insulation in an attic.

If I place R38 batt insulation in my 1,500 SF attic the material cost will be 1,500 SF x $0.90/SF or $1,350. Labor to install the batts into the attic will be two men one day or 16 hours. 16 hours x $20/hours is $320. Total labor and material cost is $320 + $1,350 for a total of $ 1,670 or $0.56/SF of floor area.

Total cost for insulation for both walls and attic is $0.67 + $0.56 or $1.23 per SF.

$3,690 or $1.23/SF to install R19 insulation in the walls and R38 batt insulation in the attic for a 3,000 SF house.

6. Drywall/sheetrock; tape & mud, PVA coating, texture. Drywall or sheetrock is placed on the interior surfaces of your house to cover the studs and insulation and present a flat wallboard surface. PVA coating is used to prime the drywall after it is installed so it will be sealed and paint will stick to it. Texture is then sprayed on the drywall to give it depth.

Drywall or sheetrock is made out of gypsum which is a soft mineral that is processed to make drywall. It is very inexpensive compared to wood paneling or basically any other wall covering. It comes in 4' x 8' or 4' x 12' sheets and is typically one half inch thick. The drywall sheets are nailed and screwed to your interior walls to form the surface that you will see everyday.

Drywall is heavy and when it is cut to fit the walls it gives off a lot of dust which makes for hard, dirty, work. To install it properly narrow cardboard butt strips are needed to shim the drywall due to uneven studs. When the studs are really bad a power plane is needed to shave off wood to make the drywall fit properly. Not all drywall contractors install butt strips or power plane the studs. Find one that does.

The numbers for material do not tell the whole story though because with drywall there are multiple trips made at the taping stage. This is because it takes time for the tapers mud to dry in-between layers. This means that the contractor will be spending some of their time driving from job to job. That cost needs to be captured in each of the jobs. Another factor is whether the longer 12' boards can be brought into the space thereby reducing taping labor hours.

I have found a drywall company in Seattle that only does 'smooth wall'. This means that the surface of the drywall after taping and mud is applied and sanded will be free of ridges, grooves, and tool marks. It is not, however, perfectly smooth. It just looks perfectly smooth from about two feet away. If the homeowner would get within 3 or 4 inches they would be able to see some sand and groove marks. This is not a problem and not the issue. Remember construction is not perfect. If the flat surfaces have grooves or tool marks that can be seen from 2' away and the edges are not clean or sharp but have grooves that can be seen from 2' away they will need to be fixed before PVA coating and texture is applied. Texture will not hide any imperfections.

The smooth wall drywall contractor with whom I have been discussing quality and price is running about $2.78 per SF of wall surface area. The run of the mill drywall companies will be less than $2 per SF. I recommend smooth wall before texture goes on because texture will not hide any mistakes.

Drywall is the first stage of the finishes that go into your house, therefore, I am willing to pay top dollar to an excellent drywall contractor. However, the homeowner must look at the contractor's previous work to be sure that a smooth wall surface is actually being delivered

The way to figure wall surface area is to take the SF of the floor area to be drywalled and multiple it by 3.5 not 5 (a ceiling and 4 walls). This is because of openings that are not drywalled reduces the actual amount of sheetrock. For example, in a 3000 SF floor area house the amount of drywall is 3000 SF x 3.5 or 10,500 SF of wall area. At 2.78/SF x 10,500 SF is equal to $29,190 or $9.73 per SF for a 3000 SF of floor area. There is enough money in this price of $9.73/SF of floor area to also cover the cost of PVA coating (seals the drywall and mud so texture and paint will adhere) and texture. $9.73 is a fat number but I will pay that for actual smooth wall with texture.

$29,190 or $9.73 per SF for 3000 SF of floor area or $2.78 per SF of wall area.

7. Roofing & flashing. Roofing is the material that is placed on the roof to waterproof our homes so they stay dry. There are many roofing materials available. They are aluminum, composition asphalt shingles, clay tiles, and cedar shakes to name a few. In comparison to composition asphalt shingles, aluminum costs about twice as much and clay tiles cost about three times as much.

The scope of work for roofing a new house is to install tar paper on the roof sheathing, install flashing (around chimneys and vents to prevent water infiltration), and then install the roofing material. If demolition is involved then the old roof has to be removed.

I mentioned earlier in this book that I hired the Home Depot to replace my old rental house roof in 2002 I will use the numbers from that project to determine an actual SF cost.

The scope of work was to tear off and dispose of the old cedar shakes, install ½" plywood sheathing on the roof, install tar paper, install all flashing around the chimney and vents, aluminum trim around the fascia boards, install a medium priced (50 year warranty) 3-tab asphalt composition roofing, install a rotating roof ventilator, install ridge cap vent at the peak of the house (for better attic ventilation) at a price of $7,200.

My rental house roof has a roofing surface area of 1,854 SF. $7,200 divided by 1,854 SF or $3.88 per SF of roof surface area. The square footage of this house is 2400 SF which means a cost of $7,200 divided by 2400 SF or $3 per SF. Roofing is also described in terms of squares. One square is equal to 100 SF. This means my 1,854 SF roof divided by 100 SF has 18.54 squares. $7,200 divided by 18.54 squares is $388 per square of roofing.

$7,200 or $3.00/SF for a 2,400 SF house where the scope of work is to remove old shingles, install plywood sheathing, flashing, and 3-tab composition asphalt shingles.

If the roofing is to be placed on a brand new house then the cost will be less than the above example because there is no removal and the plywood sheathing will be part of the framing cost. Some quick calculations will tell us that 1854 SF divided by 32 SF per sheet of plywood means that 58 sheets would be needed. At $30 each that is $1,740. Labor to install is ½ hour each or 29 hours x $35/hour is $1,015. Give an allowance of $1,000 for the removal cost of the old cedar shingles and the dump fees. Therefore the total reductions due to reduced scope of work is $1,740 + $1,015 + $1,000 = $3,755. $7,200 - $3,755 = $3,445 to install just tar paper and asphalt shingles.

$3,445 divided by 1,854 SF or $1.86 per SF of roof surface area. It is also $186 per square ($3,445 divided by 18.54 squares).

$3,445 or $1.44/SF for a 2,400 SF house where the scope of work is to install tar paper an asphalt shingles.

7. Gutters & downspouts. Gutters are the troughs that are attached at the bottom edge of a roof to catch rainwater. This is so the rainwater doesn't just flow off the house, onto the ground and find its way into your foundation. This is why we collect and direct the rainfall away from the house foundation through gutters and downspouts.

A trip to your local super store will reveal that a 4" wide x 4" deep x 10' long white (aluminum) gutter costs $7 each. Plastic is even cheaper. A 10' long downspouts also cost $7. On my 3000 SF house I have 120' of gutters. Round this up to 200' for budgetary estimating or 20 each 10' sections of gutter. The material cost for gutters is 20 each x $7 each is $140.

There are about 112' of downspouts but I will also round this up to 200' or 20 pieces of downspout also for $140. Add $200 for miscellaneous materials such as nails, clips, brackets and the various parts one needs for gutters and the total material cost is $140 + $140 + $200 = $480.

Labor to install the gutters and downspouts is only 2 men 1 day or 16 hours. 16 hours x $35 hour is $560. But there may be problems at the site so I will add a second day of labor or $560/day x 2 days is $1,120. Also needed is a lift of some kind. Use an allowance of $400 for this equipment. It will be less than this because a gutter company will need to have purchased this equipment if they are serious about their business. However, the $400 is a good equipment allowance.

The total cost of the gutters is $480 for material, $1,120 for labor and $400 for equipment for a total of $2,000.

$2,000 or $0.67/SF for the installation of gutters and downspouts for a 3000 SF house.

8. Exterior siding. Exterior siding is what is placed over the exterior sheathing on your house. It is there to keep the elements out of your house and to look beautiful. Once the plywood sheathing is placed on the exterior studs a layer of waterproofing material is installed. This can be tar paper or one of the many plastic products available. The siding materials are many. Typically they are wood, vinyl, aluminum, or fiberglass. Wood can be cedar boards, cedar shingles, redwood, or plywood.

The steps needed to side a house are to install scaffolding, install waterproofing material, install appropriate flashing and install the siding. A minimum crew size is three persons. Two are used to install the siding and the third is used to man the saw.

The cost of scaffolding is from section 1 and is $504 for one month.

My 3000 SF house was sided in five days by a crew of 3 men. That is 3 men x 8 hours per day x 5 days or 120 hours. Carpenters earn $35 per hour so $35/hour x 120 hours is $4,200 for the labor to install the tar paper and the siding. On my house I also had a thermal bubble wrap installed over the tar paper to provide extra thermal insulation. This was not required but I like to exceed the requirements of the building code if it means a cooler house.

My 3000 SF house has 2 floors with peaks at the elevations. My elevations are 40 feet wide by 25 feet tall. The rectangular section of one elevation will be 40 feet x 16 feet or 640 SF. The peak will be a triangular section with the base at 40 feet and the height of 9 feet or 180 SF for a total of 820 SF. Add about 35% to the SF for the time consuming work of fitting siding around windows and doors and I have an effective square footage of 820 SF x 1.35 or 1,100 SF per elevation. Do not subtract for windows and doors because of waste. With 4 elevations per house the total SF to side is 1,100 SF x 4 sides is 4,400 SF.

A trip to your local super store will show that a roll of #15 tar paper/felt will cost $19.55 each. This roll will cover 432 SF (36" wide x 144' long). 10.2 rolls are required to cover a wall surface of 4,400 SF. Budget for 12 rolls for waste and the cost of tar paper is $19.55 x 12 rolls is $237.

Appropriate flashing is the metal flashing that is installed on the exterior wall elevations to prevent water infiltration. If you look closely at a good siding job you will see that there is metal flashing at the base and edges of dormers. This is so that water cannot seep into the house where some architectural feature does not go extend out as an adjacent section of building. A reasonable allowance for this is $500 in material and 4 hours of labor or $140. This is because this is all it takes to put this flashing in place on a 3000 SF house. Total flashing cost is $640.

Clear cedar is the most expensive of the siding types so I will use that here to be sure I am high. A call to cedar siding suppliers in the Seattle area gives a price of $.90 per lineal foot for ½" thick x 6" wide clear cedar siding. Aluminum, vinyl, plywood, and other wood sidings cost about $1/3^{rd}$ the cost of clear cedar. Fiberglass costs about $2/3^{rd}$ the cost of cedar. However, this 90 cents per foot is a good price for Seattle where we have forests nearby but it is too low for the southern United States, therefore, to be high I will add 50% to the price of cedar siding to $1.35 per lineal foot.

There is overlap of the siding so one does not actually get 6" of coverage per a 6" board. My estimating experience tells me that if I have a 4,400 SF of wall to side then I actually need 11,440 lineal feet of siding to cover the house. A factor of 2.6. 11,400 feet x $1.35/feet is $15,390 for clear cedar siding.

Summarizing the siding costs gives $504 for scaffolding. Tar paper cost is $237. Flashing cost is $640. Labor cost is $4,200. Siding material cost is $15,390. Therefore the total cost to side my 3000 SF house is $504 + $237 + $640 + $4,200 + $15,390 equals $20,971 or $6.99 per SF for a 3000 SF house.

There is a second SF number needed for siding. It is the cost per SF of wall surface area. There is 4,400 SF of wall surface area to side. The cost per SF of wall surface area is $20,971 divided by 4,400 SF or $4.77 per SF of wall surface area.

$20,971 or $6.99/SF for installing clear cedar siding on a 3000 SF house.

9. Finishes; doors & hardware, windows, flooring, kitchen cabinets, counters. Finishes are all the interior work that makes your house beautiful and functional.

Doors & hardware. There are many shapes and types of doors but I will reduce the complexity to expensive solid core wood doors. Hardware means hinges and a lockset. The cost of the hardware is included in the following door costs. Sizes of doors is a basic 2'-8" (32") x 6'-8" (80") and all doors are pre-hung which means they come with a door frame and hinges already installed and the hole pre-drilled for the lockset. Labor to install is the time to install, shim, level the door frame and hang the door. Framing in the door frame is a framing cost.

Labor to install doors. Pre-hung doors are not difficult or time consuming to install. If the homeowner were to watch an experienced carpenter install a door the would see that the carpenter would have the door frame installed level and square with shims, door installed with hardware but without trim in about 30 minutes. This includes moving the door from the garage or wherever the door delivery person left them. I will be allowing one hour per door so that my estimates are high. The one hour per door covers all the different types of doors; exterior, interior, bi-fold and sliding. A main entry door is heavier and usually bigger with glass frames so I will use 2 hours per main entry door.

Therefore, one hour x $35/hour is $35 in labor to install one door. 2 hours x $35/hour is $70 per main entry door for labor.

To prove the assumption that an experienced carpenter will only take half an hour to install a 32" wide by 80" tall door I did a time study by observing an engineer installing a new pre-hung door in September 2006. I was the engineer. I was remodeling one of my rental houses at that time. I had previously removed the existing doors so the door opening was as if it was just framed.

I have only installed a few doors in my life but have watched it done many times. The pre-hung door was sitting in the garage and it had to be moved into the house. I set my stop watch as I was standing in front of the new door in the garage.

It took me 3 minutes to remove the hinge pins. I had trouble removing them and had to go look for a small diameter punch to help drive out the 3 hinge pins. Once they were out I then removed the door from the frame and set it aside. I then carried the door frame around the front of the house, into the house, and tried to set it in the door opening. It wouldn't fit.

The wood frame was not square and I had to chip out some wood. This is the sort of thing that happens in a remodel. I took a wood chisel and chipped out some of the wood at the top of the frame so the pre-hung door frame would fit. 6 minutes had now passed.

I set the door frame in place and started shimming it to get it square and even. I set it in place with 3 wood screws. The timer said 20 minutes. I went downstairs to the garage and carried the door inside and set it into the hinges. The timer now said 23 minutes and 20 seconds.

With the door in the frame I went about doing the final shimming of the door frame so that the door was square and that the gaps around the edge of the door to the frame were somewhat even. I also made sure the door, when opened to any open position, would stay in that position and not try to open or shut by itself. The timer now said 44 minutes.

I added more screws and trim nails to solidly set the door frame in place. This took to 48 minutes. The last task was to install the lockset and door strike. When completed the timer said 52 minutes.

If an engineer playing at being a carpenter can install a solid core wood door with hardware in 52 minutes then an experienced carpenter can easily do the same job in 30 minutes! The allowance for one hour per door is fat.

Exterior entry door. These generally are in the $1,000 range or less. But to be on the high side I will use a budgetary amount of $2,500. This amount will cover a very nice entry door. Labor is two hours to install. Two hours because entry doors are typically bigger and heavier than standard doors. 2 hours x $35/hour is $70. Total cost is $2,500 + $70 is $2,570.

Exterior French doors. French doors means they are mostly glass. I recently purchased a pair of steel framed double French doors. They cost $980 including the hardware and delivery. Therefore, $500 is a good budgetary number to use to buy a single French door. Labor to install is one hour at $35. Total cost for a single French door is $535.

Interior solid core door. I recently purchased 3 solid core wood doors with 3 heavy duty hinges per door, locksets and delivery for $630 or $210 per door. Labor to install is $35 each. Therefore, the cost to purchase and install one solid core door is $210 + $35 or $245.

Bi-fold doors. The cost of a bi-fold door is less than a standard door because they are typically hollow core. The reason for this is because the tracks and rotating hinges do not work well with the weight of a solid core door. However, to be on the high side I will use the same price for a bi-fold door as a solid core door. Since there are two bi-fold doors per opening then the cost of an installed bi-fold door is 2 x $245 or $490.

Windows. Windows come in many materials. The glass of course is just melted and refrozen silicon (which freezes at room temperature). The feature of windows that makes a big difference in price is if the glass is wrapped in metal, wood or vinyl. Pricing for vinyl windows will be used here because they are the best looking, longest lasting, and the least expensive.

The building code was recently changed in regards to how many windows a house could have. Now houses can have as many windows as the homeowner desires as long as they are low E.

I recently purchased ten vinyl windows for a house remodel. They were sliders, swing crank out, and a picture window. These were all fairly standard size windows one would expect to put into their homes. Some were 24" wide x 67" tall and others were 32" wide x 53" tall.

I will show the dollar per SF cost to simplify pricing. The high cost for the sliders was $21/SF; the high cost for the crank type windows was $31/SF. The picture window was the lowest at $14/SF. That makes sense because it has no motion components.

When the homeowner is determining the price of a particular window all they need do is determine the SF (width times height) and then multiple the SF times the cost of the type of window listed in the previous paragraph.

Flooring; carpet, vinyl, hardwood. There are many types of types of flooring but I will be giving costs for just the basic three; carpet, vinyl, and hardwood.

Carpet. Carpet material costs vary depending on the quality. I will use nylon carpet as the basis of this estimate. Wool is the best of course and costs 2 to 3 times as much as nylon. Carpet is spoken of in square yards. One square yard (SY) is 3' x 3' or 9 SF. A high budgetary number for nylon carpet is $30/SY with pad included. A good budgetary number for installation is $4/SY. $4/SY is for the scope of work where old carpet has to be removed and furniture has to be moved and put back. Therefore, a budgetary cost for nylon carpet and a good pad is $34/SY.

Sheet vinyl flooring. A trip to your local superstore will show that sheet vinyl comes in 12' lengths and many rolls are set in a tall, rotating rack. It costs from a low of $4 per square yard (SY) to a high of $14/SY. Installation cost is also $4/SY. Therefore, a budgetary cost for vinyl sheet flooring is $18/SY.

Hardwood floor, refinish. I recently had a hardwood floor refinished at my rental house. The floor dimensions are 17'-9" x 13'-8" with an area of 242.58 SF. I looked in the yellow pages and called 10 flooring contractors for pricing. The prices quoted over the telephone and confirmed by separate site visits ranged from $2.25/ to $3.50/SF. The lower prices were for 2 coats of Swedish finish and the higher price was for 3 coats. Also, there was a $1/SF premium for a floor area of less than 300 SF. This premium is not unreasonable because smaller jobs do not bring enough profit for the contractor. I paid $1,095 or $4.51/SF to have my hardwood floor refinished. Did I pay too much? Perhaps. I could have shaved a couple hundred of dollars by bidding the job out rather than just phoning the companies. However, in the Pat Fay Method we are not trying to pay the lowest price but a reasonable price. An unreasonable price would be having a general contractor coordinate the refinish of the floor (in a house remodel project) and pay the subcontractor $3.50 but charge me, the homeowner, $12/SF.

Note about hardwood floor finishes. The finishes come in 4 grades; matt, satin, semi-gloss, and gloss. Gloss has the shiniest finish and matt is the dullest. The flooring contractors and general contractors prefer to use the duller range of finishes because they do not show scratches. I do not like the matt or satin finishes because they are so dull looking. I prefer the high gloss and longer lasting sheen of gloss and semi-gloss finishes.

Hardwood floor, buff and refinish. Buff and refinish is where the homeowner has hardwood floors in their house. I spoke to a Glitsa rep (supplier of Glitsa Swedish Floor materials) about when to sand an existing hardwood floor down to bare wood and when to just take a buffer to clean and prep the hardwood floor and apply a top coat of Swedish finish. Buff and recoat can be very successful when the floor has lost its sheen and there are minor scratches. Many homeowners are misled into thinking that the only way to refinish hardwood floors is to sand them down to bare wood. The homeowner only wants this done when the surface of the hardwood floor is heavily scratched, there is cupping of the boards due to water damage or the color has darkened to an unattractive color by age. If the hardwood floor has just lost its shine then the homeowner can hire a finisher to clean, machine buff, and apply the finish coat of Swedish finish for $1 to $2 per SF.

Hardwood floor, install. While I was gathering prices for the refinishing of my hardwood floors I asked the companies with whom I was negotiating for pricing for new hardwood oak floors. The pricing I was quoted ranged from a low of $7/SF to a high of $15/SF. $15/SF is too high a price! A reasonable amount to pay to for good oak flooring installed, sanded and then 3 coats of Swedish finish is $8 to $12/SF.

Ceramic tile on floors and walls. During our new house construction we had tile installed on the floor and part of the walls in our master bathroom. The contractor we hired had a showroom for flooring materials (and as I later learned) used independent tile installers. This means the tile installers were not employees but that the contractor had a list of local tile installers that they used as needed. They were basically a tile supplier and a broker for tile installers.

Our master bathroom has dimensions of 8' wide x 12'-10" long. The entire floor is tile and the walls around the bathtub are also tile. The walls opposite the bathtub are sheetrock. This gives you an idea of how big the room is and how much tile is installed. More specifically there are 71 SF of floor tile (no floor tile at the bathtub and shower) and 37 SF of wall tile for a total of 108 SF. It took one man 3 days to install the concrete board, apply thin set grout, tile and then grout to fill in the gaps around the edges of the tile. The tile installer was not really there for 8 hours each day, however, for this estimate I will assume 3 days at 8 hours. Therefore, at 2006 rates the labor cost would be 24 hours x $35/hour or $840.

Tile, like all finishes, varies much in price due to quality. A trip to a super store will show the material cost for a good ceramic tile will cost from $1.50/SF to $6.00/SF. $6/SF x 108 SF is $648. Add to this the cost for the backer board. They come in 3' x 5' (15 SF) sheets for $11.00. 108 SF divided by 15 SF per sheet is 7.2 sheets. Use 9 sheets for budgeting due to waste. 9 sheets x $11 per sheet is $99. Add $50 for grout and the spacers needed to hold the tile at the correct space from each other. The total material cost is $648 + $99 + 50 equals $797.

The total cost to purchase and install tile is $840 for labor and $797 for material or $1,637. $1,637 divided by 108 SF is $15.16 per SF to install ceramic tile on floor and walls.

Kitchen Cabinets. Kitchen cabinets are one of the items for which homeowners are charged way too much money. The home construction industry has convinced the American homeowner that they need to spend excessive amounts of money on kitchen cabinets.

When my wife was gathering prices for kitchen cabinets the prices ranged from a low of $11,000 to a high of $60,000 depending upon the supplier. We decided to risk going with the $11,000 cabinet maker because we liked the quality of the cabinets this cabinet maker produced. He had (and has) a small shop located in one of the outlying towns north of Seattle. The cabinets were all maple wood, stained nicely, and the price included installation. We paid an additional $2,400 for granite on the island counter top and plastic laminate for counters on the remainder of the base cabinets. Total kitchen cabinet cost was $11,000 + $2,400 or $13,400.

Kitchen cabinets are either base cabinets or uppers. The base cabinets are set on the floor and act as the support for the counter tops. The uppers are set against the wall and are installed up against the ceiling or just below the ceiling for added shelf space on top of the upper cabinets. Standard height of base cabinets is 36" with a depth of 24". Uppers are 32" to 36" tall with a depth of 12" or 18"depending on the kitchen design.

Our base kitchen cabinets are the standard dimensions and have a total length of 46'-10". Our upper cabinets are 32" tall and 12" deep and have a total length of 12'. The total length of cabinets is 46'-10" + 12' or 58'-10". This means we paid $13,400 divided by 58'-10" or $227.76 per lineal foot for cabinets and counter tops in 1994.

In 2006 I was assisting a couple in the planning and preliminary design for their kitchen remodel. Their scope of work included removing the old cabinets and installing all new cherry wood cabinets and plastic laminate countertops. They had a total of 45' of base and upper cabinets. The price from a variety of commercial suppliers was about $25,000 or $556 per lineal foot ($25,000 divided by 45') to remove the old cabinets and install new cabinets including plastic laminate. The cabinet maker who did the cabinets for my house had a price of $15,000 for the same work or $334 per lineal foot.

Therefore, a reasonable price to pay for kitchen cabinets with plastic laminate countertops installed is $334 to $556 per lineal foot in 2006.

Counter tops. Counter tops can be made form many different materials. We have a combination of plastic laminate, granite, marble, and tile. Tile costs are covered in a previous paragraph.

Plastic laminate, costs from $2 to $5/SF for material depending on the quality. Labor to install consists of applying glue to the counter surface, laying the plastic laminate, and cutting the edge to be flush with the counter. Plastic laminate goes on fast by an experienced and skilled craftsman with the right tools.

Our plastic laminate counter top has dimensions of 2'wide x 38' long. It took the installer 6 hours to install it. $35/hour x 6 hours is $210 or $3.5 per lineal foot (LF).

The total cost to install plastic laminate is $5/SF for material and $3.5/LF for a total of $8.50 per lineal foot.

Granite and marble is, of course, more expensive than plastic laminate. I recently remodeled a bathroom and worked with a good marble/granite supplier/installer in Seattle. I discussed budgetary pricing with them. A high budgetary number for granite and marble installed on kitchen or bath countertops is $100 per SF. If the counter is 2' wide then the cost is $200 per foot. This price will allow the homeowner to select and budget for the nicest marble and granite.

10. Appliances; stove/oven, cook top, dishwasher, microwave, refrigerator/freezer, washer, dryer. General contractors will not typically include appliances in their cost of construction but in the Pat Fay Method it is included in the overall cost. This is because it is a legitimate cost to build. You can't live in a house without appliances.

Of course, the cost of appliances will vary depending on the brand and quality. However, I can determine a good budgetary amount to include in an estimate. A trip to your local appliance or super store will show the following appliance pricing. I only list the medium to high priced appliances. The homeowner can find many lower priced and on sale appliances that will serve their needs Ill.

Stoves/oven. $548 (medium) to $980 (high).
Cook top $400 (medium) to $900 (high)
Dishwasher $248 (medium) to $648 (high)
Microwave $198 (medium) to $500 (high)
Refrigerator/freezer $800 (medium) to $2,500 (high)
Washer $497 (medium) to $895 (high)
Dryer $450 (medium) to $848 (high)

To be on the high side I will only use the high cost for all of the above listed appliances. $980 + $900 + $648 + $500 + $2,500 + $895 + $848 = $7,271 for material cost. The labor to install these appliances is one hour each or 7 hours at $40/hour or $280. I assume that the cost for power and gas to be brought to each of these appliances is covered in the electrical and plumbing sections. Total cost is $7,271 for material and $280 for labor for a total of $7,551.

$7,551 or $2.52/SF for a 3000 SF house.

11. Plumbing; underground plumbing, above ground rough-in plumbing, finish plumbing: kitchen sink with garbage disposal, all other sinks, kitchen appliances, toilets, showers, bathtubs, laundry room, hot water tank, and hot water recirculation system. Plumbing is the piping that distributes fresh water (the industry term is potable water) throughout our houses and then gives a path for the sanitary sewer to be drained away and also to vent the unwanted gases to the atmosphere. That is basically the principal by which all plumbing is installed in a house.

There are more details than this but the details are the concern of your plumber. The homeowner just needs to define the location of the sinks and devices that use water and drain.

The building and plumbing codes covers the kinds of materials that are acceptable for all of these processes, as well as how they are to be installed. The code allows for a range of materials for water distribution but my opinion is that the simplest and best is copper pipe. Drainage and vent pipe must meet the drain, waste, vent standards (DWV). ABS plastic pipe (black plastic) meets these requirements. I believe that ABS is the best because it is so simple to install. It cuts easily, glue is all that is needed to assemble it and it rarely leaks. The only disadvantage to ABS is that it has to be supported every 4 feet compared to metal pipe. However, that is a minor problem just requiring a little more labor to support it more often.

The costs that are in the following sections are for inside the house only and they are for copper pipe for water distribution and ABS for DWV. The cost to bring the water and sanitary sewer to the house is in section 3 on underground utilities.

Plumbing costs inside the house can be broken down into 3 main sections; underground plumbing, above ground rough-in plumbing, and finish plumbing. Finish plumbing is made up of 9 detailed sections that cover the costs to buy and install the plumbing parts. They are; kitchen sink with garbage disposal, all other sinks, kitchen appliances, toilets, showers, bathtubs, laundry room, hot water tank, and hot water recirculation system. For these 9 sections I assume the rough in is already complete and the work needed to be done is to install and connect the particular sink, tub or other item here listed.

Underground plumbing. Underground plumbing is the below grade (underground) drain and waste piping that receives the above ground piping from the bathrooms, kitchens, and appliances. This pipe is at slopes of 1/8" per foot for 3" diameter pipe or smaller and ¼" per foot for pipe 4" or larger in diameter. We do not run water lines underground inside the house but in the walls.

The scope of work for this section is just the below grade pipe and their fittings including a 4' stack to keep dirt out of the pipe.

The underground plumbing at my house has a 4" diameter main that runs east west for a length of 40'. Into this pipe runs the drains from the hot water tank (10' of 2.5" pipe), from the laundry room (10' of 2.5" pipe), from the upstairs children's bathroom (10' of 3" pipe), from the powder room (10' of 2.5" pipe), from the kitchen sink (20' of 2.5" pipe), and from the master bathroom (20' of 3" pipe). I need to also add 4' of pipe for each respective stack. This is a total of 75' of 2.5" pipe or 8 ten foot pieces, 38' of 3" pipe or 4 ten foot pieces, and 40' of 4" pipe or 5 ten foot pieces (one more for waste). Note: in reality I ran the master bath drain line outside the house and had a separate drain line for this because I did not want the sound of draining water inside the house. So I show the cost of running this drain line to the 4" main for cost purposes here.

The pipe is ABS plastic which comes in 10' lengths at the super stores. A ten foot piece of 2 ½" ABS pipe costs $12. 8 pieces x $12 each is $96. A ten foot piece of 3" ABS pipe costs $14. 4 pieces x $14 each is $56. A ten foot piece of 4" ABS pipe costs $17. Five pieces x $17 each is $85. This adds up to a material cost is $237. There are also couplings, wyes, and elbow fittings to buy, as well as glue. I could count fittings but if I have $237 in pipe a good estimate of fitting costs is $200. Therefore, the material cost to do the underground plumbing at my 3,000 SF house is $237 + $200 or $437.

The labor to do this work is two men two days. That is all it takes because that is all it took at my house. There was one plumber and a helper. After the foundation is poured the plumber will come in and dig trenches, lay the pipe, install the fittings, have the pipe inspected (requires a 10' head water test), and then cover the pipe. My plumber even had to use a small jackhammer to cut a couple of holes through the concrete footings to allow the pipe to be placed properly. Two men x 8 hours/day x $40/hour is $640. The total labor and material cost is $640 + $437 or $1,077. Total labor and material is $1,077 + $437 is $1,514.

Above ground rough-in plumbing. Above ground rough in piping is made up of the drain, waste, vent (DWV) piping and the hot and cold water copper lines. The DWV piping in this section is just the horizontal runs from the sinks and appliances down to the underground plumbing and the vent piping.

Above ground DWV piping. There are 80' of 2.5" & 40' of 3" ABS drain line from the kitchen and bathrooms. There are another 140' of 2.5" vent line in my attic. I had the vent lines from the kitchen and powder room (which are in the front of the house) routed to connect with the vents from the two upstairs bathrooms at the back of the house. The reason I did this was because I did not want any vents protruding through the roof at the front of the house where they could be seen. A ten foot piece of 2 ½" ABS pipe costs $12. 8 pieces x $12 each is $96. A ten foot piece of 3" ABS pipe costs $14. 4 pieces x $14 each is $56. The pipe cost is $152. There are also couplings, wyes, and elbow fittings to buy, as well as glue. I could count fittings but if I have $152 in pipe a good estimate of fitting costs is $100. Therefore, the material cost to do the above ground DWV plumbing at my 3,000 SF house is $152 + $100 or $252.

Hot and cold water piping. In my opinion, copper pipe is really the best water distribution system to have in your house. It is not that expensive and it cuts easily and is sweated together with lead free solder. Copper pipe comes in three types with varying pipe wall thickness; M, L, and K. K has the thickest walls and is for industrial applications, L has medium thickness walls and M has the thinnest. Both type L & M are available for purchase at the super stores but I believe there is no point to spending the extra money for type L (50% more expensive) because it is a waste of money. This is because house water systems operate at about 60 psi (pounds per square inch). Type M copper pipe can easily operate with pressures to 120 psi with no leakage. We don't want anymore than 60 psi of water pressure in our houses because at higher pressures all the seals in our faucets and appliances would fail. On the other hand I know engineers who are willing to go to the expense of Type L because they want the extra wall thickness in case a sheetrock nail grazes the pipe or for just that little bit of extra thickness. You are the project manager and you must make up your own mind on which pipe to use.

In my house, there are a few feet of 1" diameter copper pipe from the point of entry for the city water to the pressure regulator and to the hot water tank. After that I had my plumber run ¾" diameter pipe for both the hot and cold water mains from the hot water tank to the kitchen, master bath and children's bathroom. The branch lines were reduced to ½" diameter. There are 10' of 1" pipe, 200' of ¾" pipe, and 260' of ½" diameter copper type M pipe for the hot and cold water distribution. Add an additional 80' of ½ diameter pipe for the return line on the hot water recirculation system and the ½" diameter pipe total is 340'. 1" copper pipe is $60 for 10', ¾" copper pipe costs $40 for a 10' piece or 20 pieces x $40 each is $800 and ½" copper pipe costs $20 for a 10' piece or 34 pieces x $20 each is $680. Total pipe cost from a super store is $1,540. Add $1,000 for fittings, solder, pipe clamps and brackets and the total material cost is $1,540 + $1,000 is $2,540.

The labor to install the rough plumbing, both DWV and water piping is one plumber and one helper for 64 hours. I hired a plumber who had a plumbing day job and then came to work at my house construction project in the evenings and weekends. I was the helper. However, in your case the plumbing cost would be 64 hours x $40/hour or $2,560 for the plumber and 64 hours x $30/hour or $1,920 for the helper. Total labor cost is $2,560 + $1,920 or $4,480. Total labor and material cost for the above ground DWV and water piping is $4,480 (labor) + $252 (DWV piping) + $2,540 (copper water pipe) is $7,272.

$7,272 or $2.43/SF for the above ground rough in plumbing for a 3,000 SF house.

Finish plumbing. Kitchen sink with garbage disposal, all other sinks, kitchen appliances, toilets, showers, bathtubs, laundry room, hot water tank, and hot water recirculation system.

Kitchen sink with garbage disposal. It only takes about 4 hours to install a kitchen sink but to be high to cover unknowns I will use 6 hours. 6 hours will cover one trip to go buy the parts, cut the opening for the sink (if wood/laminate), install the garbage disposal and the faucet on the sink, install the sink, install the angle stops/valves and water supply hoses, and a P-trap drain assembly. 6 hours x $40/hour is $240.

Material costs are: sink $400, kitchen faucet $300, ¾ HP (horsepower) garbage disposal $160, 2 angle stops $16, 2 water supply hoses $20, P-trap assembly $15, and $40 for miscellaneous parts. Total material cost is $951. Total labor and material cost to install a kitchen sink with garbage disposal is $240 + $951 is $1,191.

All other sinks. All other sinks are basically the bathroom sinks and a laundry room sink. These sinks only take 2 hours to install. The scope of work is to install the faucet and drain assembly into the sink, set the sink, install the angle stops, and install the water supply hoses.

I recently installed a sink in my rental house and it took me less than 2 hours to do all this work. 2 hours x $40/hour is $80. Material cost for a bathroom or laundry room utility sink is $250, faucet $160, 2 angle stops/valves $16, 2 water supply hoses $20, P-trap assembly $15, and $10 for miscellaneous parts. Total material costs are $471. Total labor and material cost to install a bathroom or utility room sink is $80 + $471 is $551.

Kitchen appliances. The refrigerator will need a water supply for the ice maker. This water is typically run through ¼" copper tubing. It is connected to one of the ½" cold water pipes in the kitchen. One hour or $40 is all that is needed to do this work because all that need be done is to drill holes in the studs to allow passage for the tubing, install a valve at the cold water pipe, and connect the flex hose to the refrigerator. 50' of ¼" copper tubing costs $45, a ball valve is $8, and the flex hose costs $8. The material cost is $61. Total labor and material cost to install a water supply to a refrigerator is $40 + $61 is $101.

The dishwasher needs a hot water supply and a drain line. I watched my plumber install these items recently at my rental house and it took about 90 minutes which included cutting into an existing hot water line and sweating (soldering) in a tee and a valve. I will allow 2 hours for this work or $80. Material cost is $8 for one ½" ball valve connected at a nearby hot water line. The hot water supply pipe is ½" diameter copper pipe which costs $20 for 10'. Allow 20' for piping which is $40. Allow $10 for fittings and lead free solder. The hose drain assembly that goes from the drain on the dishwasher to the garbage disposal is $15. Total material cost is $73. Total labor and material cost to connect a drain and hot water to a dishwasher is $80 + $73 is $153.

Toilets. The scope of work to install a toilet is to assemble and set the toilet (on the already roughed in toilet hold down ring set in the floor), install an angle valve on the roughed-in water supply, and install the water supply hose to the toilet.

I recently purchased a Kohler toilet for $188 at my local super store. Included in the $188 were the toilet, toilet seat, wax ring, and hold down bolts with trim. It took me 45 minutes to assemble the toilet, install the wax ring, install and bolt down the toilet, install the angle valve and connect the water supply hose and caulk around the base of the toilet. Labor therefore is one hour to install a toilet or $40. An angle valve is $6, and the water supply hose costs $8. Total material cost is $202. Total labor and material cost to install a toilet is $40 + $202 is $242.

Showers. For this estimate I will assume a one piece fiberglass shower corner insert will be installed. The scope of work is to install the shower water control valve, install pipe to the shower head, install the shower insert, install the drain fitting to the already roughed in drain line, and install the shower water control trim and the shower head.

My plumber took about 3 hours to do this work. Therefore, I will allow 4 hours to be high. 4 hours x $40/hour is $160.

If your framing is not square where the shower insert is to be installed then add an allowance of 4 hours for a carpenter to fir out the wall. If the corner where the insert is to be placed is not square then the shower insert will not fit properly. 4 hours for the carpenter x $35/hour is $140. Also add $50 for lumber and nails.

A well known manufacturer of bathroom fixtures and showers has some very nice one piece shower insert modules for $825. Add $150 for the shower water control valve including shower head and $15 for the drain fittings. Add an allowance of $40 for copper pipe, fittings, teflon tape and the total material cost is $1,030. Total labor and material cost to install a shower insert is $160 + $1,030 is $1,190.

Bathtubs. For this estimate I will assume a bathtub without the swirling water features and a shower head. The scope of work is to install the bathtub water control valve assembly (sometimes just a faucet), install copper pipe to a shower head, install the bathtub, install the drain fitting to the already roughed in drain line, install the shower water control trim and the shower head.

My plumber took about 5 hours to do this work. It took awhile because of multiple trips from the second floor to the main floor to work on the water and drain lines beneath the bathtub. I will allow 6 hours. 6 hours x $40/hour is $240.

The super stores have 30" x 60" bathtubs for as low as $240 up to $1,000. I will use $1,000. Add $350 for the bathtub water control valve/faucet, $60 for a shower head and $15 for the drain assembly. Add an allowance of $60 for copper pipe, fittings, teflon tape and the total material cost is $1,485. Total labor and material cost to install a bathtub is $240 + $1,485 is $1,725.

Laundry room. A laundry room will need water and drain for the clothes washer and a utility sink. For a washing machine the only cost would be to install two angle stop/valves on the hot and cold water lines (already roughed in) and install the hoses from the valves to the clothes washer.

Labor to install two angle valves is 15 minutes each. Add another few minutes for connecting the supply hoses and the washer drain hose and labor is actually less than one hour. One hour or $40 to install a clothes washer.

Material cost will only be the 2 angle valves ($16) because the water supply hoses and drain line usually come with the washing machine. Total labor and material cost to install a washing machine is $40 + $16 or $56.

Hot water tank. The scope of work to install a hot water tank is to set the hot water tank, secure it to structure, install valves at the inlet and discharge hot and cold water pipes, and install a ¾" diameter pipe from the relief valve to drain.

Labor to do this work for an electric hot water tank is two hours. 2 hours x $40/hour is $80. If you think this is too light (too few hours) just watch a plumber do this work. They will have it installed in a little more than an hour. Add one additional hour for the gas connection for a gas hot water tank for 3 hours or $120.

A 50 gallon electric hot water tank will cost $340 and a 50 gallon gas hot water tank will cost $430. A one inch brass ball valve costs $15, and 20 feet of 1" copper pipe Type M costs $60. Allow $25 for fittings and lead free solder and the material cost for a 50 gallon electric hot water tank is $440. The material cost for a 50 gallon gas hot water tank is $530.

Total labor and material cost to install a 50 gallon electric hot water tank is $80 + $440 is $520. Total labor and material cost to install a 50 gallon gas hot water tank is $120 + $530 is $650.

Hot water recirculation system. Hot water recirculation systems are installed to cut down on the time for hot water to reach a sink. Without a hot water recirculation system sinks that are a long way away from the hot water tank will have to wait a minute or two for the hot water from the tank to reach the faucet. This can prove to be very irritating. Fortunately the solution is really quite inexpensive.

The principal behind a hot water recirculation system is to have a small pump with low flow and low pressure circulate the hot water through a return pipe connected to the hot water supply pipe at the farthest points of the house and run the return line back to the hot water tank. The hot water then just slowly circulates through the hot water supply and return pipe so the water in the supply pipe is always hot. When the homeowner opens a faucet there is hot water immediately available.

We installed a Lang recirculation pump and it cost $120 with two ½" diameter ball valves at $8 each or $16. The length of ½" diameter pipe depends on how long a run of pipe there is. I will select 80' because that is how long the return pipe is on my recirculation system. At $20 for a 10' long pipe then 8 pieces of pipe x $20 each is $160. Add $60 for fittings, extra pipe and solder. The total material cost is $356.

It would take about an hour to install the pump and valves. I would allow 8 hours for a plumber to install the 80' of ½" diameter pipe through the joists and floors to the farthest point of the hot water main because sometimes it is difficult to snake the pipe through. 9 hours x $40/hour is $360. Total labor and material cost to install an 80' long copper pipe with a recirculation pump is $360 + $356 is $716.

12. Heating Ventilating and Air Conditioning (HVAC). Heating and ventilating is basically our furnaces with the ductwork needed to convey the conditioned air (heating or cooling) to the registers or vents. Ventilating is also the exhaust fans that are needed in bathrooms and the whole house fan.

It cost us $12,400 to have two gas fired furnaces installed in our house. We had a furnace in the basement to feed the first floor and a furnace in the attic to feed the second floor. The reason I did not have just one is because the common ductwork would have connected the house and allowed sound from the main floor to be heard in the bedrooms. This price included the whole house fan, the ductwork, and the wiring to make it work. That is $4.13/SF for our 3,000 SF house back in 1992.

A furnace will cost in the range of $2,000 to $5,000 installed. An air conditioning unit will also cost that amount. Ductwork will cost about $10/LF to be fabricated and installed in your house. Estimate 100' of ductwork or $1,000. A whole house fan will cost about $350 and 3 hours labor to install and wire or $120 for a total of $470. Add another $1,000 for fittings, registers, vents, and flexible hose. Don't forget to add the cost of a 240V circuit or

$370 (from section 13). The total cost for HVAC is $5,000 (furnace) + $1,000 (ductwork) + $470 (whole house fan) + $370 (power) + $1,000 (registers and parts) or $7,840.

$7,840 or $2.61/SF for one furnace and ductwork in a 3,000 SF house.

13. Electrical and Communications. Detailed costs; electrical panel, dedicated 120V outlet for a microwave or furnace, 6 outlets on one circuit, light switch, light, stove, electric clothes dryer, air conditioning compressor, hot water heater, telephone/data outlet. It cost $16,000 to have our new house and garage wired (material and labor) by an electrical contractor. $16,000 divided by 3,500 SF is $4.57/SF.

I have recently discussed pricing for construction projects with home electrical contractors and the pricing varies from a low of $3/SF to a high of $8/SF depending on both the size of the house and the company doing the work. I will use the higher number here for estimating and budgeting purposes.

The scope of work is to have a new house wired per the code and have Category 5 telephone wire installed. The budgeting range for wiring is $3/SF x 3,000 SF is $9,000 to $8/SF x 3,000 SF is $24,000.

$24,000 or $8.00/SF to wire a new 3,000 SF house.

Detailed costs; electrical panel, dedicated 120V outlet for a microwave or furnace, 6 outlets on one circuit, light switch, light, stove, electric clothes dryer, air conditioning compressor, hot water heater, telephone/data outlet.

Electrical panel. I recently had the old glass fuse style changed out to new modern 200 amp panel in one of my rental houses. There were two men for one day or 16 hours of labor. Material cost of a 200 amp panel with 16 circuit breakers, grounding wire, and small parts was approximately $400. A new 200 amp electrical panel cost $1,485.

Dedicated 120V outlet for a microwave or furnace, 6 outlets on one circuit. The cost of a 120 volt outlet will depend on if it is one outlet at the end of a long run or if it is just one of many outlets on a particular circuit. However, the highest cost will be a dedicated 120V outlet (aka receptacle) such as is required for a microwave. The outlet box, outlet and cover will all cost less than $5. The wire used to wire 20 amp circuits in a house is 12/2 wire. This means there are three #12 gauge wires in the electrical cord. One is colored black for the hot 120V from the circuit breaker, one white for the neutral lead, and one ground wire. The super store price for 250 feet of 12/2 wire is $80 or 32 cents per foot. A really long dedicated circuit will take 100' of wire. 100' x 32 cents per foot is $32 for wire. Total material cost is $32 + $5 or $37. The labor to run a circuit 100' is 2 men 2 hours each or 4 hours of labor. 4 hours x $40/hour is $160. Total labor and material cost to install is $160 + $37 or $197 for a dedicated 120V outlet.

If there are 6 outlets on one circuit that would add another 2 hours of labor or $80 + $25 for material. $197 + $80 + $25 is $302 for the 6 outlets or $50.33 per outlet.

Light switch. A light switch box, switch and cover will cost $5. The wire run will be short because it is going to control some light or device. If I use 30 feet of wire that is 30' x 32 cents per foot is $10. Labor is 30 minutes or $20 to drill the studs, pull the wire, wire the switch, and install the cover plate. Total labor and material is $20 + $15 or $35 for a light switch.

Light. A light will consist of the light, the light box to land the wires, and the wire. Lights vary in cost so I will use $50 for a light fixture. Adjust the cost for your project depending on the fight fixture you select. Use 50' of wire x 32 cents per foot is $16 for wire. Labor will be one hour to install the fixture the wire and connect the light or $40. Total labor and material cost is $40 + $66 or $104 for a light fixture.

Stove, electric clothes dryer, air conditioning compressor, hot water heater. These devices require 240V which means running two hot 120V wires plus a neutral wire plus a ground. The worst case is a 60 amp load which would require 6/3 wire which is three #6 wires and a ground. There would be a red and a black for the hot 120V, white for neutral and copper for ground. This wire could cost as much as $1.20 per foot at the super stores. Use 100' for the length and the cost of the wire is $120. Add $10 for an outlet box, the outlet and cover plate. The total material cost is $130. Since #6 wire is harder to handle I will use 2 men 3 hours each or 6 hours or $240 of labor to run one of these circuits. Total labor and material cost is $240 + $130 or $370 to run one 240V 60 amp circuit.

Telephone/data outlet. Telephone and data lines use wire called category 5e (aka Cat 5 wire) which is basically a number of twisted wire pairs. The super store price for 1000' of category 5e wire is $90 or 9 cents per foot. Use 100' of wire for an outlet x 9 cents per foot is $9. Add $15 for the box and telephone/data connectors and the material cost is $24. Labor is one hour per box or $40. Total labor and material is $40 + $24 or $64 per box.
Telephone and data systems will require a control box. The phone company usually provides the control box and it is mounted on the outside of the house. However, most data systems are owner provided so add $750 for material cost and 2 hours or $80 to provide, install and wire the control box for a total of $830.

14. Concrete flatwork; sidewalks, driveways, patios. Concrete flatwork is our driveways, patios, and sidewalks. The concrete is just the standard 3,000 psi mix that is purchased from a concrete supply company. The typical thickness of flatwork is 4 inches.
The scope of work is to grade and compact the area, set the forms, install expansion strips, place and finish the concrete. The cost of the grade and compact will have to be determined by the homeowner from the information in section 2. This section will be just the formwork, expansion strips, place and finish the concrete.
I will do two examples; a 4' wide x 10' long sidewalk and a 10' wide x 40' long driveway. A patio will cost the same as a driveway

Sidewalk, 4' wide x 10' long. Forms for sidewalks are typically 2 x 4's or long strips of plywood. A 10' long 2 x 4 will cost about $5. Three 2 x 4's are required. Two will be used on the long sides and one will be cut to form the ends. 3 each x $5 is $15 for forms. Expansion strips are placed about every 10' in a sidewalk and they cost about $5 each or $10 for two; one at each end of the 10' long sidewalk. I do not show a cost for stakes to brace the forms because they will already be owned by the concrete company. The volume of concrete is 4' wide x 10' long x 4"/12" thick concrete sidewalk is 13.34 cubic feet. Divide by 27 cubic feet per cubic yard and .5 CY (one half of a cubic yard) of concrete is needed.

Small loads are very expensive because the larger concrete companies must add surcharges and trip fees for this small a load of concrete. I have found a small company in Seattle that delivers small loads but they are not cheap either. Budget $200 for this half a CY of concrete.

Labor to form, install the expansion joints, place and level the concrete, and then finish the concrete for this size sidewalk is 8 hours for one concrete finsiher. It will look like less than this but there will be time to set the forms and then wait time for the concrete truck to arrive. Placing and leveling the concrete for a 10' sidewalk will be done in about 30 minutes. Then the concrete finisher will begin to float the concrete to smooth it out. Then there is wait time for the concrete to set up. The first phase after floating it level is to wait until water comes out of the concrete and then is absorbed back in. Once that happens then the concrete must be worked by hand with concrete finishing tools to get the concrete to take a uniform look and flat surface. Once that is done the concrete must set some more to harden a little more and then a broom will be lightly pulled across the surface to give it a rough surface so people do not slip on the sidewalk when it is finished and covered with rainwater. Then the concrete is allowed to cure for a few days and the concrete finisher must come back and strip the forms. 8 hours is a minimum for a 4' wide x 10' long sidewalk. 8 hours x $34/hour is $272.

Total labor and material cost is $272 (labor) + 25 (forms) + $200 (concrete) or $497 for 4' wide x 10' long sidewalk or $497 divided by 40 SF is $12.45 per SF for sidewalk.

Driveway, 10' wide x 40' long. The driveway will be formed up a little differently than a sidewalk. The driveway will be formed in sections typically in 10' x 10' sections. Imagine the 40' long driveway in 10' squares and numbered from 1 to 4. The first and the third would be formed and concrete placed and finished first. A day or two would go by and then the remaining two would be poured. The first two sections poured would act as forms for the remaining two. This is because you do not want one long continuous 40' section of concrete driveway because it would crack very badly.

Forms for the driveway would also be 2 x 4's or long strip of plywood. A 10' long 2 x 4 will cost about $5. 8 each 2 x 4's would be required for the first two pours and then they would be stripped and reused for the second two pours where needed. 8 each x $5 is $40 for forms. Expansion strips could be placed between each section and a cost of $40 would be a good budget. I do not show a cost for stakes to brace the forms because they will already be owned by the concrete company. The volume of concrete for a 10' wide x 40' long x 4"/12" thick concrete driveway is 133.34 cubic feet. Divide by 27 cubic feet per cubic yard and 4.94 or 5 CY of concrete is needed.

5 CY of concrete is still considered a small load by some concrete supply companies and others give the homeowner a better rate for 3 CY or more. I will use a cost of $150 per CY of concrete or 5 CY x $150/CY or $750 for concrete.

Labor to form, install the expansion joints, place and level the concrete, and then finish the concrete with several trips is 24 hours for at least two concrete finishers. 24 hours x $34/hour is $816.

Total labor and material cost is $816 (labor) + $80 (forms) + $750 (concrete) or $1,646 for 10' wide x 40' long driveway or $1,646 divided by 400 SF is $4.12 per SF for a driveway or patio.

15. Decks. The deck cost here is for a basic deck that is attached to an entrance or wraps around a house.

Decks have an outside framework made up typically of 4" x 6" wood beams with interior 2x4 stringers at 16" on center to support the decking material. The wood beams are supported off the ground by steel support brackets with a wooden post set in a concrete block.

Often the material is made from treated wood but not always. The reason for this is in areas like Seattle where I do not have a lot of bug problems I can just use pine or fir and coat is with a good water sealer. The pricing here is with pine/fir wood covered with a wood sealer. The decking material is 2" x 4" clear cedar. Also purchased were 4 three step precut stair risers.

I recently had an 8' wide x 8' deck built with the above materials. A 4"x 6" x 8' long Douglas fir wood beam costs $18. There were 4 each or 4 x $18 is $72. There were 5 interior 2" x 4"s at 8' each that were cut down a little. These cost $6 each or a total of $30. The steel support bracket and concrete post cost $10 each and since there were 4 of them the total is $40. The stair risers cost $25 each or $100 for the 4. The clear cedar 2x4x8' decking cost $17 each. There were 26 of them or 26 x $17 each is $442. Add $60 for nails, hangers, sealer and stain and the total material cost is $72 + $30 + $40 + $100 + $442 + $60 = $744. I hired a carpenter who finished the job in 12 hours but I had agreed on 16 hours. Therefore, the labor cost was 16 hours x $35/hour is $560. Total cost is $744 + $560 = $1,304. Divide this value by 64 SF and the unit cost is $20.38/SF. This is a good number to use for a small deck. However, $15/SF is a more reasonable number to use if the deck is 200 SF or more.

$1,304 or $20.38/SF for a 64 SF deck. Use $15/SF for a 200 SF or larger decks due to economy of scale.

Chapter 16- Lessons Learned from Homeowners

Situation 1: Planning for a kitchen remodel
      Lesson learned #1-Do not hire a designer before deciding what you want
      Lesson learned #2-Do not remove scope of work to reduce cost of project
      Lesson learned #3-Get pricing from 6 to 10 contractors
      Lesson learned #4-Homeowner's mistaken feelings of trust
      Lesson learned #5-Homeowner's mistaken feelings of obligation
      Lesson learned #6-Homeowner not wanting to hurt the contractor's feelings
      Lesson learned #7-Homeowner is afraid to say "No, I will not use you on this project!"
Situation 2: Work on a backyard garden structure
      Lesson learned #8- Do not pay the contractor until project is complete
      Lesson learned #9- Do not give contractor any money to buy materials
      Lesson learned #10-Homeowner mistakenly concerned about being fair to the contractor
      Lesson learned #11-Trust in the Pat Fay Method

Chapter 16- Lessons Learned from Homeowners

Situation 1: Planning for a kitchen remodel. In situation one I assisted a married couple in their planning, preliminary design, as well as, analysis of one contractor's bid proposal. The husband of this couple attended one of my evening classes on how to manage your home remodel without a general contractor. The wife did not attend.

    After the husband attended my class he and his wife did some planning and preliminary design. Before they completed this process and before I came into the picture the husband hired a design build general construction company to produce a set of kitchen remodel drawings for $500. The wife recommended against doing this because they had not yet decided on what exactly to do.

    He ignored her objection and signed a contract with the design build company for the kitchen remodel design. I looked at the drawings and they were not very good. However, they were adequate if that design build contractor were to get the work. They were totally inadequate for bidding out the project to other contractors because they had poor detail with few dimensions.

    The company also provided a cost proposal of $76,000 to do the kitchen remodel and wall removal work. The scope of work was to remove the old cabinets, sink, and appliances. The appliances would be stored in the owner's garage and be reused. The refrigerator was to be moved to a new location and a new microwave installed. The sink would be reinstalled in the same location thereby limiting the amount of plumbing work required. The appliance location change required new electrical outlets to be installed at the new locations of the microwave and refrigerator. An island cabinet would also be installed as a cooking prep area with no sink. An existing wall separating the kitchen from the living room would be removed and the sheetrock would be repaired and the whole area repainted. My estimate to do this work was in the $30,000 to $40,000 range, depending on the quality of the new cabinets.

    My role with this couple was to assist them in the process but they would be in charge. My role was completely advisory and uncompensated. My fee for my time was witnessing how a typical, middle class, well educated couple approached, planned, dealt with contractors and construction, and most importantly how they thought.

Lesson learned #1-Do not hire a designer before deciding what you want. During our meetings it was clear that the couple had not yet decided on the actual scope of work or the floor plan modifications they wanted. I asked why a design build company had been hired if they were undecided on the scope of work. The husband stated that he felt it would be useful in his planning process. The wife stated that she had not wanted to hire the company.

After meeting with this couple for several months it was clear that they would have to have the design work redone once they decided on their final revised scope of work.

The lesson to be learned is that the homeowner who follows the Pat Fay Method must not hire an architect or designer until they have decided on their basic scope of work and floor plan modifications. There can even be two to three options but the homeowner must know what they want.

This is the homeowner's responsibility. The homeowner can spend all the time they want on different options, however, do not spend money on a designer or architect until the homeowner has decided what they want. Otherwise it is money wasted.

Lesson learned #2-Do not remove scope of work to reduce cost of project. The homeowners received a price proposal for $76,000 from the design build firm who did their design drawings. I reviewed the proposal and then asked the homeowners what they thought of the proposal and what were they planning to do?

They replied that they did not want to spend that much money. Now a very interesting thing happened in their thought process. The first thing they thought of to do was to reduce the scope of work so the price would come down! They even started to make a list of all the things they could live without!

I stopped them and we had a discussion about why the first thing they started with was removing scope of work. I pointed out that they only had one price from one contractor and in the Pat Fay Method the homeowner is to have from six to ten prices from as many contractors. The homeowner really had no idea whether the $76,000 was a good price or not.

Lesson learned #3-Get pricing from 6 to 10 contractors. I also pointed out that the three-page price proposal from their contractor looked reasonable when one looked at each individual line separately. However, the overall price of $76,000 was about double what my estimate was.

This is a very common problem in home construction when the contractor knows they have no competition! They will list everything they can on a proposal relying on the inexperience and naiveté of the homeowner. If the contractor knew they were competing against other contractors their price would have been much lower and not every item that could be imagined listed on their price proposal.

Therefore, their best first move was to get 6 to 10 other contractors to give them a price proposal for the same work.

Lesson learned #4-Homeowner's mistaken feelings of trust. A second very interesting statement occurred when I suggested getting pricing from six to ten contractors; the husband said, "Oh no, we don't need to do that. We trust this builder. We saw his other work and it was excellent. We really feel that he is trying to do a good job for us and we want to work with him".

I pointed out that there was no basis for trust between the homeowner and the contractor because the two had not worked together before. The small amount of interaction they had had with the contractor could not be construed as prior experience. Therefore, there was no basis for trust.

However, the homeowner wanted to trust the contractor. Pat Fay believes there is a human trait problem occurring when a homeowner deals in an unknown subject and activity and a contractor comes along who says reassuring things of how they will help the homeowner. This, for some reason, deludes the homeowner into wanting to use the unknown contractor even if their price is too high.

Lesson learned #5-Homeowner's mistaken feelings of obligation. I then asked why they would feel trust for a contractor when my estimate for the exact same work was about $40,000 less than the contractor's? The husband then stated that he felt an obligation to work with this contractor because he was working with them.

I asked the husband to clarify what he meant when he said the contractor was working with them? He stated that the contractor had spent all this time making their drawing and generating a cost proposal for them.

I reminded him that he and his wife had paid $500 for the drawing and that since they had paid that fee there was no further obligation. As far as the price proposal was concerned, they had no obligation to the contractor because making price proposals is what contractor's do and it is just a cost of doing business.

A false sense of obligation is a pitfall that all homeowners must be aware of and take mental steps to harden themselves to not feel an obligation to any contractor just because they have provided a drawing or a cost proposal.

The homeowner has no obligation to hire any contractor unless the contractor will work according to what the homeowner wants and for a price that is acceptable to the homeowner.

Lesson learned #6-Homeowner not wanting to hurt the contractor's feelings. I have thought long and hard on what I learned from these normal, thoughtful, kind, well educated, middle class homeowners. My conclusion is that the normal homeowner worries that they will hurt a contractor's feelings if they do not hire them.

I conclude this based on my months with this middle class American family, as well as listening to the experiences of hundreds of homeowners who have attended my classes. They evaluate home construction contractors based on how they interact with their friends and associates. However, to apply the same feelings and concerns to home construction contractors is a grave mistake.

The contractors the homeowner deals with are first and foremost businessmen. In fact, they are ruthless businessmen who will not smile on the job the way they did sitting across the kitchen table from the homeowner before they got a contract. They will think nothing of the feelings of the homeowner when it gets time to complete the work and get on to the next job.

Therefore, in the Pat Fay Method, the homeowner must not have mistaken feelings of trust, obligation, or a mistaken concern that they may hurt a contractor's feelings. This is business. The homeowner must act and conduct themselves as hard nosed business people with their number one concern being the completion of their home construction project on time and within budget. The homeowner can be polite, easy to speak to and deal with, but the homeowner must not be concerned about the contractor's feelings.

Lesson learned #7-Homeowner is afraid to say "No, I will not use you on this project!" Another thing the homeowner must learn is how to tell a contractor that you will not be using them on their project. The reasons will be many. For example, the pricing is too high, the contractor cannot get started soon enough, they will not sign your contract or your addendum per the Pat Fay Method or it may be as simple as you do not like them.

Whatever the reason the homeowner's has a right to pick whomever they want to work on their project.

If the homeowner is hesitant to look the contractor in the eye over the kitchen table and say, "no, I will not use you on this project" then say it over the telephone. Or just never call them back. If the contractor does get the homeowner on the phone and complains that they spent a lot of time preparing price proposals just be truthful and state that you decided not to use them because they were just too expensive. Also, tell them that preparing price proposals is a cost of their doing business. Then wish them good luck, say goodbye, and hang up.

Situation 2: Work on a backyard garden structure. In situation 2, I assisted a close personal friend, Mary, in her planning phase and while she was hiring a contractor to build a garden structure in her backyard garden.

The scope of work was to go to the lumber store, buy the materials, deliver them to her backyard, seal the ends of posts with sealer, install four posts into the ground in concrete, install cross bars both directions at the top (to give shade), and wrap the posts in cedar.

The contractor had worked previously for an acquaintance of hers. Mary had been told he had done a good job. The contractor was a sole proprietor contractor. Basically, a 40 year old man with a pickup truck and carpenter tools. When I met him I assessed him as a hard luck character but probably a skilled carpenter. He had previously told Mary that he worked for $20 per hour. However, on this project he would have to give her a lump sum fixed price bid.

Mary asked me how much the project should cost. I did a cost estimate and concluded that the material cost was approximately $600. The posts were to be 6" x 6" x 10' long and they would be very difficult for one person to handle. I told her that 2 men would be needed for the job (which the contractor later confirmed). I estimated two men two days or 32 hours would be a reasonable time to work the project. The price to pay at $20 per hour for 32 hours would be $640. However, since I was not involved in the negotiations I told Mary not to agree to any more than two men for three days or 48 hours of labor. At $20 per hour for 48 hours would be $960. She ignored me and agreed to the contractor's price of $1,200.

The contractor asked for the $600 so he could buy the materials plus 50% of the $1200 up front. I told her not to pay any of the $1200 until the project was complete because in the Pat Fay Method we pay for completed work not partially completed work.

She later told me what happened. She did give the contractor $600 in cash to buy the materials and agreed to pay $400 of the labor at the end of the first workday. The contractor took the $600, went to the lumber store, bought all of the materials, delivered them to her back yard, dug the 4 post holes, installed the posts with braces, and mixed and placed the concrete. They then quit for the day while the concrete set up overnight.

Mary paid the contractor $400 in cash for their labor for the day. He told Mary he and his assistant would be back tomorrow morning at 8 AM. The contractor left with a smile and a wave and a parting promise to be back bright and early the next morning.

An hour passed and Mary noticed the top of the posts were not at the same height. She called me and I came over to inspect the work. I found that three of the posts would have to be trimmed off at the top to be level. That is pretty typical though because the contractor will want to wait until the second day to do this after the concrete sets. However, the posts were in perfectly level in both directions, the posts were installed per the drawings, and they had cleaned up the site before leaving. I concluded these men were good carpenters based on their workmanship.

Mary wanted to be sure that they knew about the posts having to be trimmed off. She had the carpenter's cell phone number so she called him. I listened in on the extension. He answered the phone and it was immediately obvious from the background noise that he was in a bar. He said he was planning to trim the posts off and not to worry. See you in the morning. He never showed up again!

Lesson learned #8- Do not pay the contractor until project is complete. In the Pat Fay Method, the homeowner does not want to make partial payments to the contractor. This is because the homeowner wants a completed project. When one reads through this entire book it is easy to see the only real leverage the homeowner has with contractors is the power of money. Do not give your only power away before the project is complete!

This contractor was a good carpenter and I believe he would have finished this project in one more full day of work. He then would have received an additional $800 in fee. However, he could not avoid going to the bar once he had $400 burning a hole in his pocket. It is sort of a sorry situation when one steps back and thinks about it. However, my concern is with homeowners and how to prevent the situation where a homeowner is left with a pile of lumber and no contractor to install it.

If Mary had refused to pay the contractor any partial payment and used the carrot of full payment once the work was completed her project would have been completed in one more day.

Lesson learned #9- Do not give contractor any money to buy materials. Mary made another mistake that could have gone bad. This was handing the contractor $600 in cash to buy the materials for her job.

This contractor could just as easily driven off and never returned and would have been $600 richer. Mary was just lucky.

In the Pat Fay Method, there are two reasons why we do not give money to the contractor to buy the material for your project. First, if the contractor cannot come up with $500 to $5000 to buy the materials to build your project then they are a financially unstable company. If the contractor has no financial resources to buy the materials then the chances are the money the homeowner gives to the contractor to buy materials will go to finish another project, make a truck payment, buy a gift for their girlfriend or go to the bar.

The second reason why the homeowner wants the contractor to buy or provide the materials is because this is their bond (see contractor chapter 11). In the home construction world there is no bonding of the contractors. In the Pat Fay Method the way we get a bond from the contractor is to have them invest their money in the material. Their bond is their financial investment in the homeowner's project so they can earn the fee they are charging.

In this situation the contractor should have been required to buy $600 in material thereby providing a $600 bond to gain a fee of twice that amount or $1200. The contractor would have gotten his $600 back when the final payment was made.

Lesson learned #10-Homeowner mistakenly concerned about being fair to the contractor. I discussed this situation with Mary and told her she was really not in such bad shape. She had received about $400 in labor from the contractor and the contractor had not skipped with her $600 in cash but had actually purchased and delivered the material needed to build her garden structure. The only thing she was out was a completed project. She just had to find another carpenter to finish the work.

Once she realized that she had not really lost any money she calmed down and we discussed what she had been thinking during her negotiations with the contractor. I asked why she had decided to ignore my advice about not paying the contractor any money until he completed her project.

She told me that she thought the Pat Fay Method was unfair to the contractor. She felt that this nice young man should have a partial payment at the end of the day because he had worked so hard on her project. She felt that he deserved it.

I then asked her how she felt now that the contractor had taken her partial payment and left her with a pile of lumber? She said she hated him. What would she do the next time I asked? Mary said, "I'm following the Pat Fay Method next time. I'm mad at that contractor. I'm very angry. He lied to me! He should not have treated me that way. He hurt my feelings and he embarrassed me! Next time I won't care about being fair to the contractor. The contractor can work according to my terms. Period! If they don't like it, I'll tell them I'll find someone else!"

Lesson learned #11-Trust in the Pat Fay Method. The overall lesson to be learned in both situation 1 and 2 is to trust in the Pat Fay Method. The homeowner who follows the Pat Fay Method will win in their home construction project. The homeowners that follow the contractor method will lose.

Chapter 17-Summary of the Advantages and Disadvantages of the Pat Fay Method

Advantages
- Cost savings
- Reduced stress
- Better quality material and workmanship

Disadvantages
- Planning and scheduling
- Coordination
- Time
- Length of construction

To use the Pat Fay Method or not?

Chapter 17-Summary of the Advantages and Disadvantages of the Pat Fay Method

Advantages. The chapters of this book cover the many reasons why the homeowner is better off managing their home remodel or new construction project themselves rather than having a general contractor do it for them. This chapter summarizes the major advantages and disadvantages to help the homeowner decide whether it is worth the extra effort by the homeowner to use the Pat Fay Method in managing the construction of their home construction project.

Cost savings. The number one advantage of the Pat Fay Method is that the homeowner can significantly reduce the cost of their project. By following the Pat Fay Method the homeowner can remodel or build for about $100 per square foot (SF) or less.

The general contractors of America will typically quote a price of about $150 per SF to do a typical remodel or new construction project. However, by the time the project is complete the actual cost will be closer to $200 per SF due to change orders and other innumerable unexplained reasons.

Then there are the high end general contractors who will tell the uninformed homeowner that to have any kind of quality they need to spend at least $250 per SF.

One of the reasons I wrote this book is because I hate to see good people pay too much for their home construction projects. There is just no good reason for middle class American families to have to pay the high prices for home construction that are being charged by the general contractors of America.

Why give a general contractor too much of your money when you can manage the process yourself for about $100 per square foot? Follow the Pat Fay Method and you won't have to.

Reduced stress. Pat Fay contends and teaches that hiring a general contractor is very stressful. The general consensus is that when the homeowner hires a general contractor they will take care of all the details for you and the process is easy and stress free. I disagree. The constant request for additional money and statements that this or that part of the work was not included in the cost will cause the homeowner more stress than if they took care of the whole process themselves.

Fighting with a general contractor over the quality of materials and workmanship will be a constant source of stress. This is why it is less stressful to manage the whole process yourself without a general contractor than to put up with the stress of dealing with the typical general contractor.

Better quality material and workmanship. By following the Pat Fay Method the homeowner can require that the best materials be used because they are willing to pay for that value. Once you hire a general contractor for a fixed price they will constantly try to build with the cheapest materials they can find because whatever they save on material costs will be extra profit for them.

The quality of the workmanship can also be better by following the Pat Fay Method than with a general contractor because the homeowner will only hire experts in their phase of construction, pay them very well for their skill, and still pay far less than a general contractor will charge the homeowner.

The general contractor will hire the contractors with the lowest price they can find to install the materials so that they save on the total cost of each craft. This then increases the general contractor's profit by reducing the quality of the product, which is ultimately to the homeowner's detriment.

Disadvantages. There are disadvantages to the Pat Fay Method, but they are manageable. The homeowner should know what the Pat Fay Method requires before they embark on managing a home construction project themselves.

Most homeowners have more time than they have money. Typically the only thing holding the homeowner back from managing their project themselves is knowledge and experience.

The disadvantages listed are all things that the typical homeowner is more than capable of handling themselves. This book provides the technical information that will help the homeowner overcome a lack of experience and industry-specific knowledge, which is the greatest obstacle to managing their own project.

This book shares Pat Fay's decades of experience in the construction industry with the homeowners of America. With this book, the homeowner has the experience and knowledge with which to save more money than they thought possible on their remodel or new construction project. It is not just possible; it is very doable.

Planning and scheduling. The homeowner must be responsible for planning what they will have built, when they will have it built, what quality they are willing to accept, and to schedule it in the correct sequence.

The chapters on planning and scheduling will greatly assist the homeowner in these endeavors. Now that it is written down in black and white and in plain English the homeowner does not need to rely on general contractors to do this work for them. However, the homeowner must commit to planning and scheduling the project, which requires time, energy and patience.

Coordination. Coordinating all the different contractors is not easy but it is manageable. This is part of the work that will now fall on the homeowner's shoulders instead of the general contractor's.

Remember in the Pat Fay Method we reduce stress and problems by having only one contractor on site at a time. You will find that this is a good rule to follow. Also, with adequate planning and good project management skills, you will reduce the burden of this responsibility.

Time. The homeowner will have to spend a lot more time managing their project without a general contractor. This is only logical though, isn't it? If the homeowner is willing to save a lot of money then they should be willing to spend something to gain it.

In home construction the currency needed to save money is time. The homeowner exchanges their time for their savings of tens of thousands to hundreds of thousands of dollars on their remodels and new construction.

It is true that not all homeowners are willing to spend their time doing this activity. That is their decision to make.

For those that want to save serious money and have better quality materials and construction the Pat Fay Method is just what they need.

Length of Construction. The time needed to complete a construction project is longer when a homeowner manages their own project than if they hired a general contractor. This is because the homeowner will have to find the contractors themselves, coordinate with them as well as the building inspector, and pick and choose the materials they want in their home.

To use the Pat Fay Method or not? This is the question each homeowner must answer for themselves. The advantages of the Pat Fay Method far outweigh the disadvantages because the cost of hiring a general contractor to manage the homeowner's remodel or new construction project is just too high.

The financial cost savings are so large and significant that it is easy to overlook the value of reduced stress on the homeowner's mind and attitude. To me this reduction in overall stress experienced by following the Pat Fay Method is the number one reason why the homeowner should manage their home construction project themselves.

The normal homeowner is more than capable of coordinating and managing their home construction projects if they just know what to do, when to do it, how to do it, and what the rules are. Now you know because you have the Pat Fay Method to guide you.

I hope you find this book to be what you need to successfully manage your home remodel or new construction project yourself without a general contractor, to save serious money and still stay married.

Chapter 18-Contractor Licensing and Control by State

The homeowner will find each state's contractor licensing requirements in the following pages. Listed are phone numbers, websites, mailing address and notes. Some states require contractors to be licensed and some do not. It should be noted that all states require contractors to be registered as a business. This is because each state wants their tax revenue.

The homeowner that follows the Pat Fay Method must protect themselves against unethical contractors whether they are licensed or not. Obtaining a license typically consists of passing a skills test and paying a fee. Being licensed by a state is no guarantee that a contractor is ethical. Screen all contractors, licensed or not, per the Pat Fay Method.

Alabama. 800-304-0853, 334-242-2230, 'www.hblb.state.al.us, Home Builders Licensure Board, 400 S Union St, STE 195, Montgomery, AL 36130-3605. Note: Alabama licenses general contractors, electricians, plumbers, and HVAC contractors.

Alaska 907-465-4508, 'www.dced.state.ak.us/occ/pcon.htm, Alaska Contractor Licensing Board, PO Box 110806, Juneau, AK 99811-0806. Note: in Alaska all construction contactors need a license.

Arizona 602-542-1525, 'www.rc.state.az.us/, Industrial Commission Bldg, 800 W Washington St, Phoenix, AZ 85007. Note: In Arizona all construction contractors need a license.

Arkansas 501-372-4661, 'www.arkansas.gov/clb/, State of Arkansas Contractor's Licensing Board, 4100 Richards Rd, North Little Rock, AR 72117. In Arkansas all construction contractors need a license.

California 800-321-2752, 'wwww.cslb.ca.gov/, Contractors State License Board, 9821 Business Park Dr, Sacramento, CA 95826. Note: In California all construction contractors need a license.

Colorado 303-894-7855, 'www,dora.state.co.us/, Colorado Dept. of Regulatory Agencies, 1560 Broadway, STE 1550, Denver, CO 80202. Note: Colorado requires plumbers and electricians to be licensed.

Connecticut 860-713-6050, 'www.ct.gov/dcp/site/, Department of Consumer Protection License Services Division, 165 Capitol Ave, Hartford, CT 06106-1630. Note: In Connecticut all construction contractors need a license.

Delaware 302-577-8200, 'http://www.state.de.us/revenue/, Division of Revenue, State of Delaware, 800 N French St, Wilmington, DE 19801. Note: Delaware requires plumbers and electricians to be licensed.

Florida 850-487-1395, 'http://www.myflorida.com/dbpr/pro/cilb/cilb_index.shtml, Department of Business and Professional Regulation, 1940 N Monroe St, Tallahassee, FL 32399-1039. Note: Florida licenses all contractors. It is a felony in Florida to do home construction work without a contractor's license.

Georgia 478-207-1300, 'http://www.sos.state.ga.us/plb/, Georgia Professional Licensing Boards Division, 237 Coliseum Dr, Macon, GA 31217-3858. Note: Georgia started licensing requirements for home construction contractors in 2005.

Hawaii 808-586-3000, 'http://www.hawaii.gov/dcca/areas/pvl/boards/contractor/, Department of Commerce and Consumer Affairs-PVL, Att: CLB, PO Box 3469, Honolulu, HI 96801. Note: In Hawaii all construction contractors need a license.

Idaho 208-334-3233, 'https://www.ibol.idaho.gov/, Idaho Bureau of Occupational Licenses, 1109 Main St, STE 220, Boise, ID 83702-5642. Note: Idaho licenses plumbers and electricians.

Illinois 217-785-0800, 'http://www.ildpr.com/, Department of Financial and Professional Regulation, 320 West Washington, Springfield, IL 62786. Roofing contractors need to be licensed in Illinois.

Indiana 317-234-3022, 'http://www.in.gov/pla/, Indiana Professional Licensing Agency, Indiana Government CTR S, W072, 402 W Washington St, Indianapolis, IN 46204. Note: Indiana requires plumber to have a license.

Iowa 800-562-4692, 515-281-5387, 'http://www.iowaworkforce.org/labor/contractor.htm, Iowa Workforce Development, 1000 E Grand Ave, Des Moines, IA 50319-0209. Note: Plumbers and electricians are licensed at the local level.

Kansas Note: Kansas has no State Contractor Licensing Agency. The homeowner must contact the local county clerk for information.

Kentucky 502-573-0365, 'http://hbc.ppr.ky.gov/, Kentucky Office of Housing, Buildings and Construction, 101 Sea Hero Rd, STE 100, Frankfort, KY 40601. Note: Kentucky licenses plumbers, electricians, and HVAC contractors.

Louisiana 225-765-2301, 'http://www.lslbc.louisiana.gov/, Louisiana State Licensing Board for Contractors, PO Box 14419, Baton Rouge, LA 70898. Louisiana licenses plumbers and all residential building contractors. **Note:** The State of Louisiana does not allow homeowners to act as their own general contractor. By law residents must hire a licensed general contractor to build their entire project. The only exception is if the homeowner states they will personally install all the construction work.

Maine 207-624-8603, 'http://www.state.me.us/pfr/olr/index.htm, Maine Office of Licensing & Registration, #35 State House Station, Augusta, ME 04333-0035. Note: Maine requires plumbers and electricians to be licensed.

Maryland 888-218-5925, 410-230-6309, 'www.dllr.state.md.us/license/occprof/homeim.html, Department of Labor, Licensing & Regulation, 500 North Calvert St, Baltimore, MD

21202-3651. Note: Maryland licenses home improvement contractors, electricians, plumbers, and HVAC.

Massachusetts 617-727-3200, 'http://www.mass.gov/bbrs/, Massachusetts State Board of Building Regulations and Standards, McCormack State Office Building, One Ashburton Pl, Rm 1301, Boston, MA 02108. Note: Massachusetts licenses plumbers, electricians and all home improvement contractors.

Michigan 517-241-9280,'http://www.michigan.gov/cis/0,1607,7-154-10575---,00.html, Michigan Labor and Economic Growth, Licensing Division, PO Box 30018, Lansing, MI 48909. Note: Michigan licenses plumbers, electricians, HVAC, and all residential contractors.

Minnesota 651-296-6319, 'https://www.state.mn.us/cgi-bin/portal/mn/jsp/content.do?programid=536884659&id=-536881350&agency=commerce/, Minnesota Department of Commerce, 85 7th Pl East, STE 500, St. Paul, MN 55101. Note: Minnesota licenses plumbers, electricians, and residential contractors.

Mississippi 800-880-6161, 601-354-6161, 'http://www.mississippi.gov/ms_sub_sub_template.jspp?Category_ID=20/, Mississippi Contractor Licensing Board, 215 Woodline DR, STE A, Jackson, MS 39232. Note: Mississippi licenses electrical, mechanical, residential and remodel contractors.

Missouri Missouri has no state contractor licensing Agency.

Montana 406-444-1446, 'http://erd.dli.state.mt.us/wcregs/iccu.asp, Independent Contractor Central Unit, 1805 Prospect Ave, PO Box 8011, Helena, MT 59604. Note: Montana licenses plumbers and electricians.

Nebraska 402-595-3189, 'www.dol.state.ne.us, Nebraska Department of Labor, 5404 Cedar St 3rd FL, Omaha, NE 68106. Note: Nebraska licenses electricians.

Nevada 702-486-1100, 'http://www.nscb.state.nv.us/, Nevada State Contractors Board, 2310 Corporate Circle, STE 200, Henderson, NV 89074. Note: Nevada licenses all contractors.

New Hampshire 603-271-3748, 'www.state.nh.us/plumbing, State Board Licensing & Regulation, Two Industrial Pk DR, Concord, NH 03302. Note: New Hampshire licenses plumbers and electricians.

New Jersey 888-656-6225, 'www.njconsumraffairs.com/contractor.htm, New Jersey Office of the Attorney General, Regulated Business Section, 124 Halscy St, 7th FL, Newark, NJ 07107. Note: New Jersey licenses plumbers, electricians, and home improvement contractors.

New Mexico 505-827-7030, 'www.rid.state.nm.us/, New Mexico Construction Industries Division, 725 St Michaels DR, Santa Fe, NM 87504. Note: In New Mexico all construction contractors need to be licensed.

New York In New York the homeowner must contact the city or county for contractor license requirements.

North Carolina 919-875-3612, 'www.nclicensing.org, State Board of Examiners of Contractors, 1109 Dresser CT, Raleigh, NC 27609. Note: North Carolina licenses plumbers, electricians, and general contractors.

North Dakota 701-328-9979, 'http://www.governor.state.nd.us/boards/boards-query.asp?Board_ID=83, North Dakota State Board, 204 West Thayer Ave, Bismarck, ND 58501. Note: North Dakota licenses plumbers and electricians.

Ohio 614-644-3493, 'http://www.com.state.oh.us/dic/dicocieb.htm, Ohio Construction Industry Board, 6606 Tussing RD, Reynoldsburg, OH 43068. Note: Ohio licenses plumbers, electricians and HVAC contractors.

Oklahoma 877-484-4424, 405-271-5217, 'http://www.cib.state.ok.us/, Oklahoma Construction Industries Board, 2401 NW 23rd ST, STE 5, Oklahoma City, OK 73107. Note: Oklahoma licenses plumbers, electricians and HVAC contractors.

Oregon 503-378-4133, 'www.oregonbdc.ort, Oregon State Licensing Board, 1535 Edgewater St NW, Salem, OR 97309-0404. Note: Oregon licenses plumbers and electricians.

Pennsylvania It seems that Pennsylvania does not license home construction contractors.

Rhode Island 401-462-8580, 'www.dlt.state.ri.us/profregs, Rhode Island Department of Labor and Training, 1511 Pontiac Ave, Cranston, RI 02920. Note: Rhode Island licenses plumbers, electricians, and HVAC contractors.

South Carolina 803-896-4696, 'www.llr.state.sc.us/POL/ResidentialBuilders/, Department of Labor, Licensing, & Regulation, 110 Centerview DR, STE 306, Columbia, SC 29210. Note: South Carolina licenses residential builders and almost all home construction trades.

South Dakota 605-773-3429, 'http://www.state.sd.us/dol/boards/plumbing/Plum-H.htm, South Dakota Plumbing & Electrical Commission, 308 S Pierre St, Pierre, SD 57501. Note: South Dakota licenses plumbers and electricians.

Tennessee 615-741-8307, 'http://www.state.tn.us/commerce/boards/contractors/index.html, Board for Licensing Contractors, 500 James Robertson Pkwy, STE 110, Nashville, TN 37243. Note: In Tennessee all construction contractors need to be licensed.

Texas 512-458-2145, 'http:/www.tsbpe.state.tx.us/index.html, Texas State Board of Examiners, 929 E 41st St, Austin, TX 78765. Note: Texas licenses plumbers, electricians, and HVAC contractors.

Utah 801-530-6628, 'http://ww.dopl.utah.gov/, Division of Occupational and Professional Licensing, PO Box 146741, Salt Lake City, UT 84114-6741. Note: In Utah all construction contractors need to be licensed.

Vermont 802-479-7561, 'http://www.vermont.gov/doing_business/profession.html, Vermont Department of Public Safety, 1311 US Route 302-Berlin, STE 600, Barre, VT 05641. Note: Vermont licenses plumbers and electricians.

Virginia 804-367-8500, 'http://www.state.va.us/dpor/, Virginia Department of Professional and Occupational Regulation, 3600 W Broad St, Richmond, VA 23230. Note: Virginia licenses plumbers, electricians, HVAC and all home improvement contractors.

Washington 800-547-8367, 360-902-5800, 'http:www.lni.wa.gov/TradesLicensing/default.Asp. Washington State Department of Labor and Industries, PO Box 4000, Olympia, WA 98504-4000. Note: Washington licenses plumbers and electricians.

West Virginia 304-558-7890, 'http://www.labor.state.wv.us/consumer/default.html, West Virginia Contractor Licensing Board, Bldg 6, Rm B-749, State Capital Complex, Charleston, WV 25305. Note: In West Virginia all construction contractors need to be licensed.

Wisconsin 608-266-2112, 'http://drl.wi.gov/index.htm, Wisconsin Department of Regulation & Licensing, 1400 E Washington Ave, Rm 173, Madison, WI 53703. Note: Wisconsin licenses plumbers, electricians, and all residential contractors.

Wyoming 307-777-7991, 'http://wyofire.state.wy.us/prevention/lfees.asp, State of Wyoming, Department of Electrical Safety, Herschler Bldg 1 W, Cheyenne, WY 82002. Note: Wyoming licenses electricians.

Chapter 19-Pat Fay Method Home Construction Management Forms.

Project Log-Planning. This form is used to log any and all details, issues, notes, or action items in regards to the homeowner's planning and preliminary design process.

Project Log-Construction. This form is used to log any and all details, issues, notes, or action items in regard to the homeowner's construction issues at hand in a particular phase of construction.

No Verbal Changes (NVC). The NVC form is for use in defining a change at the time the change is made. It eliminates the surprise change order bill at the end of the job. Its use must be defined in the contract.

Cost Control. The cost control form is used to record when the homeowner pays any money to a contractor, supplier, or for any service on the project. This simple form allows the homeowner to accurately track their project costs.

Contract for Construction Services. This is the contract form to use for those homeowners who follow the Pat Fay Method. Rather than signing a contractor's contract the contractor signs the homeowner's contract.

Addendum to the Contract for Construction Services. If the homeowner signs the contractor's contract then the homeowner can modify that contract to include language and terms that are important to the homeowner by attaching the homeowner's addendum to the contractor's contract.

Daily Construction Record. The daily construction record is used when the homeowner inspects their project. Use one form per day. It is invaluable in documenting the work and its progress. The use of this form has an unexpected consequence; it improves the quality of the contractor's workmanship. When the workers know that you are inspecting their work they increase the quality of their work without a word being said.

Request for Information (RFI). The homeowner uses this form when they need to document something that is an issue or a problem. The issue could range from the quality of the workmanship to the materials being used. If you go to arbitration you will have a record that you notified the contractor in writing. Also, if your relationship has gotten to the adversarial level it would be wise to mail a copy to the contractor's business address with proof of delivery.

Telephone Conversation Record. This form is used to keep a record of when and what was said in your telephone conversations.

Transmittal Form. The transmittal form is used when giving documents or material to the contractor. It provides a written record of when and what was transmitted.

Meeting Minutes. This is a sample form the homeowner can use to record a meeting minutes report.

Contractor Information Sheet. This form is used to take down pertinent information about the contractor, their address, their identification, and their qualifications.

Lien Release and Claim Waiver Form. The lien release and claim waiver form must be signed by the contractor before the final payment check is given to the contractor.

Contractor Bid or Price Review Form. The homeowner will use this form to write down the prices from different contractors so that all prices can be seen at a glance. Also included in the form is what the contractor includes and excludes from their price.

Schedule Form-High Level. This schedule form is used to show the entire project at a glance on one page. See schedules SCH-1 & SCH-2 in Chapter 5 for examples.

Schedule Form-Low Level Detailed. This schedule shows the entire project with more detailed construction steps. See schedule SCH-3 in Chapter 5.

Project Log-Planning

Planning Issue: _____

DATE	Description of Activity/Notes

Project Log-Construction

Project Title/Phase of Construction:_____
_____

DATE	Description of Activity/Notes

No Verbal Changes Form

NVC No. _____ **to Contract**_____

Date & Time:_____   Increase   Decrease   No Cost Change (circle one)

Reason for Change:
_____
_____
_____

Description of Change:
_____
_____
_____
_____
_____
_____
_____
_____

Cost of Change: (The cost must be determined before authorizing the change. Estimate all materials and their cost, labor hours and the rate of pay per hour, and list any equipment and their cost)
_____
_____
_____
_____
_____
_____
_____
_____

This No Verbal Change, when signed by the homeowner and the contractor, is hereby made a part of the contract and authorizes the contractor to proceed with this change.

_____   _____
Contractor   Date   Homeowner   Date

Cost Control

TITLE:		
DATE	DESCRIPTION	Balance

The Pat Fay Method Contract

The _____**Contract for Construction Services** for
(homeowner's last name)

_____, (homeowner's full name) herein referred to as the homeowner, needing an expert in the field of _____
_____ (define type of construction) hires
_____(company or contractor's name) referred to as the 'contractor, to perform this work according to this contract.

1. Schedule of Work. The work will start on _____ and be completed on _____.

2. Scope of Work. The contractor is to provide all labor, material and equipment to build the following scope of work:

_____
_____
_____
_____
_____
_____
_____

The contractor is required to build per this scope of work, according to the requirements of the building code, have the work inspected and have the permit signed off by the city inspector (if required), to rework at no additional cost any exceptions noted by the building inspector, and clean up all construction debris. The homeowner requires that the contractor provide exceptional workmanship and high quality materials in the construction of this project.

3. Payment Schedule. -The homeowner will make payment in full upon completion of the work defined in paragraph 2, the scope of work, receipt by the homeowner of a lien release from the contractor and any supplier, and the permit signed off by the building inspector.

4. Changes in Scope of Work and Change Orders. All changes in scope of work and/or cost, whether an increase, decrease or no cost change, will be in writing on the homeowner's No Verbal Changes (NVC) form and when signed by the homeowner and the contractor are made a part of the contract. No payment will be made to the contractor for any change or change order that is not written on the NVC form at the time of the change. The labor rate for change orders is $35 per hour. The material cost and the number of hours to execute the change in scope will be defined on the NVC form at the time of the change.

Initials _____ _____

The Pat Fay Method Contract

5. Respect. The homeowner and contractor, including the contractor's representatives and subcontractor's, will deal with each other in a professional manner and when speaking will use a polite, respectful tone of voice. The homeowner has the right to discuss all construction issues with the contractor such as, but not limited to, progress, quality of workmanship, quality of materials used on the project, safety, and site cleanup.

6. Construction Safety. The contractor is responsible for safety on this project. All appropriate construction safety rules are to be followed.

7. Appointments and communication. The contractor will keep all scheduled appointments with the homeowner. If the contractor is unable to keep an appointment the contractor will call the homeowner in a timely manner. Communication between the homeowner and the contractor is important. The homeowner's cell phone number is _____.

8. Arbitration. If the homeowner and the contractor cannot come to a mutually agreed upon resolution to a problem then the homeowner and the contractor will use an arbitrator to resolve the impasse. The cost will be divided equally between the homeowner and the contractor.

9. Failure to Perform. The homeowner wants to have a win-win relationship with the contractor. The homeowner pledges to make prompt payment to the contractor upon completion of the work defined in this contract. However, the contractor must work with all due diligence to complete the work per the mutually agreed upon schedule in paragraph one and to the terms of this contract. Failure to perform is reason to terminate the contract.

_____   _____
Homeowner   Date   Contractor   Date

_____   _____
Street Address   Street Address

_____   _____
City, State, Zip Code   City, State, Zip Code

_____   _____
Home & cell phone   Office & cell phone

                                 _____
                                 Contractor license or business number

The Pat Fay Method Addendum to the Contract

Addendum no. ____ **to the** _____ **Contract for Construction Services** for
(homeowner's last name)

_____, (homeowner's full name) herein referred to as the homeowner, needing an expert in the field of _____
_____ (define type of construction) hires
_____(company or contractor's name) referred to as the contractor, to perform this work according to this contract.

1. Schedule of Work. The work will start on _____ and be completed on _____.

2. Scope of Work. The contractor is to provide all labor, material and equipment to build the following scope of work:

_____
_____
_____
_____
_____

The contractor is required to build per this scope of work, according to the requirements of the building code, have the work inspected and have the permit signed off by the city inspector (if required), to rework at no additional cost any exceptions noted by the building inspector, and clean up all construction debris. The homeowner requires that the contractor provide exceptional workmanship and high quality materials in the construction of this project.

3. Payment Schedule. -The homeowner will make payment in full upon completion of the work defined in paragraph 2, the scope of work, receipt by the homeowner of a lien release from the contractor and any supplier, and the permit signed off by the building inspector.

4. Changes in Scope of Work and Change Orders. All changes in scope of work and/or cost, whether an increase, decrease or no cost change, will be in writing on the homeowner's No Verbal Changes (NVC) form and when signed by the homeowner and the contractor are made a part of the contract. No payment will be made to the contractor for any change or change order that is not written on the NVC form at the time of the change. The labor rate for change orders is $35 per hour. The material cost and the number of hours to execute the change in scope will be defined on the NVC form at the time of the change.

Initials _____ _____

page 1 of 2

The Pat Fay Method Addendum to the Contract

5. Respect. The homeowner and contractor, including the contractor's representatives and subcontractor's, will deal with each other in a professional manner and when speaking will use a polite, respectful tone of voice. The homeowner has the right to discuss all construction issues with the contractor such as, but not limited to, progress, quality of workmanship, quality of materials used on the project, safety, and site cleanup.

6. Construction Safety. The contractor is responsible for safety on this project. All appropriate construction safety rules are to be followed.

7. Appointments and communication. The contractor will keep all scheduled appointments with the homeowner. If the contractor is unable to keep an appointment the contractor will call the homeowner in a timely manner. Communication between the homeowner and the contractor is important. The homeowner's cell phone number is _____.

8. Arbitration. If the homeowner and the contractor cannot come to a mutually agreed upon resolution to a problem then the homeowner and the contractor will use an arbitrator to resolve the impasse. The cost will be divided equally between the homeowner and the contractor.

9. Failure to Perform. The homeowner wants to have a win-win relationship with the contractor. The homeowner pledges to make prompt payment to the contractor upon completion of the work defined in this contract. However, the contractor must work with all due diligence to complete the work per the mutually agreed upon schedule in paragraph one and to the terms of the contract and this addendum. Failure to perform is reason to terminate the contract and any addendum.

_____   _____
Homeowner   Date   Contractor   Date

_____   _____
Street Address   Street Address

_____   _____
City, State, Zip Code   City, State, Zip Code

_____   _____
Home & cell phone   Office & cell phone

                                                              _____
                                                              Contractor license or business number

Daily Construction Record

Date:_____ Time:_____ Weather_____

Construction
Phase:_____

This is the _____ day of construction for this contractor. Contract completion date is
_____

The contractor is _____% complete with the work. The contractor should be complete with _____% of the work.

Description of the work:_____
_____
_____
_____
_____
_____
_____
_____
_____
_____
_____
_____
_____
_____
_____
_____
_____
_____
_____
_____
_____
_____

Issues:_____
_____
_____
_____
_____
_____
_____

Request for Information (RFI)

RFI no._____ Date:_____ Time:_____

Construction Phase/Contractor:_____

Homeowner issue or subject: _____
_____
_____
_____
_____
_____
_____
_____
_____
_____

Contractor response:_____
_____
_____
_____
_____
_____
_____
_____

Resolution to the issue or action required:_____
_____
_____
_____
_____
_____
_____

_____   _____
Contractor   Date   Homeowner   Date

Telephone Conversation Record

Date:_____

From:_____Telephone number:_____

To:_____Telephone number:_____

Subject(s):_____

_____

_____

_____

Transmittal Form

Date:_____

From:_____

To:_____

Method of transmittal to the contractor or supplier:_____

Reason for transmittal: _____
_____
_____
_____
_____

Subject(s):_____
_____
_____
_____
_____
_____
_____
_____
_____
_____
_____
_____
_____
_____
_____
_____
_____
_____
_____
_____
_____
_____

Meeting Minutes for Our Project

Date:_____

Attendees: _____
_____

Review last meeting minutes: _____
_____

Review the Agenda for this meeting: _____
_____
_____

Design Review:_____
_____
_____

Permit Issues: _____
_____
_____

Construction Planning: _____
_____
_____

Project Schedule: _____
_____
_____

Field Work at the job site: _____
_____
_____

New Topics of Discussion: _____
_____

Finances/Budget/Costs: _____

Action Items: _____

Round Table: _____

Next Meeting date and time:_____

Contractor Information Sheet

Contractor type:_____

Contractor Company Name:_____

Contractor's personal name:_____

Address:_____ City_____ State___Zip_____
Office phone: _____ Cell phone: _____ Fax no. _____

Contractor license/business info:_____
Drivers license no._____ Vehicle license no._____

How was this contractor located?_____

Does this contractor have a 3-ring binder with pictures of previous work?_____

Who will do the actual work? _____

Does their previous work indicate they should be considered for this project?_____

Does this contractor have written recommendations from previous clients? _____

Will the contractor show the homeowner prior or present work locations and previous homeowner clients?_____

What is your opinion of their previous work?_____
_____
_____

What is the homeowner's gut feeling about this contractor?_____

Will this contractor work according to the Pat Fay Method?_____

Notes:_____
_____
_____
_____
_____
_____
_____

Lien Release and Claim Waiver

The following contractor, subcontractor, individual or material supplier:(list name of contractor, individual or supplier)_____
_____
_____
_____,

hereinafter called 'the contractor', having done work or supplied material to _____
_____(homeowner's full name),
hereinafter called 'the homeowner, for the homeowner's home construction project located at: (list full address with city and county) _____
_____

hereby receives final payment in the amount of $_____.
This payment constitutes the final and only payment to the contractor and effective upon receipt of said final payment, the contractor hereby waives, releases and forever discharges any and all liens and rights of lien of any form, sort or nature whatever, including mechanic's or materialmen's lien, equitable lien and any and all liabilities, obligations and claims of any form, sort or nature whatever against the homeowner and the homeowner's above mentioned project or property.

The undersigned does hereby acknowledge that the undersigned has been paid in full and willingly signs this unconditional claim waiver and lien release upon receipt of the homeowner's final payment for any labor, services, equipment or materials furnished to the above mentioned project.

Signature of the contractor:_____

Dated _____, 20__ at _____(write in location, city & state)

Note: The homeowner is to check the contractor's signature against their driver's license signature.

Contractor Bid or Price Review Form

Date: _____

Construction Phase: _____

Contractor Name	Price	Includes	Excludes	Notes

Schedule-High Level

Project: _____

Project Timeline	
Planning	
Preliminary Design	
Final Design	
Permitting	
Contractor Selection	
Construction Timeline	
Inspection	
Lien Release & Payment	

Schedule-Low Level Detailed

Project: _____

Project Timeline	
Planning	
Preliminary Design	
Final Design	
Permitting	
Contractor Selection	
Construction Timeline	
Inspection	
Construction Activities	
Survey property	
Install temporary power pole	
Layout footprint of house	
Excavation	
Install underground utilities	
Form/pour foundation footings & walls	
Waterproof basement walls	
Install footing perimeter drain	
Install below grade drain, waste, vent pipe	

Place basement slab on grade	
Deliver lumber package	
Install floor joists and subfloor	
Back fill around foundation	
Frame house	
Install outside wall sheathing	
Install exterior doors and windows, caulk	
Install roofing, flashing	
Install rough plumbing, bathtub, HW tank	
Install furnace and ductwork	
Install fireplace & vents	
Install natural gas pipe	
Install rough electrical, main electrical panel	
Install telephone, cable, communication wiring	
Install vapor barrier on exterior sheathing	
Install siding & masonry	
Stain/paint siding	
Vacuum out spaces between studs	
Install wall insulation	

Turn on furnace, heat house for 3 days	
Install drywall, tape, mud, sand, PVA coating	
Spray texture, knock down all high points	
Paint interior walls	
Install all flooring	
Install kitchen cabinets	
Install countertops	
Install sinks, toilets, & trim out, finish plumbing	
Electrical finish work	
Install interior doors and trim	
Paint doors and trim	
Install door and cabinet hardware	
Install carpets	
Final finish on hardwood floors	
Install mirrors and shower door	
Final occupancy permit signed off by inspector